START AND RUN A PROFITABLE
BUSINESS USING YOUR COMPUTER

START AND RUN A PROFITABLE
BUSINESS USING YOUR COMPUTER

Douglas Gray

Self-Counsel Press
(a division of)
International Self-Counsel Press Ltd.
U.S.A.   Canada

Printed in Canada.

Self-Counsel Press acknowledges the financial support of the Government of Canada through the Book Publishing Industry Development Program for our publishing activities.

First edition: May 1998

Canadian Cataloguing in Publication Data
Gray, Douglas A.
    Start and run a profitable business using your computer

    (Self-counsel business series)
    ISBN 1-55180-067-5

    1. Computer service industry. 2. Electronic data processing.
3. New business enterprises. 4. Home-based businesses. I. Title. II. Series.
QA76.25.G72 1998   658.1'141   C98-910316-1

Self-Counsel Press
(a division of)
International Self-Counsel Press Ltd.

1704 N. State Street
Bellingham, WA 98225
U.S.A.

1481 Charlotte Road
North Vancouver, BC V7J 1H1
Canada

CONTENTS

ACKNOWLEDGMENTS   xix

INTRODUCTION   xxi

PART I: COMPUTER BUSINESS OPPORTUNITIES

1 101 MONEY-MAKING COMPUTER BUSINESSES   3

A. DESKTOP PUBLISHING   3
    1. Newsletter design and layout   3
    2. Magazine and catalogue design and layout   4
    3. Business form and stationery design and layout   5
    4. Booklet and vanity publication design and layout   5
    5. Annual report design and layout   6
    6. Menu design and layout   7

B. RESEARCHING, WRITING, AND EDITING   7
    1. Word processing   7
    2. Freelance writing   8
    3. Freelance editing   9
    4. Technical writing   9
    5. Technical editing   10
    6. Genealogy research   10
    7. People tracing   11
    8. Product and service tracing   12

9.	Transcribing	12
10.	Translating	13
11.	Foreign-language word processing	14
12.	Electronic clipping service	14
13.	Bid and grant proposal writing	15
14.	Résumé writing	16
15.	Annual report writing	17
16.	Copywriting	18
17.	Specialty magazine writing and editing	18
18.	On-line magazine writing and editing	19
19.	Information broker	21

C. GRAPHIC DESIGN — 21

1.	Graphic design	21
2.	Image scanning and digitizing	22
3.	Document scanning	23
4.	Image enhancing	24
5.	Architectural and computer-aided design	25
6.	Interior design	25
7.	Garden and landscape design	26
8.	Clip art service	27
9.	Web and business presentation clip art service	28
10.	Web sound and video clip service	29
11.	Sign, banner, and poster design	30
12.	Customized gift and promotional product creation	31
13.	Print and prepress consulting	31

D. MULTIMEDIA — 32

1.	Multimedia genealogy publishing	32
2.	Multimedia kiosk design and consulting	33
3.	Multimedia business presentation design	34
4.	Desktop video editing	35

E. BUSINESS ACCOUNTING, PLANNING, AND MANAGEMENT — 35

1.	Business plan writing	35
2.	Billing service	36
3.	Bookkeeping	37

	4.	Collection service	37
	5.	Expense analysis	38
	6.	Inventory service	38
	7.	Utility bill auditing	39
	8.	Accounts payable and payroll system service	40
	9.	Client database service	40
	10.	Property management	41
	11.	Estate management	41
	12.	Event planning	42
F.	FINANCIAL		42
	1.	Financial planning and management	42
	2.	Investment analysis	43
	3.	Sales analysis	44
	4.	Statistical analysis	44
G.	FAX AND PRINTING		45
	1.	Fax time rental	45
	2.	Fax-on-demand service	45
	3.	Laser printer time rental	46
H.	FAMILY AND HOUSEHOLD		47
	1.	Home inventory cataloguing	47
	2.	Tax preparation	47
I.	MAINTENANCE AND REPAIR		48
	1.	Computer repair and maintenance	48
	2.	Computer cleaning	49
J.	TRAINING AND CONSULTING		50
	1.	Computer setup and training	50
	2.	On-line setup and training	51
	3.	Telecommuting consulting	52
	4.	Videoconferencing consulting	53
	5.	Computer consulting for people with disabilities	54
	6.	Occupational therapy	55
	7.	Ergonomics consulting	56
	8.	On-line teaching and tutoring	57
	9.	Computer and on-line training for children	58

	10.	On-line research training	59
	11.	Job hunting training	60
	12.	Employer on-line hiring training	61
K.	DATA BACKUP, ARCHIVING, AND SECURITY		62
	1.	Data backup service	62
	2.	Data archiving	63
	3.	Data conversion	64
	4.	Data security consulting	64
	5.	System security consulting	65
L.	DATABASE SERVICES		65
	1.	Database management	65
	2.	Database creation	66
	3.	Database conversion	67
M.	E-MAIL SERVICES		67
	1.	Mailing list service	67
	2.	Electronic mailbox service	68
	3.	Anonymous re-mailer service	68
	4.	Junk e-mail filter service	69
N.	INTRANET AND NETWORK SERVICES		69
	1.	Network consulting	69
	2.	Intranet administration	70
O.	WEB SITE DESIGN AND SERVICES		70
	1.	Web site design	70
	2.	Web site administration	71
	3.	On-line form design	71
	4.	On-line catalogue creation	72
	5.	Electronic mall service	72
	6.	Bulletin board service	73
P.	SALES AND MARKETING		73
	1.	Mail order sales	73
	2.	Direct-mail marketing	74
	3.	Computer accessory sales	75
	4.	Used PC sales	75
DEFINITIONS OF ABBREVIATIONS			77

PART II: GETTING STARTED IN YOUR SMALL BUSINESS

2	**SELF-ASSESSMENT**	**81**
	A. ASSESSING YOURSELF AND YOUR MARKETABLE SKILLS	81
3	**SETTING UP YOUR BUSINESS**	**87**
	A. START-UP COSTS AND MONTHLY EXPENSES	87
	1. Start-up costs	88
	2. Monthly overhead expenses	88
	3. Personal expenses	88
	B. SELECTING A NAME	88
	1. General considerations	88
	2. Fictitious name	88
	C. SELECTING AN OFFICE	92
	1. Home office	92
	2. Office outside of home	93
	3. Equipping an office	96
	4. Office supplies	96
	5. Personnel	97
	D. SELECTING A TELEPHONE SYSTEM	97
	1. Separate telephone at home	97
	2. Business line terminating at answering service	98
	3. Business line terminating at home and answering service	98
	4. Overline	98
	5. Measured business line	98
	6. Shared line	99
	E. OTHER COMMUNICATION OPTIONS	99
	1. Telephone answering devices	99
	2. Voice mail	100
	3. Toll-free number	100
	4. Generic telephone number	101
	5. Fax on demand	101
	6. Pager	101

7.	Cellular telephone	102
8.	Electronic mail (e-mail)	102

4 LEGAL FORMS OF BUSINESS STRUCTURE — 103

A. SOLE PROPRIETORSHIP — 104
 1. Advantages — 104
 2. Disadvantages — 104
B. PARTNERSHIP — 105
 1. Advantages — 105
 2. Disadvantages — 105
 3. Partnership agreement — 106
C. CORPORATION — 106
 1. Advantages — 106
 2. Disadvantages — 108
 3. Corporate purposes — 108
 4. Shareholders' agreement — 108
D. S CORPORATION (SUB-CHAPTER OR SUB-S) (UNITED STATES) — 109
E. LIMITED LIABILITY CORPORATION (LLC) (UNITED STATES) — 109

5 SELECTING BUSINESS AND PROFESSIONAL ADVISERS — 111

A. GENERAL CRITERIA FOR ADVISER SELECTION — 111
 1. Recommendations — 112
 2. Credentials — 112
 3. Clientele — 112
 4. Fees — 112
 5. Technical competence and industry knowledge — 113
 6. Style and personality — 113
 7. Confidence — 113
 8. Communication — 113
 9. Commitment — 114
 10. Availability — 114
 11. Length of time in practice — 114
 12. Ability to aid growth — 114

	13. Small firm versus large firm	114
	14. Comparison	114
B.	LAWYER	115
C.	ACCOUNTANT	115
D.	BANKER	116
E.	INSURANCE	117
F.	CONSULTANTS	117
	1. Private consultants	117
	2. Consultants subsidized by the government	117

6 PREPARING YOUR BUSINESS PLAN — 119

A.	WHY PREPARE A PLAN?	119
B.	FORMAT	120
C.	ESTIMATING YOUR START-UP FUNDS	121
	1. Assessment of personal monthly financial needs	121
	2. Estimated business start-up cash needs	121
D.	SUMMARY	121

7 HOW TO OBTAIN FINANCING — 138

A.	TYPES OF FINANCING	138
	1. Equity	138
	2. Debt	139
B.	SOURCES OF FINANCING	141
	1. Equity	141
	2. Debt	142
C.	COMPETITION BETWEEN LENDERS	143
D.	TIPS ON APPROACHING YOUR LENDER	143
E.	WHY LOANS ARE TURNED DOWN	144
F.	TYPES OF SECURITY A LENDER MAY REQUIRE	146
	1. Endorser	146
	2. Co-maker	146
	3. Guarantor	146
	4. Promissory note	147

	5.	Demand loan	147
	6.	Realty mortgage	147
	7.	Chattel mortgage	147
	8.	Assignment of accounts receivable	147
	9.	Postponement of claim	147
	10.	Pledge of stocks or bonds	147
	11.	Assignment of life insurance	147

8 HOW TO LEGALLY MINIMIZE PAYING TAX — 148

A.	TAX AVOIDANCE AND TAX EVASION	148
B.	CASH OR ACCRUAL METHOD	149
C.	FISCAL YEAR-END	149
D.	CORPORATIONS, PROPRIETORSHIPS, OR PARTNERSHIPS	150
E.	MAXIMIZING DEDUCTIBLE EXPENSES	150
	1. Home office	151
	2. Automobile	151
	3. Entertainment	152
	4. Travel	152
	5. Bad debts	152
	6. Insurance	152
	7. Education and professional development	152
	8. Salaries	153
	9. Equipment	153
	10. Furnishings	153

9 INSURANCE — 154

A.	OBTAINING INSURANCE	154
	1. Agencies	154
	2. Insurance brokers	154
	3. Clubs and associations	155
B.	PLANNING YOUR INSURANCE PROGRAM	155
C.	TYPES OF BUSINESS AND PERSONAL INSURANCE	156
	1. General liability	156

2.	Products or completed operations liability	156
3.	Errors and omissions liability	156
4.	Malpractice liability	156
5.	Automobile liability	156
6.	Home office insurance	157
7.	Fire and theft liability	157
8.	Business interruption insurance	157
9.	Overhead expense insurance	157
10.	Personal disability insurance	157
11.	Key person insurance	157
12.	Shareholders' or partners' insurance	157
13.	Business loan insurance	158
14.	Term life insurance	158
15.	Medical insurance	158
16.	Group insurance	159
17.	Workers' compensation insurance	159

10	**CREDIT, BILLING, AND COLLECTION**	**160**
A.	DISADVANTAGES OF EXTENDING CREDIT	161
B.	ASSESSING THE CLIENT	161
C.	AVOIDING CLIENT MISUNDERSTANDINGS ON FEES	162
	1. Communication	162
	2. Written contract	162
	3. Invoice	163
D.	MINIMIZING RISK OF BAD DEBTS	163
	1. Advance retainer	163
	2. Prepaid disbursements	163
	3. Progress payments	163
	4. Regular billing	163
	5. Billing on time	164
	6. Accelerated billing	164
	7. Monitor payment trends of clients	164

		8.	Follow-up of late payments	164
		9.	Accepting credit card payments	164
	E.	BILLING FOR SERVICES		164
	F.	WHY CLIENTS PAY LATE		165
	G.	COLLECTING LATE PAYMENTS WITHOUT LEGAL ACTION		165
	H.	LEGAL STEPS IF ACCOUNT REMAINS UNPAID		166
		1.	Collection agency	167
		2.	Small claims court	167
		3.	Lawyers	167
	I.	BAD DEBTS AND TAXES		167

11	DETERMINING MARKET OPPORTUNITIES			168
	A.	PRIVATE SECTOR		169
		1.	Individuals	169
		2.	Small businesses	169
		3.	Medium-sized businesses	169
		4.	Large companies	169
	B.	PUBLIC SECTOR		170
		1.	Making contacts and obtaining information	170
		2.	Understanding the government approval system	171

12	MARKETING YOUR SERVICE OR PRODUCT			173
	A.	WHY YOU NEED TO MARKET YOUR SERVICE OR PRODUCT		173
	B.	MARKETING PLAN		174
	C.	MARKETING TECHNIQUES		174
		1.	Newspaper	175
		2.	Advertising in trade or professional journals	175
		3.	Directories	175
		4.	Brochures	175
		5.	Direct mail	175
		6.	Contact network	177
		7.	Membership in professional, trade, or business associations	178
		8.	Lectures	178

9.	Teaching	179
10.	Seminars and workshops	179
11.	Free media exposure	180
12.	Radio and television talk shows	180
13.	Writing articles	180
14.	Have articles written about you	181

PART III: GETTING PREPARED FOR YOUR COMPUTER BUSINESS

13	OFFICE SETUP AND DESIGN	185
A.	CHOOSING YOUR WORKSPACE	185
B.	SETTING UP YOUR WORK ENVIRONMENT	186
	1. Lighting	186
	2. Ventilation	186
C.	SETTING UP EQUIPMENT	187
	1. Desk	187
	2. Keyboard, pointing devices, and wrist rests	187
	3. Monitor	188
	4. Document holder	188
	5. Chair	188
	6. Telephone	188
	7. File cabinets, shelves, and storage	189
D.	ERGONOMIC TERMS AND COMMON INJURIES	189
	1. Repetitive strain injury and cumulative trauma	189
	2. Carpal tunnel syndrome	190
	3. Neck strain	190
	4. Back strain	190
	5. Eye strain	190
	6. Time is key	191
14	PURCHASING HARDWARE, SOFTWARE, AND SERVICES	192
A.	RESEARCHING YOUR PURCHASE	192
B.	HARDWARE	193

C. COMPUTER COMPONENTS   193
    1. Central processing unit (CPU)   193
    2. Motherboard   194
    3. Random-access memory (RAM)   194
    4. Hard disk   194
    5. Sound cards   194
    6. Video cards   195
    7. Expansion slots   195
    8. Monitors   195
    9. Keyboard   195
   10. Pointing device   196

D. PERIPHERALS   196
    1. Printers   196
    2. Modems   196
    3. Scanners   197
    4. Drives   197
    5. Uninterruptible power supply (UPS)   198

E. PORTABLE COMPUTERS   198

F. HANDHELD COMPUTERS   198

G. SECURITY   199
    1. Backing up data   199
    2. Virus protection   199

H. BUYING SOFTWARE   200

I. BUYING SERVICES   201

SAMPLES

#1	Start-up Expenses	89
#2	Monthly Expenses	90
#3	Personal Monthly Expenses	91
#4	Business Plan Format	122
#5	Opening Balance Sheet (New Business)	131
#6	Cash Flow Budget	132
#7	Income and Expense Statement Forecast (New Business)	134
#8	Personal Net Worth Statement	135
#9	Statement of Accounts Receivable	137

TABLES

#1	Articles in a Partnership Agreement	107

NOTICE TO READERS

ACKNOWLEDGMENTS

I would like to thank Megan Johnston for helping, through her excellent research, editorial, and computer skills, make this book a reality.

A special thanks to Ruth Wilson, Lori Ledingham, and Judy Phillips of Self-Counsel Press who made the production of this book an enjoyable and satisfying professional experience.

INTRODUCTION

Whether you are a computer beginner or a computer pro, this book will help you attain your objectives of starting your own business using your computer. The tools and techniques needed to get you started in the right direction are explained in an easily understandable fashion. A new and exciting career using your computer skills awaits you! If you don't already have computer skills but would like to learn them, there are many opportunities to do so through private or public educational institutions.

If you have ever thought of being self-employed using your computer skills, whether from your home or from an office outside your home, now is the time to take the step and be your own boss. You can start your own business part-time to see if you like it, if it is a good fit, challenging, and financially attractive. Although you may start part-time, you may find that you are soon making more money with your computer than you are working at your current job. You might then decide to use your computer skills on a full-time basis in your own business.

The personal computer is a vital tool for today's entrepreneur. It is the great enabler.

It allows you to compete against and beat larger companies in many aspects of business. With today's relatively low cost of powerful computers, with all the features and benefits available, and with an extensive array of easy-to-use but sophisticated software, you can be all you can be and do whatever you wish in business.

Computers have also revolutionized the way we work. They increase efficiency, improve time management, reduce repetitive tasks, and give a tremendous sense of power and control over business operations. Computers also enhance business image, demonstrate professionalism, and provide a competitive edge. Computers have created a level playing field in business by providing affordable technology a small business can use to compete with big business.

This book has been structured in three main parts. Part I profiles 101 money-making mini-business plans of businesses that use a personal computer to generate revenue. The format is the same for all the businesses so that you can compare them easily. Each business profile refers to other complementary businesses, in case you wish to consider multiple business activities. Most of these businesses can be started from home. As you can see, there is a wide range of small business opportunities available to the entrepreneur equipped with a computer, personal drive, imagination, resourcefulness, and a sense of direction and purpose.

The 101 computer-related businesses are categorized. However, it is a good idea to read or skim over all 101 opportunities rather than limit yourself to the ones that initially interest you. That way you can be creatively stimulated by all the ideas.

The choices are many, varied, and constantly changing. Look on these businesses as a starting point to all the opportunities that await you: other computer business opportunities will likely come to mind as you read through Part I.

After you have short-listed the ideas that interest you, get candid feedback from friends, family, and business associates on the business you are considering. Complete the process of self-evaluation covered in chapter 2. If you are still keen, complete the business plan discussed in chapter 6 to see how viable the concept is. If you still want to proceed, do so on a step-by-step basis following the process outlined in Part II and Part III, to test the idea to see if you like it and if it is a good business and personal fit.

Part II discusses getting started in your own small business. It includes tips on doing a self-assessment and on business start-up basics. There are also various sample forms to assist you.

Part III discusses the steps you need to take to be prepared for your computer business. This includes setting up your office and avoiding common computer-related injuries. Part III also offers tips on purchasing computer hardware, software, and services.

After you have finished reading this book, check out all the other sources of additional information available to you, such as books, magazines, seminars, courses, and conferences. The Internet alone is a veritable gold mine of information to boost your learning curve and confidence. You may wish to visit my Web site at *http://www.smallbiz.ca*.

Computer technology is always developing, so you will find that the process is one of constant learning and challenge. It is also exciting and dynamic. Best of all, being your own boss means that you reap all the benefits of your time while developing skills and talents.

Best wishes to you, and may you have a rewarding and fulfilling journey ahead.

Part I

COMPUTER

BUSINESS

OPPORTUNITIES

1

101 MONEY-MAKING COMPUTER BUSINESSES

For suggestions on how to benefit from the following discussion of business opportunities, please refer to the Introduction. If you are not familiar with some of the technical terms in this chapter, please see the Definitions of Abbreviations on page 77, as well as chapter 14.

A. DESKTOP PUBLISHING

1. Newsletter design and layout

Description: Many businesses and organizations publish newsletters for employees, customers, or members.

As a desktop publisher, you are provided with the copy (articles and headlines, images and company logos) and are responsible for laying it out in a readable format. This service can also involve creation of graphics or charts to illustrate the text.

Skills: Good layout and design skills. Knowledge of industry formats and experience working with service bureaus and printers.

Equipment: Desktop publishing software and a computer with enough processing power, RAM, and storage capacity to run it; a flatbed and/or slide scanner for inputting images and graphics; a large-screen monitor; and a high-quality inkjet printer for producing drafts or proofs of the newsletter. For output, have the final version printed on a high-quality laser printer at a service bureau.

The better the quality of the original, the better the quality of the copies.

Photocopying, collating, and stapling can also be done at a service bureau. If the output involves a number of pages, or a high volume of copies, consider using a printing plant.

For delivering electronic files to service bureaus or printers, you will also need some form of high-capacity media drive, such as MO, Zip, CD-R, or CDRW. Make sure your choice is compatible with that of the service bureau and printer you are using.

Potential customers: Medium- to large-sized businesses or organizations that publish newsletters but do not have staff qualified to do this type of work.

Promotion: Contact your potential clients directly to find out if they publish a newsletter and ask how it is currently handled — by staff or contracted out. Ask if you may submit a bid on publishing the newsletter along with a portfolio containing samples of your work. Advertise your services in a publication that targets business, marketing, and human resources professionals. Contact the executives of organizations, such as alumni or professional societies, and ask what newsletter production arrangements they currently have.

Associated businesses: Magazine and catalogue design and layout, Booklet and vanity publication design and layout.

2. Magazine and catalogue design and layout

Description: This design and layout service can target the same types of businesses as the newsletter service, since internal corporate or organization magazines are usually just a high-end newsletter on glossy paper, with a better quality of writing and images, and possibly advertising.

You could expand this service by producing catalogues of products or services sold by a company or organization.

Skills: Good design and layout skills. Knowledge of industry formats and experience working with service bureaus and printers. Knowledge of conventions of magazine design.

Equipment: Desktop publishing software and image-editing software and a computer with enough processing power, RAM, and storage capacity to run it; a flatbed and/or slide scanner for inputting images and graphics; a high-resolution, large-screen monitor; and a high-quality color inkjet printer for producing drafts of the magazine.

For delivering electronic files to service bureaus or printers, you will also need a high-capacity media drive, such as MO, Zip, CD-R, or CDRW. Make sure your choice is compatible with that of the service bureau and printer you are using.

Potential customers: Medium- to large-sized businesses or organizations that publish newsletters but do not have staff qualified to design and lay out the publication.

Promotion: Contact your potential clients — businesses or organizations such as alumni or professional societies and clubs — directly to find out if they produce or are planning to produce a magazine or catalogue. If the answer is yes, ask if you may submit a bid on producing the publication along with a portfolio containing samples of your work. Advertise your services in a publication that targets business, marketing, and human resources professionals. Contact the executives and board members of large organizations and societies and ask what magazine or catalogue production arrangements they currently have.

Associated businesses: Newsletter design and layout, Business form and stationery design and layout.

3. Business form and stationery design and layout

Description: Desktop publishing software can be used to design a range of customized items for businesses, service providers, and organizations, including applications, order forms, message pads, schedules, calendars, stationery, and even checks. This type of service is a good adjunct to other graphic design and layout services.

Skills: Good design and layout skills. Knowledge of industry formats and experience working with service bureaus and printers.

Equipment: Desktop publishing software and a computer with enough processing power, RAM, and storage capacity to run it. A high-quality inkjet printer for producing drafts or proofs of the forms.

If you have the forms or stationery output by a printing service, you will need a high-capacity media drive, such as MO, Zip,

CD-R, or CDRW. Make sure your choice is compatible with that of the service bureau and printer you are using.

Potential customers: Any business, organization, or institution that does not have an in-house design department.

Promotion: Create a brochure with samples of your work and describing your services, and distribute copies to potential clients. Advertise your services in a publication that targets business professionals, small business owners, or executives of organizations and institutions.

Associated businesses: Graphic design, Newsletter design and layout, Magazine and catalogue design and layout.

4. Booklet and vanity publication design and layout

Description: This type of service targets individuals or organizations that are producing small-run, commemorative family histories or vanity booklets and publications.

You are provided with the copy or text as well as any images or graphics. This service involves the design and layout of the interior and cover of the publication and can also involve arranging prepress and printing services.

Skills: Good design and layout skills, and knowledge of the graphic conventions of book publishing (e.g., which fonts to use for body text; placement of headers, footers, and footnotes; location of index and table of contents; and design of opening page).

Equipment: Desktop publishing software and a computer with enough processing power, RAM, and storage capacity to run it, and a high-quality inkjet printer for producing drafts.

If you arrange for the book to be output by a printing service, you will need a high-capacity media drive, such as MO, Zip, CD-R, or CDRW. Make sure your choice is compatible with that of the service bureau and printer you are using.

Potential customers: Businesses and organizations, amateur writers, and genealogy enthusiasts.

Promotion: Advertise your service in magazines targeting writers, researchers, and genealogy enthusiasts, or in publications for marketing and public relations professionals.

Associated businesses: Newsletter design and layout, Magazine and catalogue design and layout.

5. Annual report design and layout

Description: Many businesses as well as nonprofit organizations and societies produce reports for shareholders and other stakeholders describing achievements in the past year and including projections and plans for the next year or next few years. Because this is done only once a year, these businesses or organizations may not have staff with the skills or time to design and lay out a professional-looking report.

Annual reports come in many forms, from basic spiral-bound text-only booklets to more elaborate publications that incorporate exotic designs and unusual materials.

This work involves the design and layout of text and images you are supplied with but can also involve taking photographs and creating charts and graphics to illustrate the report.

Skills: Excellent design and layout skills.

Equipment: Desktop publishing, graphic, and image-editing software; a computer with enough processing power, RAM, and storage capacity to run it; a flatbed and/or slide scanner for inputting images and graphics; a high-resolution, large-screen monitor; and a high-quality color inkjet printer for producing drafts of the publication.

For delivering electronic files to service bureaus or printers, you will also need a high-capacity media drive, such as MO, Zip, CD-R, or CDRW. Make sure your choice is compatible with that of the service bureau and printer you are using.

Potential customers: Any business, organization, or society that produces an annual report.

Promotion: Target potential clients directly with a portfolio of your work. Advertise in publications targeting business executives. If there is a board of trade in your area, consider advertising in its newsletter, magazine, or on-line publication. The latter could link to your own Web site describing your services.

Associated businesses: Newsletter design and layout, Magazine and catalogue design and layout, Annual report writing.

6. Menu design and layout

Description: Yet another specialty desktop publishing service, menu design and layout involves laying out the names, descriptions, and prices of menu items but can also include creations of illustrations, graphics, and photographs to illustrate the menu or complement the restaurant decor. Designing a menu template that the restaurant alters and prints daily as its menu changes is another option.

Your service can also include arranging and supervising the printing of the menu, especially if it is printed on special paper or involves lamination or folding.

Skills: Good design and layout skills.

Equipment: Desktop publishing and graphics software and a computer with enough processing power, RAM, and storage capacity to run it; a flatbed and/or slide scanner for inputting images and graphics; a large-screen monitor; and a high-quality inkjet printer for producing drafts or proofs of the menu. For delivering electronic files to service bureaus or printers, you will also need some form of high-capacity media drive, such as MO, Zip, CD-R, or CDRW. Make sure your choice is compatible with that of the service bureau and printer you are using.

Potential customers: Owners and managers of restaurants, hotels, or clubs with restaurants or dining rooms.

Promotion: Advertise your services in a publication targeting restaurateurs or other service industry managers and owners. Target potential customers directly with samples of your work and perhaps a draft design of their menus.

Associated businesses: Newsletter design and layout, Business form and stationery design and layout.

B. RESEARCHING, WRITING, AND EDITING

1. Word processing

Description: This type of service can involve taking raw text and editing and formatting it, or inputting it from other paper-based documents. Word processing is like a low-end version of desktop publishing but is less graphically oriented.

Consider specializing in an area of business in which you have a background, for example, medicine, marketing, or agriculture. Promote your familiarity with the jargon of that particular field. Although this narrows the field of clients in your geographical area, it will help distinguish you from other similar services if you promote your business on-line. And because word documents can easily be transferred electronically, your potential clientele is not necessarily limited by geography.

Skills: Good writing and editing skills, fast and accurate typing. Knowledge of the common word-processing programs, such as Microsoft Word and WordPerfect. Knowledge of other office suite applications is an asset because it will allow you to create and incorporate tables and spreadsheets into the finished documents.

Equipment: You will need a computer capable of running office suite software, a high-quality inkjet printer, a sheet-fed or flatbed scanner, and OCR software if you are inputting paper-based documents. An Internet connection if you are working with clients who are not in your geographical area is also necessary.

Potential customers: A business or organization that needs documents created on an intermittent basis and does not have the staff, equipment, or time to do this task in-house.

Promotion: Create a brochure describing your services and distribute copies to small- and medium-sized businesses. Advertise in business publications or in the business section of your local newspaper. If you have a specialty, consider promoting your services on a Web site.

Associated businesses: Transcribing, Desktop publishing services, Résumé writing.

2. Freelance writing

Description: There is a wide range of opportunities for writers, including promotional writing or creating journalistic material, such as writing a history of a company or organization on its fiftieth anniversary or ghost writing an autobiography. Most magazines and newspapers, as well as on-line publications, commission freelance writers.

If you have an area of interest or specialized knowledge, consider focusing on it when promoting your business. Although this narrows the field of clients in your geographical area, it will help distinguish you from other similar services on-line. And because your written material can easily be transferred electronically, your potential clientele is not necessarily limited by geography.

Skills: Excellent writing, editing, and research skills.

Equipment: A computer capable of running word-processing software, and a high-quality inkjet printer if the client requires a paper-based copy of your written material.

Potential customers: A business or organization that needs promotional material created on an intermittent basis and does not have the staff or time to do this task in-house.

Promotion: Contact businesses or organizations directly to promote your services. Provide samples of your work in addition to a résumé. If you are interested in promotional writing, send your résumé and samples of your work to advertising agencies.

If you are soliciting a commission from a magazine or newspaper, find out the name and correct title of the editor who handles freelance submissions. Publication directories or writers' markets references are not reliable sources for this type of information, and an editor is going to be suspicious of the quality of your research if you can't get his or her name and title right. Once you have the information, send a résumé, cover letter, and two to three samples of your work.

Writing is a competitive business and requires some aggression on your part to succeed at it. No matter what type of writing you plan to do, follow up your résumé and samples of your work with a telephone call: your client is unlikely to call you.

Associated businesses: Freelance editing, Technical writing.

3. Freelance editing

Description: As with freelance writing, there is a variety of opportunity in this service area. This can include editing promotional material or other in-house documents for businesses. As well, you can use your knowledge of grammar, punctuation, and sentence structure to edit books (especially vanity or short-run books), academic theses and research, and commemorative or specialty publications.

If you have an area of interest or specialized knowledge, consider focusing on it when promoting your editing services. This will help distinguish you from other similar services on-line. And because text-based material is easily transferred electronically, your potential clientele is not necessarily limited by geography.

Skills: Excellent knowledge of grammar, spelling, and sentence structure.

Equipment: You will need a computer capable of running word-processing software, a high-quality inkjet printer, and an Internet connection if you are doing work for clients who are not in your geographical area.

Potential customers: Magazines and newspapers creating special sections or publications, businesses that do not have the staff or time to edit in-house, on-line magazines, and graduate students and other academics.

Promotion: If you are targeting magazines, newspapers, and businesses, follow the advice for promoting freelance writing services (section **B.2.**). If you are targeting academics and graduate students, create a brochure describing your services and distribute copies to university department offices, libraries, and service bureaus (desktop publishing or photocopying centers). Consider creating a Web site describing your services to promote your services beyond your geographical area.

Associated businesses: Freelance writing, Word processing, Technical writing, Technical editing.

4. Technical writing

Description: Technical writing is currently much in demand as software and hardware manufacturers and service providers need people to create the documents and manuals to go with their products. The degree of technical knowledge you need, depends on the type of products or services your client is offering.

The readers of the documentation can be technological sophisticates or computing neophytes. For the latter, your ability to clearly translate technical information into concise, plain English (or other language) will keep the client coming back for more.

This business can be supplemented by your ability to create diagrams and illustrations as software and hardware documentation often employs these.

Skills: Strong writing skills and technical knowledge.

Equipment: A computer capable of running word-processing software and a high-quality inkjet printer. If your clients are not in your geographic area, an Internet connection is an asset.

Potential customers: Hardware and software manufacturers and providers of technical services.

Promotion: Contact your potential clientele directly and provide samples of your work with your résumé. There are several on-line forums and associations for technical writers; joining them may provide you with leads for this type of work.

Associated businesses: Freelance writing, Freelance editing, Technical editing.

5. Technical editing

Description: As with technical writing, this skill is currently in demand as software and hardware manufacturers and service providers need people to edit existing documentation and manuals. You may be required to simplify a highly technical document or update a manual for a new or modified version of a product or program.

Skills: Strong knowledge of grammar, spelling, and sentence structure in addition to technical knowledge.

Equipment: A computer capable of running word-processing software and a high-quality inkjet printer. If your clients are not in your geographic area, an Internet connection is an asset.

Potential customers: Software and hardware manufacturers, providers of technical services, and technical writers.

Promotion: Contact your potential clients directly and provide samples of your work with your résumé. Promote your services with the various on-line forums and associations for technical writers.

Associated businesses: Technical writing, Freelance writing, Freelance editing.

6. Genealogy research

Description: Increasing interest in the field of family histories can be seen in the number of genealogy Web sites, on-line forums, and software now available.

Because of the surge of interest, some countries, for example, Ireland, have put databases of birth, death, and marriage records on-line. Some small towns in Ontario and Quebec, which saw early waves of European immigration, are also making town and church records accessible over the Internet. Years ago, researchers would have had to travel to these places and wade through dusty volumes and archives.

Many people have the interest in tracing their family trees but not the time, patience, or familiarity with new technology to do a proper job.

This type of business, like other forms of research, still involves wading through vast amounts of information, but much of this can now be done from your computer.

Genealogy research involves taking the bits of information a client has about his or her ancestors and grafting it together to create a bigger picture. It includes locating documents, such as birth, death, and marriage certificates, and interviewing family members and friends of the client.

Skills: Research, interviewing, and writing skills and a familiarity with genealogy Web sites, forums, and on-line databases of information.

Equipment: You'll need a computer with a high-speed Internet connection so time on-line is spent researching and not waiting for Web pages to download. Your system must also be capable of running the software you select. If you are planning to present the client with a finished manuscript or book of your research, you will need a high-quality inkjet printer and flat-bed scanner (you won't want to use a sheet-fed scanner to digitize old photographs and documents).

A wide range of genealogy software is available which includes research advice, some on-line links, and methods of organizing the information you collect. Most of the consumer-oriented programs also include some form of desktop publishing and image-editing software to help create finished documents. This software is available in stores, but much of it is on-line or available through genealogy organizations. An unexpected source of professional genealogy software is the Mormon Church. Knowledge of ancestors is integral to this church's belief system. To aid Mormons in tracing family trees, church genealogists created software. Personal Ancestral File is a consumer version of this program.

Potential customers: Anyone with an interest in genealogy.

Promotion: Advertise in one of the many genealogy publications or on-line Web sites where you will reach people interested in this topic. The latter will be particularly effective since your potential clientele is not limited by geography.

Associated businesses: On-line research training, Multimedia genealogy publishing.

7. People tracing

Description: This type of business has many applications. Individuals may need to find someone, such as an old school friend or long lost family member, for personal reasons. Lawyers need to contact potential witnesses or experts, and bill collectors need to track down debtors. From the Internet you can search for telephone numbers and e-mail addresses, as well as databases of more personal information. Much of this information is readily available, but your marketing edge will be speed, familiarity with the sources, and knowing what kind of trails people leave on-line. A lot of time can be wasted sifting through the sheer volume of data available on-line. Knowing where to look first will give you an advantage.

Skills: Research skills and familiarity with on-line databases and search engines.

Equipment: A computer with a high-speed Internet connection. As your edge is speed, you want to spend your time researching, not waiting for Web pages to download.

Potential customers: Individuals, lawyers, bill collectors.

Promotion: Advertise on an on-line search engine or in publications for professionals such as lawyers.

Associated businesses: Genealogy research, Product and service tracing, Collection service.

8. Product and service tracing

Description: Like genealogy research and people tracing, much of this type of research can be done on-line. And like these other services, it is done for people who are short on time.

Product and service tracing involves tracking down hard-to-find or out-of-production goods, and providers of unusual services. It can also be a consulting service, assisting clients with needs who don't know much about the products or solutions that are available.

You can specialize in a particular area, such as software and hardware for businesses, finding collectibles or antiques for

individuals, or tracking down an expert in repairing mildew-damaged artwork.

Skills: Research skills, familiarity with on-line databases and search engines. If you are focusing on a particular area such as software, you'll need to keep up with the latest advances in the field.

Equipment: You will need a computer with a high-speed Internet connection so you spend time on-line researching and not waiting for Web pages to download.

Potential customers: Expanding businesses that cannot devote staff to this task, individuals who are avid collectors or are in search of a service but are short on time or are unfamiliar with on-line research techniques.

Promotion: If you are appealing to businesses, advertise in business-oriented publications or the business section of your local newspaper. If you are targeting individuals with special collections or interests, try advertising in such specialty publications. High-end home design or renovation magazines, for example, are good places to target readers interested in antiques or rare china who can afford this type of service. You can also promote your services via a Web site, as your clientele is not limited by geography.

Associated businesses: People tracing, Genealogy research.

9. Transcribing

Description: Transcribing services are required by a wide range of businesses and organizations. Transcribing involves taking recorded material and translating it into text.

You can supplement this service by offering to record the events yourself and laying out and publishing the recorded material in a format the client chooses, for example, a bound booklet or HTML document that can be viewed on the Web.

Skills: Fast and accurate typing, as well as knowledge of grammar and editing skills.

Equipment: A computer with word-processing software, a high-quality inkjet printer, and a tape recorder to play back the recorded event are the minimum equipment requirements for this type of service. You may also want to consider voice recognition software (and the requisite sound cards and hardware), which translates speech into text. This will save you having to type everything in, but keep in mind that voice recognition applications currently available are not 100% accurate and will necessitate thorough editing of the material. (This technology is rapidly improving, so keep an eye on advancements if you are considering this type of business.) If your services include creating a finished document, you'll need desktop publishing software. You will also need to purchase or rent the necessary recording equipment if you are recording the event in addition to transcribing it.

Potential customers: Associations and business organizations that take minutes of meetings, seminar and conference organizers.

Promotion: Create a brochure describing your services and target your potential clientele directly. Promoting your services on-line is an option, but as you are likely limited by geography, a Web site alone is not sufficient. You might consider it as an addition to other advertising, for example, you could include the Web site address in your promotional material as a place to go for more information.

Associated businesses: Translating, Word processing.

10. Translating

Description: If you are literate in two or more languages and have good writing and editing skills, consider this type of service. Depending on the languages in which you are literate (if your second language is widely used in business areas, it will be more valuable), your skills may be much sought after.

This work involves taking foreign-language documents and translating them into English or another language, or translating text created by the client into another language for use in promotional material or other documents, including spreadsheets and databases. It can also involve transcribing services.

Skills: Literacy in two or more languages, writing and editing skills.

Equipment: You will need a computer that can run office suite software (e.g., spreadsheets, databases, and word-processing applications), and a high-quality inkjet printer. An Internet connection if you are working with clients who are not in your geographical area is also necessary.

Potential customers: Import/export businesses or other companies doing business internationally.

Promotion: Contact foreign embassies or consulates as well as import/export businesses in your area. Register with translation agencies that already have a pool of clients. Consider on-line promotion with a Web site describing your services. The latter is a good option, because your potential clientele is not limited by geography.

Associated businesses: Transcribing, Word processing.

11. Foreign-language word processing

Description: Foreign-language word processing is one of the specialties mentioned in the description of word-processing services. This type of service involves all the aspects of word processing but is done in a language other than the native language of your geographical area.

Skills: Literacy in the language you are working, excellent writing and editing skills, as well as fast and accurate typing. Knowledge of the word-processing programs commonly used in the language you are working in. Knowledge of other office suite applications is an asset because it would allow you to create and incorporate tables and spreadsheets into the finished documents.

Equipment: You will need a computer capable of running office suite software, a high-quality inkjet printer, a sheet-fed or flatbed scanner, and OCR software if you are inputting paper-based documents. An Internet connection if you are working with clients who are not in your geographical area is also necessary. Depending on the characters used in the written form of the language your services are in, you will need some additional software that can recognize and create those characters.

Potential customers: Import/export businesses or other companies doing business internationally. Nonprofit or government agencies that create documents for foreign-language immigrants.

Promotion: Contact foreign embassies or consulates, nonprofit services and government agencies for immigrants, and companies that do business internationally. Register with translation agencies. Although you will not be performing translation services, their clients may at some time be in need of your services. Consider creating a Web site describing your services, which would promote your services beyond your geographical area.

Associated businesses: Transcribing, Translating, Word processing.

12. Electronic clipping service

Description: A traditional clipping service tracks articles about people, products, services, events, or trends that appear in newspapers, magazines, and journals. An electronic clipping service tracks the same topics but in on-line magazines, Web sites, and on-line forums.

The information gathered is then organized and transmitted to the client as a printed paper document or in electronic form. The latter can be a text-based document or in a format that preserves the graphical elements (including animation or video) of the Web page.

Skills: Excellent research skills, knowledge of Internet technology and Web search engines.

Equipment: A computer with a high-speed Internet connection and a high-quality inkjet printer capable of printing color are needed. If the client wants the information in electronic form, a high-capacity storage drive, such as Zip, MO, or CD-R, is an asset.

Potential customers: Any manufacturer or service provider that wants to track the reaction to a new product or find out about competitors' products. Organizations or agencies that want to track reaction to clients they represent or events they sponsor.

Promotion: Contact your potential clients directly. Advertise your services in publications produced for public relations or marketing professionals.

Associated businesses: On-line research training, People tracing, Product and service tracing.

13. Bid and grant proposal writing

Description: This type of writing involves working with nonprofit organizations trying to get funds from government agencies and private foundations, and/or businesses bidding on government contracts to supply services or products. The various levels of government or private agencies each have their own application and bid-tendering processes.

Depending on the application process, writing bids and grant proposals can also include creating a report using desktop publishing software or developing a multimedia presentation using some type of presentation graphics software.

This type of work would be a good choice for a person with experience in public service, running a business or nonprofit organization.

Skills: Excellent writing skills. Knowledge of the private and government grants that are available, and of the criteria for receiving the grants. Knowledge of the types of bids and the tendering process.

Equipment: A computer capable of running word-processing software and a high-quality inkjet printer. If your work includes desktop publishing or presentation graphics, you will need a computer with more memory, storage, and processing power.

Potential customers: Any business or organization wanting to access government tenders or grants that does not have a staff member who specializes in this type of work.

Promotion: Developing clients for this type of service requires a subtle promotional approach. Before contacting a potential client to tell him or her what you can do, you'll need some background on his or her business or organization. Your ability to network will serve you well in this type of work. Networking can provide you with information on clients you've already targeted and provide you with leads for new clients. Consider joining or speaking to associations of nonprofit organizations or to businesses seeking government contracts, such as construction companies, as a way of networking and promoting your services. If these groups have a newsletter or association magazine, consider placing an advertisement in it or ask if they would be interested in a regular column written by you.

Associated businesses: Annual report writing.

14. Résumé writing

Description: Creating a succinct, dynamic résumé and cover letter is a skill that many people do not have, despite other talents, strengths, and professional achievements.

These people are in the market for the services of someone who can extract the highlights of their professional and/or academic careers and tailor them to the requirements of prospective employers.

Different types of résumés and cover letters are required for job candidates responding to newspaper advertisements or on-line help-wanted notices, or those making cold calls, contacting employers who may or may not have positions open.

Computers and the Internet have added a few more complexities to the task of writing a successful résumé. Some employers ask applicants to respond by e-mail, which means applicants have less control over the appearance of their résumés on receipt. As well, the first eyes on these résumés are often electronic and not human. Many large companies now scan in paper-based résumés and, using some form of OCR software, search for key words and phrases to assess whether the résumés get to the next level of consideration.

These are all elements of job hunting that people who are looking for their first job or for a job for the first time in a decade are not likely to be aware of. They do not want to be experts in job hunting — they want a job.

Experience in a particular professional field, such as law, business administration, accounting, or publishing, is an asset.

This work can also include producing a finished résumé or series of résumés and cover letters using desktop publishing software, or creating résumés in a format that is viewable on-line.

Skills: Excellent writing skills. Knowledge of the way résumé scanning software works, as well as how to format e-mail and other digital documents.

Equipment: A computer capable of running word-processing software and a high-quality inkjet printer. If your service includes designing the résumé, you will need a computer with more processing power, RAM, and storage to run desktop publishing software. You should also consider investing in a laser printer depending on the number of finished résumés you will be producing. If the number is low it would probably be affordable to have the final documents printed at a service bureau.

Potential customers: Recent graduates, professionals who are already employed but desiring a change, and those who have been laid off or out of the job market for a period for various other reasons.

Promotion: Create a brochure and distribute copies to libraries, job centers, and service bureaus at educational institutions. Advertise in newsletters or other publications for professional associations. Consider creating a Web site promoting your skills and services.

Associated businesses: Job hunting training, Employer on-line hiring training.

15. Annual report writing

Description: Many businesses as well as nonprofit organizations and societies produce for shareholders and other stakeholders reports describing achievements in the past year and include projections and plans for the next year or next few years. Because this is done only once a year, they may not have staff with the skills or time to produce a professional, well-written report.

Creating an annual report involves writing about a company's or organization's successes and failures and may include a history of the organization; writing profiles of executives, board members, and directors; taking or commissioning photographs of these individuals; and creating charts and graphics.

This type of work can also include creating a multimedia presentation if, for example, the report is presented at an annual meeting.

Skills: Excellent writing and interviewing skills, knowledge of statistics, and an ability to synthesize large amounts of information into a clear, concise format.

If your service also involves designing the report, excellent design and layout skills are necessary, as is knowledge of professional printing processes.

Equipment: A computer capable of running word-processing software and a high-quality inkjet printer. If your service includes designing the report or a multimedia presentation, you will need a computer with more processing power, RAM, and storage to run desktop publishing or presentation graphics software. A laser printer, or access to a service bureau with one, is required unless you are delivering the finished report to the press in an electronic format.

Potential customers: Any business or organization that publishes an annual report.

Promotion: Target potential clients directly with a portfolio of your work. Advertise in publications targeting business executives. If there is a board of trade or chamber of commerce in your area, consider advertising in its newsletter, magazine, or on-line publication. The latter could link to your own Web site that describes your services.

Associated businesses: Desktop publishing, Copywriting, Bid and grant proposal writing, Annual report design and layout.

16. Copywriting

Description: "Copy" is the written or spoken element of any print or broadcast advertisement or other promotional or packaging material. Although advertising agencies and in-house marketing departments of large companies have their own copywriters, freelance writers are often needed when there is extra work or to provide a fresh point of view.

This type of work can be as simple as describing a service or product, or as complex as creating a campaign of print and broadcast advertising in conjunction with other marketing professionals.

Skills: Excellent writing and editing skills, and creativity. An ability to work well with clients and in conjunction with other advertising professionals, such as art directors, is also important.

Equipment: A computer capable of running word-processing software. Some form of Internet connection to submit drafts of your work to the client (so that your potential clientele isn't limited to your geographic area).

Potential customers: Advertising agencies and any business that produces its own promotional material.

Promotion: Consider joining an association of copywriters or marketing or advertising professionals to promote your skills and learn about copywriting opportunities. Send samples of your work along with your résumé to advertising agencies and in-house marketing departments at large companies, and remember to follow it up with a telephone call. If you are just getting started, consider doing work for nonprofit organizations to develop your skills, portfolio, and reputation. Also consider registering with an agency that represents freelance copywriters.

Associated businesses: Annual report writing.

17. Specialty magazine writing and editing

Description: Many professional organizations, private companies, and alumni or academic associations create magazines for their members or employees. Because production of such a publication is unrelated to their core business, they often contract out this work to freelance editors, writers, and desktop publishers.

Creating a specialty or in-house magazine involves writing, editing, image editing, and creating illustrations and graphics, or subcontracting or commissioning aspects you are not skilled in to freelance writers or artists. It can also include working with service bureaus and a professional printing plant, although this type of work can also be subcontracted to prepress and printing consultants who are versed in the quality, abilities, and prices of press plants in your area.

Putting together a specialty publication for an organization is an excellent way to gain experience in all the aspects of magazine publishing, which is otherwise prohibitive for an individual because of the paper and printing costs.

You can also supplement this work with a on-line version of the publication.

Skills: Writing, interviewing, editing, and layout skills. Depending on how much of the work you are doing yourself, you may also need to be a skilled photographer, illustrator, or graphic artist. An ability to work with clients — who will after all have the final word — is essential. You will also need knowledge of prepress and printing press services.

Equipment: A computer with sufficient RAM, storage, and processing power to run word-processing, desktop publishing, image-editing, and graphics software. Peripherals such as a flatbed scanner and laser printer are also useful. Access to a service bureau with scanners and lasers printers is an alternative if your initial budget can't stretch to include these items.

Potential customers: Professional organizations, private companies, and alumni or academic associations.

Promotion: Contact potential clients to find out whether they produce or plan to produce such a publication. If so, ask what their current arrangements are and based on their requirements, submit a proposal (including cost) to create the publication. Include samples of your work — and that of any graphic artist, photographer, or illustrator you'll be commissioning — with your submission. If you don't have experience in this area, consider doing this type of work on a volunteer basis for a nonprofit organization to develop your skills, portfolio, and reputation.

Associated businesses: Desktop publishing, Copywriting.

18. On-line magazine writing and editing

Description: This is another way of entering the publishing business, but one that gives you a little more creative freedom and opportunity to write about subjects that interest you than is possible when publishing a specialty magazine.

Unlike trade publications and specialty magazines, on-line magazines are not prohibitively expensive for the individual because you don't have to consider the cost of paper and printing. (If your on-line magazine becomes very popular, you will incur high traffic costs, but this is negligible compared to printing costs.)

With this type of publication, you don't need to please the client as you do with trade or specialty magazines, but you do need to appeal to and reach your readers, and to make any money, you need to attract advertisers.

There are many successful on-line magazines with respectable advertising revenues that were started by enthusiasts rather than by publishing professionals.

One strong advantage of on-line publications is that you can monitor the appeal of its various elements in a way that is more objective than the reader surveys paper-based publications rely on. With Web sites, you can count not only the number of hits a particular page gets but also the amount of time each reader spends before moving on to the next page. The accuracy of this type of information is very appealing to advertisers. Industry analysts also predict that the amount of on-line advertising is going to grow exponentially in the next few years.

Web publishers also have an advantage over print publishers in that they can change the content as often as they like. Longer feature stories, for example, could change weekly or monthly, but news items could be updated daily. Past issues can also be archived at the site and accessible to readers.

Skills: Excellent writing, editing, illustrating, and Web design skills and knowledge of Web image and text formats. As your publication develops, you may want to contract out some of this work. Web site design, for example, is one area where you may consider getting professional help or hiring a consultant. A site that is easily navigable, reliable, and free of glitches will be important in attracting advertisers. Web sites need constant attention and daily upkeep. Don't wait until readers let you know that things aren't working correctly.

Make sure you choose carefully when selecting the ISP to host your Web site. Find out how accessible technical help is and details of the ISP's subscriber-to-line ratio (how much incoming traffic it can handle). Changing service providers is not impossible but should be avoided.

Equipment: Computer with enough RAM, storage, and processing power to operate Web publishing, word-processing, image-editing, and graphics software, and a high-speed Internet connection. Having several different Web browsers installed on your computer is also advisable. Different Web browsers can interpret code (which includes color and placement of images) differently, and they do not all support every new Web format, such as frames. Having more than one browser installed allows you to see how people with various browsers will view your publication.

Potential customers: Readers with access to the Web.

Promotion: The key to the success of this type of publication, like any magazine, is coming up with concept, theme, or point of view that will have significant reader appeal. If you have an area of expertise or passion that you'd like to develop a magazine around, search on-line for publications with similar themes and consider how you could improve them or make your publication stand out from the crowd.

Once you are up and running, register your publication with as many search engines as possible so that on-line readers will be able to find your site easily.

Target readers with similar interests at trade shows or conferences. If your publication is about home renovation or gardening, for example, consider setting up a kiosk at a home show so visitors can check out the site and link to your advertisers' sites (your advertisers could help defray the cost of the booth and kiosk).

Associated businesses: Specialty magazine writing and editing, Web site design.

19. Information broker

Description: This type of service has similarities to an electronic clipping service and to other research services but involves sifting through and synthesizing the information you find into a form the client desires. You can tell a client who is writing or reporting on a particular person, event, product, or service, and your report will likely include an assessment of the information you found. Your appeal to clients will depend on your abilities in this area.

If your client wanted information on cost of living in U.S. cities, for example, you would probably find that statistics gathered by governments, antipoverty organizations, and real-estate institutes were dramatically different. Based on your knowledge of the biases and strengths or weaknesses of these organizations, and the differing criteria used in the studies, you will be able to provide your client with a more objective assessment.

This work will involve research in on-line and traditional newspapers, magazines, and journals, as well as delving into free and subscription-based databases.

Focusing on a particular area of expertise or interest is worth considering.

Skills: Excellent research and writing skills. Knowledge of on-line publications and databases and how to efficiently search through them to find the data you need from these vast resources.

Equipment: A computer capable of running word-processing and Web browser software and a high-speed Internet connection.

Potential customers: Businesses or organizations that do not have an in-house research department.

Promotion: If you have decided to focus on a particular type of information, consider advertising in a publication that serves professionals in this field. Advertise in publications or newsletters for business executives.

Associated businesses: On-line research training, Electronic clipping service.

C. GRAPHIC DESIGN

1. Graphic design

Description: Graphic design is a highly saleable skill, especially if you are familiar with the various software and hardware tools and formats used in computer-generated graphic design.

This type of service is required by businesses for a wide range of advertising and promotional material, to illustrate newspaper and magazine articles (both on-line and paper-based publications), for business documents such as annual reports, and for product packaging and logos.

Skills: Graphic design requires artistic skill as well as training and/or experience with the complex software and hardware required to create professional-looking illustrations and layouts.

A successful designer is also able to create a variety of styles and looks depending on clients' needs.

Equipment: A computer capable of running graphic design software, such as Adobe

Illustrator or CorelDRAW, and image-editing software such as Adobe PhotoShop or Micrografix Picture Publisher. Because this type of work can require having several programs running at the same time, the computer will need a significant amount of RAM (otherwise time is wasted closing and opening applications to avoid system crashes). For graphic design work, which involves memory-hungry files, you will need a system with a hearty processor and plenty of storage.

Graphic work also involves several peripherals, including a laser printer (unless the final output of your creations is electronic or is done at a service bureau), a high-capacity media drive (MO, Zip, or CD-R) for transferring large files to clients or service bureaus, and various input devices, such as a drawing tablet and pen.

A high-resolution, large-screen monitor is advisable for graphic design work so that you can get accurate color and are able to zoom in on fine details and see more detail on a full-screen view of your designs.

It is important to find out what the standard formats and media (e.g., tapes, diskettes, cartridges) are for the type of business you are doing if you are dealing with service bureaus or if your client requires a copy of your files to use or modify after your work is completed.

Potential customers: Advertising agencies, magazines and newspapers, any business requiring design services for product packing or promotional material.

Promotion: Contact clients directly. For this type of work, you will need to create a portfolio containing samples of your work. This can be a large, binder-style portfolio that contains full-sized samples of your work. You could also consider creating a CD-ROM containing samples of your work, in packaging you have also designed. This allows you to leave your work with the potential client in a format that is easily accessible.

Another promotional option is creating a Web site with an on-line gallery of your work. You could then include the Web site address in the résumé and cover letter you send or drop off with the client.

Consider joining an agency that represent graphic artists and designers, or a society for this type of professional where can keep up on technical advances in your area in addition to finding out about business opportunities.

Associated businesses: Image scanning and digitizing, Image enhancing, Clip art service.

2. Image scanning and digitizing

Description: This involves using various scanners (flatbed, slide, or handheld) to digitize images from paper-based formats, such as photographic prints or books, or film-based formats, such as slides.

Image scanning will also require delivering the digitized images in a format, such as CD-ROM, that clients can use.

This is an excellent side business if you already own a high-quality scanner for use in a related business, such as image enhancing or desktop publishing.

Skills: Familiarity with various graphic formats (e.g., EPS, TIFF, JPG); experience with scanning technology.

Equipment: A high-quality flatbed scanner, a slide scanner, and a computer with adequate RAM, storage, and processor power. To transfer the digitized images to clients, you will need some form of removable media drive, such as MO, Zip, CD-R, or CDRW, that can hold large image files. At 1.44 Mb, standard floppy diskettes do not have the capacity to hold large image files.

A high-resolution, large-screen monitor is also advisable for accurate color and so you can check the quality of detail in the digitized image.

Potential customers: Individuals wanting family photographs or documents in a format that can be viewed and edited on a computer — for use with genealogy software, for example. Businesses that require company logos or photographs be digitized for use on a Web site, multimedia business presentation, or for use in desktop publishing or word-processing software to create company documents.

Promotion: Create a brochure describing your services and distribute copies at public libraries and to businesses in your area. Consider advertising your service in publications for small business and entrepreneur associations. If this service is a sideline, promote it through your other business, letting clients know that this is an additional service you provide.

Associated businesses: Image-enhancing service, Document scanning, Data conversion.

3. Document scanning

Description: Like image scanning, this work involves scanning paper-based documents into an electronic format that can be edited, and in some cases archived and searched.

Creating an editable, electronic document is done with OCR software. The difficulty of this process depends on the quality of the documents being scanned and the intelligence of the software. Some OCR applications are capable of deciphering handwriting, while others are tripped up by fonts with elaborate serifs. Some software will link multiple pages together, so a multipage document can be easily scrolled through on screen as a single file.

Though this software is quite sophisticated, it is not perfect, and thorough editing is usually required (the client may be prepared to do this, however).

Because electronic text documents are smaller than image files, floppy diskettes may be sufficient for delivering the scanned documents to the client. You could also deliver this type of file electronically, via e-mail.

Skills: Familiarity with OCR software and word-processing formats. Experience with scanning technology.

Equipment: A computer capable of operating OCR and word-processing software. The type of scanner required depends on the volume of documents you will be scanning.

Flatbed scanners usually provide the best resolution but require you to lift the lid, align the document on the surface, and close the lid for each sheet you scan. A better choice for high-volume scanning is a scanner with some type of automated feeder. This type of scanner is called a sheet-fed scanner and models are available for individual use or for high-volume, professional use (some flatbed scanners do have feeder attachments).

Potential customers: Any business or organization that needs printed material transferred to a digital format.

Promotion: Create a brochure describing your services and distribute copies to businesses and organizations in your area. Consider advertising your service in magazines or newsletters published by or for professional or business organizations.

Associated businesses: Data conversion.

4. Image enhancing

Description: This work involves taking images that have been scanned or that are already in an electronic format and enhancing them. Image enhancing is the electronic equivalent of being a darkroom technician, capable of photographic tricks such as dodging and burning.

These tricks include minor changes, such as correcting overall color, contrast, darkness, and saturation. Depending on your skill, it can also include removing blemishes, adding or removing objects, and altering or enhancing the color of an individual element of an image.

It can also involve grafting elements from different images together.

Skills: Along with a good photographic or artistic eye, you will need training in or experience with image-editing software such as Adobe PhotoShop (there are many other image-editing programs, but this is currently the industry standard), which is a powerful but complex tool. Knowledge of image formats, such as JPG, TIFF, and EPS.

Equipment: A computer with the processing power, RAM, and storage capacity to operate image-editing software, and the software itself, which for this type of service can be a significant investment.

To transfer the enhanced images to clients, you will need some form of removable media drive, such as MO, Zip, CD-R, or CDRW, that can hold large image files. At 1.44 Mb, current floppy diskettes do not have the capacity to hold such files.

A high-resolution, large-screen monitor is advisable for image enhancing work, so that you can get accurate color and are able to zoom in on fine details and see more detail on a full-screen view of your enhanced images.

Potential customers: Advertising agencies or publications that use high-quality images only occasionally or that do not have staff trained in this type of work, individuals or organizations with damaged family or archival photographs they would like repaired and preserved in an electronic format.

Promotion: Distribute samples of your work — the before and after versions of the images

— directly to potential clients. Consider creating and promoting a Web site that includes samples of your work.

Associated businesses: Image scanning and digitizing, Clip art service.

5. Architectural and computer-aided design

Description: This can involve designing or creating drawings of buildings, homes, or products using computer-aided design (CAD) software.

With larger projects, architects and designers employed by architecture firms are invited to present design ideas as part of the bidding process for the project. Individuals or small businesses planning a renovation or new building, however, may want to commission an architect or designer to get some idea of what is possible within budget restrictions. The architect or designer is paid for the time taken to assess the client's needs and to create the plans, as the project may be a long way from completion.

Product design would also be done on this type of freelance basis, with the client needing accurate drawings of a completed or proposed item for copyright purposes or for negotiating production of the object with a manufacturer.

Skills: Architectural, drafting, or design training (depending on the type of work you are doing, you may require a license). Experience with CAD software and various input peripherals, such as graphics tablets, scanners, and plotters. If you are designing buildings or proposed renovations to an existing building or home, familiarity with existing municipal building codes and standards is required. Depending on the quality of rendering required, you may need a high-quality laser printer or access to a service bureau that can produce blueprints or other large-format prints.

Equipment: CAD software and a computer with the processing power, RAM, and storage capacity to run this software. A high-resolution, large-screen monitor is also a good idea, so you can zoom in on fine details and see more of the complete drawing on the screen without having to scroll. Input devices such as graphics tablets and scanners.

Potential customers: Individuals renovating or building homes. Businesses renovating or building offices or plants.

Promotion: Advertise your services in the home section of your local newspaper or in local home design or renovation publications. Advertise in publications for small- to medium-sized businesses.

Associated businesses: Interior design.

6. Interior design

Description: The skills of an interior designer are commonly sought after to give the inside of a home a unified, polished look. This same service is also required by businesses: storefront operations, offices, and even areas of a manufacturing facility may all have need for an interior designer.

This type of service can include coming up with the design ideas based on the client's requirements (including budget, of course) and presenting the ideas to the client in an electronic or paper-based format. Software is now available that allows you to create a three-dimensional image of the interior you are designing and allows you to easily alter the color and texture of walls, floors, or furniture. Some software publishers also allow you to access databases of new furniture, accessories, paint colors, and fabric designs from their Web sites to include in your presentations to clients.

Interior design can also include finding and buying the necessary materials and overseeing the work.

Skills: Some form of training or experience in this type of design.

Equipment: Interior design software, computer with processor, RAM, and storage capacity needed to run this graphic-rich software. A high-resolution, large-screen monitor is also advisable so color is accurate and you can zoom in on details in the design plans you will be presenting to clients. An Internet connection if you are accessing the software publishers' databases of furniture, accessories, and fabrics, or if you need to research unusual or hard-to-find items online.

Potential customers: Individual homeowners or businesses planning to update their interiors.

Promotion: Advertise in the home section of local newspapers or in local home magazines. If you are targeting businesses, consider placing a display advertisement in your local Yellow Pages or other directory of business services.

Associated businesses: Garden and landscape design.

7. Garden and landscape design

Description: Garden and landscape design is another service that is sought after by individual home owners and businesses of all sizes.

This work can be a basic consulting service for new homeowners who are interested in gardening but don't know where to begin, or it can involve the planning, purchasing of supplies, planting, and upkeep of the garden for an individual household or business. This type of design service nicely complements an existing gardening or landscaping business.

There are a lot of garden design and landscape software programs available, ranging from simple consumer versions to complex professional versions. The better programs have databases of flowers, shrubs, and trees for a variety of climates. They can also show you how a certain configuration of flora — based on factors such as geography and orientation to the sun — will look in spring, summer, fall, and winter, and how it will look in one, five, or ten years. Based on the water, fertilizer, and cutting or pruning requirements of the garden, this software can also help you draw up a maintenance plan for the garden or yard if you are not doing the upkeep yourself.

Skills: Some training or experience in garden and landscape design.

Equipment: You'll need garden and/or landscape design software, and a computer with a processor, RAM, and storage capacity needed to run this graphic-rich software. A high-resolution, large-screen monitor is also advisable so clients can have a clear, detailed, and accurate picture of your garden or landscape plan.

Potential customers: New homeowners, businesses, or institutions with some type of garden or grounds in need of your skills.

Promotion: Luckily, unlike interior design, you can see which businesses or institutions are in need of your services by simply driving or walking by their premises. Target these clients directly with a brochure describing your services, or even a draft plan or image of the improvements you can make based on a certain budget. (Note: don't make this proposal too detailed or they will have no need for your services!) If you are targeting new homeowners, consider advertising in the gardening section of your local newspaper, or produce a brochure describing your services and pay for it to be distributed by your local welcome wagon or other advertising vehicle that targets new homeowners.

Associated businesses: Interior design.

8. Clip art service

Description: Many newspapers, magazines, or advertising agencies use collections of stock images to enhance their publications and promotional materials. The demand for clip art is steady because a particular style of image can become quickly outdated or commonplace. Images of consumer items such as cars or computers, for example, need to be updated annually.

Clip art images can include photographs, cartoons, fonts, icons, and illustrations in a wide range of styles depicting common objects, expressions, situations, or landscapes.

This type of service is particularly suited to a computer-based business. Illustration and image-editing software gives illustrators and graphic artists powerful tools for their craft and allows them to easily correct or slightly alter an image.

Computers are also useful as a tool for delivering clip art — images can be sent on CD-ROM or downloaded from a Web site.

Skills: Graphic art, illustration, or photography training or experience. Familiarity with various image formats (e.g., JPG, TIFF, EPS).

Equipment: Graphic art and image-editing work involves large files and the use of several applications simultaneously, so you'll need a computer with a powerful processor, plenty of RAM, and large storage capacity. A high-resolution, large-screen monitor for color accuracy and detailed work. Peripherals for this type of work may include a flatbed scanner, slide scanner, and graphics tablet.

You will also need to invest in professional graphic design, illustration, image-editing, and special-effects software. This can eat up a considerable amount of your budget. Consider buying older versions of these packages, which can then be upgraded when you can afford to.

As well, a high-speed Internet connection is advisable. If clients will be ordering and downloading clip art images from your Web site, you will also need to set up an on-line payment system. Contact ISPs, banks, and other financial institutions to find out what electronic commerce services they provide. For your Web site you'll also need some form of Web site design software that is sophisticated and powerful enough to showcase your creations.

If you plan to distribute your work on CD-ROM, you'll need a CD-R or CDRW drive (both types of drives allow you to copy your work onto a disc that is readable in a regular CD-ROM drive, the latter drive allows you to reuse the disc, as you do with floppy diskettes). These types of drives are not suitable for making mass copies of a CD-ROM but are suitable for small batches or special orders for individual clients.

Potential customers: Newspapers, magazines, advertising agencies, and independent graphic artists and designers.

Promotion: Create a brochure or catalogue containing samples of your work and your Web site address and distribute copies to your target customers. Register your Web site with as many search engines as you can — this allows people who are outside of your geographical area to locate your work by typing in key words (make sure the text on your Web site clearly describes the images and service you provide).

Associated businesses: Web and business presentation clip art, Graphic design.

9. Web and business presentation clip art service

Description: This service is like a traditional clip art service: creating stock images and selling them to businesses for their use in on-line publications or promotional material.

Stock art for Web sites and business presentations includes the same photos, fonts, and illustrations created for traditional clip art but in formats suitable for use on the Web (e.g., JPG, GIF). Clip art for the Web can incorporate animation segments, three-dimensional icons and graphics, as well as sound and video clips (see section **C.10.**).

Skills: Graphic art, illustration, photography, or animation training or experience, and familiarity with various on-line image formats (e.g., JPG, GIF).

Equipment: As with a traditional clip art service, this service involves large files and the use of several applications simultaneously, so you'll need a computer with a powerful processor, plenty of RAM, and large storage capacity, and a high-resolution, large-screen monitor for color accuracy and detailed work. Peripherals for this type of work may include a flatbed scanner, slide scanner, and graphics tablet.

You will also need to invest in professional graphics and special-effects and image-editing software. If your budget is tight, consider buying older versions of these packages and upgrading them when you can afford to.

As well, you'll need a high-speed Internet connection. If clients will be ordering and downloading clip art images from your Web site, you will also need to set up an on-line payment system with a financial institution or through an ISP. For your Web site you'll also need some form of Web site design software that is sophisticated and powerful enough to showcase your creations.

Potential customers: Any on-line publication; retailers, manufacturers, or service providers that maintain a Web site or intranet (internal corporate network) for promotional purposes.

Promotion: Create a brochure or catalogue containing samples of your work and with your Web site address, and distribute copies to your target customers. Register your site with as many search engines as you can — this allows people who are outside of your geographical area to locate your work easily.

Associated businesses: Clip art service, Graphic design.

10. Web sound and video clip service

Description: The multimedia nature of the Web and presentation graphics software means businesses can incorporate sound and video clips into their Web sites. And as with other clip art, there is a demand for high-quality clips of common sights and sounds, whether natural and ambient or set up and involving some type of special effect. Sounds can include bird chirps, sirens, clapping, tires screeching, and even a variety of musical clips. Video clips can include sunsets, sailboats, people shaking hands, and facial expressions.

As this type of work can involve investment in expensive professional quality audio or video equipment, it is an excellent complement to an existing recording or video business.

Like other clip art services, you can deliver your clips on some form of high-capacity media such as CD-ROM, or have customers download the clips from your Web site.

Skills: Training or experience in recording and editing digital video or audio. Familiarity with Web and presentation graphics formats.

Equipment: In addition to the recording equipment, you'll need a computer with a powerful processor, plenty of RAM, and large storage capacity.

You will also need video or audio editing software. In recent years, several companies have released desktop versions of this type of software. This area of software development is becoming very competitive because of consumer interest in editing their own videos. While it is expensive, expect it to become easier to use and more fully featured. Also expect prices to drop as competition heats up.

As well, you'll need a high-speed Internet connection. If clients will be ordering and downloading clips from your Web site, you will also need to set up an on-line payment system with a financial institution or through an ISP. For your Web site you'll also need some form of Web site design software that allows you to showcase your audio or video sequences.

Potential customers: Any on-line publication; retailers, manufacturers, or service providers that maintain a Web site or intranet (internal corporate network) for promotional purposes, as well as designers or marketing departments that develop business presentations.

Promotion: Create a brochure describing your service and with your Web site address, and distribute copies to your target customers. Register your site with as many search engines as you can — this allows people who are outside of your geographical area to locate your work easily.

Associated businesses: Clip art service, Web and business presentation clip art service.

11. Sign, banner, and poster design

Description: Eye-catching signs, banners, and posters are in demand by businesses, institutions, or organizations to promote events, special sales, services, or even to help newcomers navigate through or around an environment or institution.

Skills: This type of design requires artistic skill as well as some type of training or experience in signage and knowledge of fonts. Training and/or experience with the complex software and hardware required to create professional-looking signs is also an asset.

Equipment: You will need a computer capable of running graphic design, font, and image-editing software; a significant amount of RAM; a hearty processor; plenty of storage capacity; and a high-resolution, large-screen monitor for accurate color representation and working on fine details.

Peripherals for this type of work include a flatbed scanner, drawing tablet and pen, and some type of high-capacity media drive, such as MO, Zip, CD-R, or CDRW (check with service bureaus you are dealing with to find out what format they prefer). Because the final output of signs, banners, and posters either involves a mass printing, or printing on a large format or with special paper or signage material, you will most likely have this done by a service bureau or at a printing plant.

The type of printer you have, therefore is less important, but a high-quality color inkjet maybe useful for printing mockups and drafts for your clients.

Potential customers: Any business, institution, or service provider that does not have an in-house graphics or signage department.

Promotion: Target your potential clients directly with a brochure that contains samples of your work and description of your services. Advertise in the business section of your local newspaper or in business or professional association publications.

Associated businesses: Graphic design, Clip art service.

12. Customized gift and promotional product creation

Description: This specialty area of graphic design used to be the exclusive territory of manufacturers, but with the advent of consumer-oriented graphic and image-editing software and reasonably priced, high-quality color inkjet printers, items such as children's books, calendars, and T-shirts can easily be customized for one-off or small scale production. Larger-scale production of these or other items including mouse pads, mugs, or key chains can be subcontracted to a manufacturer after you have done the design work.

This type of service would be a good adjunct to other graphic design services.

Skills: Some artistic skill and experience with the graphic and image-editing software and hardware required to create professional-looking products.

Equipment: A computer capable of running graphic design and image-editing software will need a significant amount of RAM, a hearty processor, and plenty of storage. As with other design work, you'll need a high-resolution, large-screen monitor for accurate color and detail work.

You'll also need a flatbed or slide scanner and high-quality color inkjet printer (while the prices of color lasers are dropping, they are still quite prohibitive) and the special paper or media (such as iron-on transfers) needed for the items you are producing. You may want to contact the manufacturer directly to see if you can buy the specialty paper and iron-on transfer products in bulk.

If you are dealing with service bureaus or printers for high-volume printing, you'll need some type of high-capacity media drive (e.g., MO, Zip, or CD-R) to transfer these large files. Find out what the printer and service bureau use so there are no compatibility problems.

Potential customers: Small- to medium-sized businesses and organizations that need customized promotional material. Individuals who want specialty gift items.

Promotion: Create a catalogue with samples of your work and target your business or institutional clients directly. Advertise in magazines, newsletters, or on-line publications targeting marketing professionals in your area.

To market customized gift items, consider renting a booth at a craft show, community fair, or shopping mall in your area, and display various customized samples of your work.

Associated businesses: Graphic design.

13. Print and prepress consulting

Description: This type of work involves being the intermediary between marketing departments, advertising agencies, or design freelancers and service bureaus and printing services. Your value is being able to match your clients with the services that suit their needs and budgets. This type of service is needed if clients are printing specialty reports and promotional material and do not have expertise in this area. It also involves press checks.

In addition to paper-based products, such as annual reports or flyers, you could consult on the printing of packaging or specialty promotional items, such as T-shirts, key chains, and mouse pads. This service can also include tracking down supplies — for example, unusual paper.

Skills: Knowledge of the services and prices of service bureaus and printing services in your area. You'll also need to know about services and prices outside your region and possibly even outside your country, if you are dealing with less common types of printing, such as CD-ROM packaging.

Equipment: As with other consulting services, your equipment is not that important since the design work is done by the client or by another freelance service. Some type of Internet connection is advisable for researching prices and unusual services or supplies.

Potential customers: Independent graphic artists, marketing departments, and advertising agencies without an in-house media buyer specializing in print.

Promotion: Contact your potential clients directly to discuss your skills and the services you can offer. Advertise in publications targeting marketing and graphic design professionals in your area.

Associated businesses: People tracing, Product and service tracing.

D. MULTIMEDIA

1. Multimedia genealogy publishing

Description: There has been a recent surge in interest in family histories and genealogy that can be seen in the number of genealogy software applications, Web sites, and on-line forums. Although many people are successfully tracking the paths of their ancestors and finding old documents and photographs, they don't know how — or don't have time — to organize the material they've gathered.

This type of service involves taking this material and organizing it into a book or CD-ROM (multiple copies can be made of both of these and distributed to family members), or some form of multimedia presentation for a family gathering.

A Web site is another good format for publishing this type of information, as it can be viewed by family members living in other regions or countries, and can serve as a forum for gathering new stories and images of family members and ancestors. A Web site can also include sound and video clips in addition to photographs and documents such as birth, death, and marriage certificates, and diplomas and other educational and professional papers.

Skills: Excellent design, layout and organization skills. Knowledge of the various media formats and standards.

Equipment: Desktop publishing, image-editing, and Web site design software (some genealogy software includes aspects of these applications, but they tend to be "lite" versions with fewer features); a computer with the processor, RAM, and storage capacity required to run these applications. A flatbed scanner (a sheetfed scanner is not suitable for scanning fragile documents or photographs), slide scanner, and high-quality color inkjet for drafts will also be needed.

Potential customers: Individuals with an interest in genealogy who have more money than skill or time.

Promotion: Advertise in one of the many genealogy publications or on-line Web sites where you will reach people interested in this topic. This is a good option as your potential clientele is not limited by geography. Create your own Web site promoting your services and register it with several search engines.

Associated businesses: Desktop publishing, Genealogy research, Web site design.

2. Multimedia kiosk design and consulting

Description: Kiosks are standalone or networked computers placed in public locations or common areas, such as hotel lobbies, bus and train stations, shopping malls, and sporting event venues. Kiosks have a simplified interface, such as a touch screen, and allow people to easily search for information.

Applications for kiosks including finding the location or availability of products in a large store; finding the name of a book, CD-ROM, or other product based on scant information; helping visitors find directions; promoting events; and showing tourists highlights of a city or other tourist destination.

Kiosks can also be set up as an advertising vehicle in public places. Some kiosks will print out the information on products or directions that the user requires.

This type of designing and consultation work includes creating a multimedia kiosk presentation from video, audio, text, and graphic material supplied by the client and can extend to gathering and creating this material yourself or commissioning other artists and writers to do so.

Skills: Experience or training in multimedia design and programming. For kiosks linked to inventory and sales databases, knowledge of database programming and networking technology is required. You also need to be familiar with kiosk hardware and technology, such as touch screens or simplified keyboards and other input devices.

Equipment: The kiosk hardware will be purchased or leased by the client. You will need a computer with the processing power, RAM, and storage capacity to create and edit the multimedia presentations. A portable computer is an asset as you will be working both in your own and the client's environment.

Potential customers: A large store or venue in which visitors or customers may need access to directions or product information. Conference or event organizers.

Promotion: Target potential clients directly and offer to demonstrate the potential of this type of technology for them. Offer to demonstrate your services to local business, tourism, or governmental organizations, such as a chamber of commerce, board of trade, or regional parks, recreation, or facilities department.

Associated businesses: Multimedia genealogy publishing, Multimedia business presentation design.

3. Multimedia business presentation design

Description: New software and presentation hardware systems make it possible to employ multimedia elements in business presentations to raise them above a series of transparencies or slide shows of charts, diagrams, and point-form lists of achievements or projections. They can now include sound, music, video, and animation clips, and even live links to Web sites or direct links to individuals in remote locations (using video-conferencing technology). As well, the presentation system can be linked to a printer so selected diagrams or notes can be printed on request following the presentation.

Although the possibilities are endless and complex, this type of work could also be as simple as helping a sales professional, or team of professionals, prepare a multimedia presentation that he or she would run on laptop computers when meeting with clients.

Skills: Familiarity with the many aspects (e.g., audio, video, image editing, and animation) of multimedia technology and specialized software and hardware. Experience in the pacing and formalities of business presentations.

Equipment: Presentation graphics software and a computer with a processor, RAM, and storage capacity sufficient to run it (a portable computer would be a wise choice for this type of service). There is a wide range of presentation software, some of which is included in office suite software, but this may not be powerful enough or have enough features for your purposes. Some examples of professional, fully featured presentation graphics programs are PowerPoint, Harvard Graphics, and Freelance Graphics. If you are including video sequences from an analog source, your computer will need a video capture board to digitize the sequence for editing.

Depending on the type of presentation you are designing, you will also need presentation peripherals, such as a multimedia projector, white board, or other form of screen. This equipment could be supplied by the client or leased on the client's behalf.

Potential customers: Any business or organization that needs to make presentations, to shareholders, employees, or members (annual general meetings, for example), or to potential clients as part of a bid on a project or contract.

Promotion: Target potential clients directly with a presentation that demonstrates the possibilities and versatility of your service.

Associated businesses: Multimedia kiosk design and consulting, Multimedia genealogy publishing.

4. Desktop video editing

Description: This is another area where professionals have benefited from the surge of consumer interest in this type of technology. Because both video cameras and computers are becoming more popular, there has been a desire for consumer-priced software that marries the two, allowing users to edit their own videos on home computers. This has resulted in video editing software becoming more fully featured, easier to use, and cheaper to buy.

A desktop video editing service can serve both business and nonbusiness clients. For business clients, you can edit the video and, using presentation graphic software, prepare a very professional, polished product for use in presentations or sales. This work could also be extended to include shooting the necessary video yourself.

For families or individuals, you could help compile and edit vacation and other personal videos into a viewable format. This could even incorporate still photographs, old 8 mm film sequences (that have been transferred to video or digital video format), and some form of narration or a musical background.

Skills: You will need some type of training or experience in video or film editing, and knowledge of current digital video formats and compression standards.

Equipment: A computer with a powerful processor, plenty of RAM, and large storage capacity, and video editing software.

If you are editing video from a VCR or nondigital camera, you will need a video capture board or a video codec (a hardware circuit) that converts analog video into digital code for editing on a computer and then back to analog for final output on video. If the edited video sequences are to be used in a digital format, such as a video CD or broadcast over the Internet, you will also need to compress the video — this can be done by the video codec.

Potential customers: Businesses that want to promote a venue, service, or product, and families that want to compile personal video tape, but don't have the time, equipment, or skill to do so.

Promotion: List your business in the Yellow Pages or other directory of business services in your area. Advertise your services in publications targeting marketing professionals. Create a brochure describing your services and target potential business clients directly. Distribute brochures to public family-oriented places, such as libraries and community centers.

Associated businesses: Web sound and video clip service, Multimedia business presentation design.

E. BUSINESS ACCOUNTING, PLANNING, AND MANAGEMENT

1. Business plan writing

Description: A clear, well-written, detailed business plan is essential in persuading investors — whether private investors or institutional investors such as banks — that a

35

proposed business is worth their consideration.

This service can be limited to writing up the information provided to you by the client, or it can extend to helping the client plan the business itself and suggesting the type of investors the client should consider approaching.

As well, a business plan service can include a multimedia presentation to potential investors.

Skills: Ability to write clearly and in an organized way about financial plans; this includes an understanding of financial projections and statistics.

Experience starting and running your own business, or some type of venture capital or investment experience is an asset.

Equipment: A computer that can run word-processing or office suite software (the latter if you are including charts and other graphics to illustrate the plan). A high-quality color inkjet printer for drafts of the plan. The final plan should be printed on a laser printer, but this can be done through a service bureau if your initial budget cannot accommodate the more expensive printer.

Potential customers: Entrepreneurs interested in starting a new business.

Promotion: Advertise your services in the business section of a local newspaper or in business or entrepreneurial publications. You could also consider creating a Web site that promotes your service. If you do develop a Web site, register it with several search engines, so potential clients doing research on-line can find you easily.

Associated businesses: Expense analysis.

2. Billing service

Description: This service involves sending out bills for a range of professionals or small service providers who don't have the staff, time, or experience to do their own billing. A billing service can also extend to consulting on setting up billing software and hardware systems for new clients or for clients whose businesses have grown and who wish to have their billing done in-house.

This service is an excellent adjunct to other accounting services.

Skills: Experience or training in basic accounting, and familiarity with any taxes on the services exacted in your province.

Equipment: A computer capable of running accounting database software, and a laser printer to output professional-looking invoices and stationery. Accounting database software and possibly some form of office suite software if form letters are required with the billing.

Potential customers: Professionals or small service providers, such as dentists, veterinarians, landscapers, house painters, or repair services.

Promotion: Advertise your services in a local newspaper. Contact your potential clients directly to promote your services. Consider offering potential clients a one-month trial of your service for a nominal fee.

Associated businesses: Bookkeeping, Collection service.

3. Bookkeeping

Description: Bookkeeping is a service you can provide for small business operators or professionals who do not have the staff, time, or experience to perform this essential task.

As with running a billing service, bookkeeping can extend to consulting on setting up bookkeeping software and hardware systems for new clients or for clients whose businesses have grown and who wish to have their bookkeeping done in-house.

Skills: Training or experience in bookkeeping.

Equipment: A computer capable of operating bookkeeping software, which can range from simple DOS-based programs to more complex and elaborate graphical interfaces that require a robust processor and more RAM. Your choice of bookkeeping or accounting software will depend on clients' needs.

Potential customers: Any small business operator, service provider, or professional. This could include the same types of businesses and services noted under billing, as well as artisans or artists who would rather devote time to their craft than keeping track of suppliers' invoices and orders and payments for their products.

Promotion: Advertise your services in a local newspaper. Contact your potential clients directly to promote your services.

Consider offering potential clients a one-month trial of your service for a nominal fee. If you are targeting a particular type of client, such as artisans, consider advertising in an association publication or newsletter.

Associated businesses: Billing service, Utility bill auditing.

4. Collection service

Description: Bill collection can take a lot of time and is essential for small business operators or service providers but is something they often do not have time to do.

Bill collectors sometimes buy the debt or outstanding amount at a reduced rate and make their money by recovering the total amount. It can also be done for a percentage of the money collected for the client.

A computer is used in this type of service for accounting purposes but is also helpful for tracing people via the Internet.

Skills: A confident and determined personality is essential for this type of service. Bill collecting experience is an asset, as well as familiarity with Internet search engines and other on-line databases.

Equipment: A computer capable of running accounting software, and an Internet connection.

Potential customers: Any small business, supplier, or service provider having difficulty collecting from clients or customers.

Promotion: Advertise your services in a local newspaper. Contact your potential clients directly to promote your services.

Consider advertising in a publication or newsletter that targets small businesses. List your service in the Yellow Pages or other directory of business services.

Associated businesses: Billing service.

5. Expense analysis

Description: This type of consulting work can be done as a one-time consultation for a business, association, or institution that is reorganizing, or as a monthly or annual consultation for these same groups that want a continuing unbiased view on how and where they can make extra savings.

Analyzing expenses includes auditing all aspects of spending by an organization, such as expense claims, vehicle use, equipment purchases, and contracts with suppliers, service providers, and subcontractors. The audit would include a final report of recommendations.

Skills: Experience or training in business management and/or accounting, and good analytical and research skills.

Equipment: A computer capable of running office suite software (including word-processor and spreadsheet applications) and an inkjet printer for the final report. An Internet connection would be helpful for researching alternative supply sources or getting quotes on various services.

Potential customers: Any business association or institution, including nonprofit organizations, that does not have sufficient management personnel for this task, or those looking for a new perspective on their operations.

Promotion: Contact potential clients directly with a letter describing your services (including, or making available on request, references from current or former clients). It will require some research to make sure you are targeting the correct person within an organization. Join or attend functions of local business associations, such as a board of trade or chamber of commerce, as a way of networking and getting leads on business opportunities.

Associated businesses: Utility bill auditing, Financial planning and management.

6. Inventory service

Description: An inventory service can include auditing a client's inventory on a regular basis. It can also extend to setting up a computerized inventory system for the client.

The former is usually done on a monthly or annual basis and requires working late evenings or over weekends during nonbusiness hours. The inventory can include the stock or supplies of a store or service provider, or even an annual review of assets (e.g., furniture, equipment, and vehicles) of a large company, institution, or organization.

Skills: Good organization skills and an ability to work quickly and efficiently. If you are setting up an inventory/sales system for the client, you will need to be familiar with all aspects of this technology, from cash registers to database technology.

Equipment: If you are reviewing the inventory of a store, it may already have a barcode system allowing items to be swiped with a handheld scanner and the information gathered to be transmitted to a database from which a report is issued. If this type of system is not in place, you could consult with the organization and arrange for them to lease or buy such equipment.

If it is a small or one-time inventory, you could set up a similar system with one or more personal digital assistants (PDAs). The inventory can be registered on these handheld computers, which have touch screen interfaces, and the information easily downloaded to a computer running spreadsheet software. An inkjet printer is needed for producing a final report.

Potential customers: Stores, restaurants, manufacturers, and organizations with large amounts of products, supplies, or furniture and equipment.

Promotion: List your business in the local Yellow Pages or other directory of business services. Advertise in the business section of a local newspaper or in business publications. Create a brochure describing your services and distribute copies directly to potential clients.

Associated businesses: Bookkeeping.

7. Utility bill auditing

Description: Utility bill auditing is another auditing service which requires you to review current spending practices and to

make recommendations for short- or long-term savings.

The recommendations can cover heating, lighting, and equipment use, and can also include suggestions on insulation or seasonal hours of operation that take advantage of natural light. There may also be tax exemptions in some regions for businesses that switch to furnaces that use a certain type or fuel, or change to a more efficient lighting system.

Skills: Excellent analytical and research skills. Knowledge of the various utilities in your area, as well as familiarity with various forms of heating, lighting, and power supplies.

Equipment: A computer capable of running spreadsheet software and an Internet connection for researching and receiving on-line quotes for various rates and services. An inkjet printer for producing a final report.

Potential customers: Companies or organizations, including government, with large office, manufacturing, or institutional facilities.

Promotion: Create a brochure promoting your service and distribute copies directly to potential clients. You could also offer a short seminar for a local business association or governmental organization on the benefits of your type of service (taking care, or course, not to give away all your secrets).

Associated businesses: Ergonomics consulting, Expense analysis.

8. Accounts payable and payroll system service

Description: This service is provided to small- or medium-sized businesses or organizations that do not have the staff, time, or experience to do this essential task.

It requires keeping track of product or supply purchases and payroll, and issuing checks to suppliers and staff.

Skills: Accounting experience; familiarity with payroll software; familiarity with municipal, provincial, and federal taxes, deductions, and exemptions that may apply to purchases and paychecks.

Equipment: A computer capable of running payroll software, which can range from simple DOS-based programs to Windows applications with more elaborate graphical interfaces requiring a powerful processor and more RAM. Depending on the number of checks issued, you may also need a printer configured for this task. Current models are similar to dot matrix printers, which feed through a continuous stack (rather than single sheets) of preprinted blank checks.

Potential customers: Small- to medium-sized businesses.

Promotion: Advertise your services in the business section of your local newspaper. List your business in the Yellow Pages or any other directory of local business services.

Associated businesses: Bookkeeping.

9. Client database service

Description: There is a wide range of database software designed specifically for tracking calls and updating information on customers and clients. This category of software, called contact management, is quite complex and can require some expertise in setting up and training users.

This type of consulting work can be ongoing as new staff needs to be trained, as software is upgraded, or if the organization wants to convert to a different program.

With new technology, databases can also be accessed remotely, or updates made from data downloaded from handheld or laptop computers. Your knowledge of these advances and ability to implement the various options will help you keep up with or ahead of the competition.

Skills: Good organization skills and experience with various forms of database software and hardware.

Equipment: Your equipment is not that important, as the work is done in the client's environment.

Potential customers: Any business with a sales force or organizations with a need to contact or track clients, customers, or patients (e.g., a medical practice).

Promotion: List your business in the Yellow Pages or other directory of local business services. Advertise your service in publications that target salespeople or business executives.

Associated businesses: Database management.

10. Property management

Description: Property management includes aspects of accounting in addition to the responsibilities related to maintaining and leasing the property, whether apartments, homes, warehouses, or office space.

The accounting aspects would cover collecting rent or lease payments, and paying taxes and expenses for upkeep of the property, as well as keeping records of all these activities. Depending on the type of property you are managing and your skills, you can do the physical upkeep and repair work yourself or hire qualified tradespeople.

Skills: Good organization skills, and a confident and determined personality (for dealing with unpaid rents or unsatisfactory work by tradespeople). Previous property management or real estate experience is an asset.

Equipment: A computer capable of running accounting software, which can range from simple DOS-based programs to Windows applications with more elaborate graphical interfaces requiring a powerful processor and more RAM. If your work requires issuing a lot of checks, receipts, and statements, you'll need a printer configured for this task. Current models are similar to dot matrix printers, which feed through a continuous stack (rather than single sheets) of preprinted blank checks or statements.

Potential customers: Owners and investment partners of apartment or office complexes, shopping malls, or vacation properties.

Promotion: List your service in the Yellow Pages or other directory of business services in your area. Advertise in the real estate section of a local newspaper.

Associated businesses: Collection service, Bookkeeping, Estate planning.

11. Estate management

Description: This work is similar to property management because it includes accounting as well as making arrangements for maintenance and repair of properties and assets belonging to an estate. Estate management includes managing homes, rental properties, and functioning businesses. Because of the latter, this work may require making decisions related to the direction of the business in conjunction with estate trustees.

Skills: Good organization skills and experience or training in property and business management.

Equipment: You will need a computer capable of running accounting and office suite software; a high-quality inkjet or laser printer for correspondence; and a printer configured for issuing checks, receipts, and statements. Current models are similar to dot matrix printers, which feed through a continuous stack (rather than single sheets) of preprinted blank checks or statements.

Potential customers: Individuals making their own estate arrangements or lawyers seeking someone to manage a client's properties.

Promotion: List your service in the Yellow Pages or other directory of business services in your area. Advertise in the real estate and business sections of a local newspaper. Consider advertising in a newsletter or publication that targets your local legal community. Contact potential clients directly with a letter describing your services. Letters of reference from current or former clients should be provided or made available on request.

Associated businesses: Property management, Collection service, Bookkeeping.

12. Event planning

Description: This service can include planning events for businesses, organizations, institutions, or individuals who do not have staff, experience, or time to do their own organizing. Events can range from a social or business cocktail party to a series of seminars or a multiday conference or meeting with attendees from other parts of the country, or from other countries.

Your service can also include designing and issuing invitations or registration forms, collecting registration fees, and handling accommodation and travel arrangements.

You are not limited to your geographical area for event planning; you can plan events for local organizations at vacation destinations or in other cities.

Skills: Good organization skills, knowledge of rates for various event venues in your area, as well as catering, travel, and hotel rates. Marketing experience is an asset.

Equipment: A computer capable of running office suite software (which includes word-processing, spreadsheet, and database applications), a high-quality inkjet or laser printer for correspondence (printing of invitations or registration packages can be done by a service bureau or printing service).

If your services include design invitations or any type of promotional material, you will need desktop publishing software and a computer with a fast processor, RAM, and storage capacity to store larger graphical files. A fax or Internet account would also be helpful for getting quotes quickly from venues or service providers.

Potential customers: Institutions, organizations, businesses, or individuals who want a well-organized event.

Promotion: List your business in the Yellow Pages or other directory of business services. Advertise in the business section of your local newspaper or in publications of business associations, such as boards of trade or chambers of commerce.

Associated businesses: Direct-mail marketing, Mail order sales.

F. FINANCIAL

1. Financial planning and management

Description: Owners of small- to medium-sized businesses whose strength and experience is in selling or manufacturing a particular product or service may welcome an independent, experienced guide when making decisions about the direction of the business. These decisions can include buying property or equipment, and selecting benefits and benefit providers for employees. Financial planning and management can include helping develop business plans and presentations to banks or other potential investors.

Skills: Experience or training in the various aspects of business management. Familiarity with spreadsheet, accounting, and/or financial management software.

Equipment: A computer (a laptop may be suitable for this service if you are working in the client's environment) with spreadsheet, accounting, and/or financial management software, and an inkjet printer for reports and proposals.

Potential customers: Small- to medium-sized businesses — especially those that are growing — that do not have an employee who specializes in business management.

Promotion: Contact potential clients directly. As this is a position of trust, be prepared to provide clients with references from former or current clients. Consider joining a local business association, such as a chamber of commerce, to develop contacts and business opportunities.

Associated businesses: Business plan writing, Expense analysis, Property management.

2. Investment analysis

Description: This type of service is similar to financial planning and management but is more oriented to individuals or families. It involves analyzing a client's income sources, expenditures, age, and goals such as purchasing a bigger house, a business, or retiring early. Based on this information, you will present the client with ideas on which investment opportunities are most suitable for him or her.

While a lot of investment information is now available on the World Wide Web and many financial institutions have discount investment services, such information may not include advice on long-term planning. As well, financial institutions have their own investment products, such as mutual funds, that they are interested in promoting. You can promote yourself as a less biased source of information.

Skills: Training and/or experience in investing, and familiarity with investment opportunities and laws that regulate income and investments.

Equipment: A computer (a laptop may be suitable for this service if you are working in the client's environment) with spreadsheet, accounting, and/or financial management software, an inkjet printer, and an Internet connection for on-line research.

Potential customers: Individuals and families, as well as charities or organizations that want to develop an ongoing or future source of income from a large donation or infusion of money.

Promotion: Publish a brochure that includes a few investment tips for your target clientele in addition to a description of the services you provide. Consider offering an one-hour evening or lunch-hour seminar on investing or planning for retirement as a way of developing new business or as an adjunct to your investment analysis service.

Associated businesses: Business plan writing, Expense analysis, Property management.

3. Sales analysis

Description: Sales analysis is a specialized area of statistical analysis and includes aspects of marketing. For this type of service you develop a profile, based on a company or service provider's records from a certain period of time, of what, when, and how many of certain products or services were sold. With your information you can put together recommendations for the client on what products or services to discontinue, promote more heavily, etc. Based on the amount of information the client gathers about their customers — age, gender, income level, or geographic location for example — you may also be able to help the client with their marketing strategy.

Skills: Training or experience in sales and/or marketing. Excellent research and analytical skills.

Equipment: A computer capable of running database software, an inkjet printer, and an Internet connection for research and communication purposes. An office software suite would be valuable for correspondence and for developing reports, which could contain graphics and tables.

Potential customers: Retailers or wholesalers, manufacturers, and service providers.

Promotion: Consider offering a seminar on sales analysis to a local business association, such as a board of trade, chamber of commerce, or manufacturing association. You may also want to develop a Web site to promote your service as your potential clientele is not necessarily limited by geography.

If you have little experience in this field, consider developing a sales profile on a volunteer basis for a nonprofit agency or charity that sells products or services to raise funds. This will help you gain needed experience and references.

Associated businesses: Statistical analysis.

4. Statistical analysis

Description: Statistics from surveys, research studies, census data, sales figures, and polls can be very valuable to a range of businesses and government agencies. The value, however, is in the correct interpretation and the job of analyzing the statistics.

Acceptable margins of error, representative samples, and leading or biased questions are all elements of statistical analysis. It is research that starts with numbers but that attempts to find out what is behind those numbers. This work requires analysis of the statistics and a report to the client detailing the value of the information.

Skills: Excellent research skills. Training and/or experience in translating and researching statistics.

Equipment: A computer capable of running database software, an inkjet printer, and an Internet connection for research and communication purposes. An office software suite is valuable for developing reports, which could contain graphics and tables to illustrate the statistics.

Potential customers: Businesses and government agencies.

Promotion: For this type of work, some research will be involved in developing clients. Consider offering a seminar on the value of statistical analysis to a business association, such as a board of trade or chamber of commerce. You may also want to develop a Web site to promote your service, as your potential clientele is not necessarily limited by geography.

Associated businesses: Information broker, Sales analysis.

G. FAX AND PRINTING

1. Fax time rental

Description: A fax time rental service can be run through an existing service, for businesses or service providers that do not have the equipment, skill, or time to send multiple faxes to clients or customers.

This is an excellent addition to an existing business, as the faxing broadcast (sending the same fax to multiple recipients) can be programmed to occur overnight or during a period when your equipment is not being used for your existing business or service.

Skills: Familiarity with faxing technology.

Equipment: A computer, or network of computers, with a high-speed fax modem and connection to a telephone line.

Potential customers: Small business operators, service providers, and event organizers.

Promotion: Promote this service through your existing business. Advertise your services in the business section of a local newspaper or in business publications. Contact your potential clients directly to promote your services. List your service in the Yellow Pages or other local directory of business services.

Associated businesses: Fax-on-demand service.

2. Fax-on-demand service

Description: This type of service involves sending out faxes requested by customers detailing specifications of a product or service provided by the fax-on-demand clients.

The requests are received via a telephone number (usually toll-free) that links customers to a menu where they select the information they want and key in their own fax numbers.

This can be linked to your fax modem to automatically send out the information, or it can simply record the requests, which you can later program to be sent out in batches or at a time when your system is not otherwise occupied.

You can also act as a consultant and set up this type of service for other businesses.

Skills: Familiarity with faxing technology.

Equipment: A computer or network of computers with high-speed fax modems and connections to telephone lines. Toll-free or toll-paid (usually a 1-900 number) telephone service.

Potential customers: Manufacturers or providers of unusual or complex services or products. Publishers of magazines or newspapers that provide recipes, plans, or some type of listing as a reader service.

Promotion: Create a brochure describing your services, and distribute copies directly to potential clients. This brochure could include a toll-free number connected to your service through which potential clients can receive more details of your service (this would also demonstrate your service).

List your business in the Yellow Pages or other directory of business services in your area.

Associated businesses: Fax time rental.

3. Laser printer time rental

Description: If you already own an expensive laser printer for an existing business, this type of service is an excellent way of recovering some of the cost. A laser printer time rental service includes printing out a range of documents and files during times when the printer is not being used for your existing service.

A laser printer that can output a wide variety of paper and envelope sizes would make this service attractive to a wide range of potential customers.

Skills: Familiarity with a wide range of software and printing technology.

Equipment: A high-quality laser printer as well as a computer with sufficient RAM and processing power to print quickly — files containing complex graphics will tie up both the printer and computer if the latter are not sufficiently powerful. You will also need the software used by clients to open and print their files.

Potential customers: Small businesses or individuals in your area who occasionally need but do not have a high-quality output printer. Your advantage is location and familiarity with potential customers.

Promotion: Advertise this service through your existing business.

Associated businesses: Fax time rental.

H. FAMILY AND HOUSEHOLD

1. Home inventory cataloguing

Description: A catalogue of home contents is valuable for insurance purposes if there is a theft or damage by flood or fire, but it is something many homeowners never get around to doing.

This service can also be valuable for people who are renting out their homes (furnished or not), to keep a record of the original condition of the building and/or contents, as well as for people who are moving or storing the contents of a house and need a record of it in case of damage or theft from the storage facility, or damage during moving.

This service would include descriptions of objects, as well as a list of serial or identification numbers on electronic devices. The inventory can also include images of the items catalogued taken with a digital camera. As these images will need to be in a digital format and could be of medium to low resolution, a fairly basic, reasonably priced digital camera is suitable for this type of work. The initial cost of the camera will quickly be recovered as you will not have film, processing, or printing costs.

You can store the completed inventory as part of your service or transfer it to CD-ROM (a format that can store more data and is more durable than a floppy diskette) for the client to store in a secure off-site location, such as a safety deposit box.

This service can be provided on an annual basis as insurance policies come up for renewal. It is an excellent adjunct to an insurance business or some type of caretaking service, such as monitoring rental properties.

Skills: You should have good descriptive writing skills and be organized and detail oriented.

Equipment: A computer capable of running database software. If you are incorporating images, you will need a digital camera, and if you are planning to output the inventory list to CD-ROM, you will need a CD-R or CDRW drive. A high-quality color inkjet printer is also a good idea for creating a paper document of the finished inventory.

Potential customers: Homeowners and people who are moving or storing the contents of a home or vacation property.

Promotion: Advertise in the home section of your local newspaper or in home- or family-oriented publications in your area. List your services in the Yellow Pages or other directory of business services in your area. As your clients will be entrusting you with a list of their assets, you should be able to supply clients with references from current or former clients.

Associated businesses: Data backup service, Data archiving, Data security consulting, System security consulting, Estate planning.

2. Tax preparation

Description: There is now quite a wide range of tax preparation software available. Much of it is oriented to individual tax preparers, fairly idiot-proof, and reasonably priced. So why would people pay to have their returns prepared? Because they don't have time, the necessary equipment, or any idea of how to begin organizing their shoe boxes full of receipts.

This is an excellent sideline to an existing service, as preparing tax returns is a seasonal service.

Skills: Training, experience, and/or certification in preparing tax returns for individuals or small business operators. This is an area where you will need to keep your ear to the ground. Tax laws change annually and the accepted method of filing returns is evolving. Just a few years ago, the Canadian government had no system for accepting electronic returns. Recently, the federal government began accepting electronic returns from certain accredited tax preparation agencies. Eventually, e-mail will be the preferred way of receiving returns as e-mail becomes more widespread (it is also a cost saving for the government if paper returns don't have to be keyed or scanned into a form that can be processed by a computer).

Equipment: A computer capable of running tax preparation software. This can be a fairly modest machine depending on the graphical requirements of the software you choose. A high-quality inkjet computer is also necessary.

Potential customers: Small businesses, organizations, or individual tax filers.

Promotion: Begin promoting your services through advertisements in local newspapers at the end of the year or beginning of the new year through to the tax deadline. Advertise in the business section of your local newspaper or in business-oriented publications if you are targeting businesses.

Associated businesses: Estate planning, Home inventory cataloguing, Bookkeeping.

I. MAINTENANCE AND REPAIR

1. Computer repair and maintenance

Description: Computer repair and maintenance involves caring for both the hardware and software of a computer or network of computers.

Many small- and medium-sized businesses have a need for this type of service as their staffing does not extend to having a full-time, in-house systems administrator.

This type of work involves emergency repairs and regular, preventative care, and can involve some type of retainer or contract for which you are on call for a certain number of hours or days a month.

The repairs and maintenance include solving software conflicts, installing RAM or storage capacity as a system or network becomes overburdened, and running virus-checking and diagnostic software on a regular basis to catch any developing problems before they become serious.

Regular maintenance of a business's system or network will take place in that business's environment, but emergency repairs can be done at your own business or home repair shop.

Skills: Thorough knowledge of a range of computer hardware and software. Training or experience in this field is an asset. You will also need a good supply of, or easy access to, replacement parts.

Equipment: Tools for dismantling a computer and peripherals, cleaning supplies, small portable vacuum cleaner, canister of compressed air, and a range of diagnostic and virus-scanning software.

Potential customers: Small or home-business operators, individuals or families with home computers.

Promotion: Create a brochure describing your services and target business clients directly. Advertise in the business section of your local newspaper or in local business publications. List your service in the Yellow Pages or other local business directory. To attract individual or home-office users, try posting a brochure describing your services in public places, such as libraries and community centers, and consider advertising your services in a local newspaper.

Associated businesses: Computer setup and training, On-line setup and training, Computer cleaning, Data backup service, Data archiving.

2. Computer cleaning

Description: Depending on the configuration of a computer and its peripherals, its location, and the type of regular care it has, it can attract dust, dirt, and food or liquids and thus work less effectively.

This type of work can involve basic cleaning, such as opening up keyboards and vacuuming or blowing pressurized air to remove dust, dirt, or food crumbs, as well as cleaning the mouse or trackball input device.

It can also be more complex — a type of disaster recovery — involving properly drying out, cleaning, and repairing a keyboard, printer, or other component of a computer into which liquid has spilled.

Computer cleaning can be done on an on-call basis when a "disaster" has occurred, or on a regular contract basis to prevent the buildup of dirt and dust for those businesses wanting to make sure their systems are running effectively.

This is an excellent adjunct to a computer repair service.

Skills: Knowledge of computer hardware and some type of training or experience in computer repair or maintenance.

Equipment: Tools for dismantling a computer and peripherals, cleaning supplies, small portable vacuum cleaner with attachments for cleaning small areas, canister of compressed air, and a hair dryer. Depending on the type of cleaning, you may also need some type of diagnostic software to make sure the cleaning is successful. If you are doing this type of cleaning at your home or at your business, you will need a computer to run the peripherals you have cleaned to make sure they are working.

Potential customers: Businesses or organizations that have a computer network or several computers but no in-house systems administrator, as well as home-business operators and individuals or families with home computers.

Promotion: Create a brochure describing your services and distribute copies directly to the business clients you are targeting. The brochure could include rates for regular cleaning based on the number and type of computers in an organization. Consider advertising in the business section of your local newspaper or in local business publications.

Rates for regular or emergency cleaning for individual and home business computer users could be included in this brochure, or you could create a separate brochure and distribute copies to public places such as libraries or community centers to target this market. A listing in the Yellow Pages or other directory of business services is also a good idea.

Associated businesses: Computer repair and maintenance.

J. TRAINING AND CONSULTING

1. Computer setup and training

Description: As the use of computers in homes and businesses continues to spread, so will the opportunity to help new computer owners and users set up and operate their systems.

This type of work can involve consulting with clients before they purchase their systems to find out what their particular needs are and helping them get the right system to fit their budgets. The work will also involve helping clients set up the computer systems in their homes or offices, and training them to install and use the software they have selected.

This work can be ongoing, especially with business clients, if clients need to upgrade the software and hardware or need their systems repaired or tuned up. Promote the fact the you are an unbiased party, unlike a salesperson who benefits if the buyer spends more money.

As well, you can promote the fact that you know where the bargains are and what the best quality components are. The individual buyer with little knowledge of computers is likely to be keen on one-stop shopping, which can be an expensive way of purchasing equipment. The new computer-using client may also not be aware of the variety of sources for software, such as the Internet (shareware and freeware).

Skills: You'll need to be well versed in both the hardware and software available for the type of market you are targeting. If you are dealing with families, for example, you should be familiar with the wide range of educational software for children, in addition to the word-processing, database, and multimedia programs parents may use. A knowledge of reputable and reasonably priced computer shops and the variety of software resources is vital.

You will also need to keep up-to-date with new technology and be able to assess whether it is suitable for your clients. Training will also demand patience and an ability to put your ideas and technical knowledge across to people who have little or no computer experience.

Equipment: Your own equipment is less important, as the training and setup will be done in the client's environment. A basic system with database and billing software, and an Internet connection to keep in touch with clients, is adequate for your own computing needs. This type of business makes a good home-based operation, though much of it won't actually take place in your home.

Potential customers: Any families or small businesses that are buying their first computer or upgrading their systems.

Promotion: Publish a brochure and distribute copies to family-oriented locations such as community centers and libraries. If you are targeting small businesses, you can distribute the brochure to your potential clients. You may also be able to leave brochures at a local computer store. If you have money for advertising, consider running an advertisement in your community newspaper or in the training section of a computer publication (one that is distributed free and is more likely to be picked up by computing novices). Since you are targeting new users who are not connected to the Internet, on-line promotion is not a good option.

Associated businesses: On-line setup and training, Computer consulting for people with disabilities, Computer repair and maintenance.

2. On-line setup and training

Description: Access to the Internet is becoming more common, and the methods of connecting more varied. The possible uses of on-line access are also becoming varied and dynamic, and people — families or businesses — with little familiarity with these possibilities are in search of guidance.

On-line setup and training can begin with helping clients choose the right type of connection, from a simple modem to high-speed and/or dedicated connections, such as ADSL (asymmetrical digital subscriber line), ISDN (integrated services digital network), cable, or satellite. Each of these technologies has its own hardware and software.

You can help your clients select the appropriate hardware, such as a modem, and then the right type of ISP, as well as e-mail and Web browser software. This can be followed by training clients to use the software and introducing them to the resources they might want to take advantage of on-line.

If your clients operate businesses and will be setting up Web sites or conducting some form of sales via the Internet, you can also advise and train them in the various forms of on-line commerce available through financial institutions and ISPs.

This type of consulting can be ongoing. As the capabilities of this technology increase, you can help your former clients upgrade their on-line equipment and practices.

Skills: Knowledge of the rapid changes and the possibilities of this area of computer technology is vital. You will need to be familiar with the reliability of ISPs in your area and what range of services they provide, as well as the hardware vendors and sources of software (which for Internet neophytes is usually the ISP). Training will require patience and an ability to explain technical ideas to people with less technical knowledge.

Equipment: Your own equipment is not that important because the training will be taking place in the client's environment.

Potential customers: Individuals or households, as well as a wide range of entrepreneurs and small businesses that want or need to explore the commercial possibilities of the Internet. This can include storefront businesses that want to expand their client base beyond their current foot traffic, as well as craftspeople or other home-based producers or service providers that want to create an on-line or electronic storefront.

Promotion: As with computer setup and training, consider publishing a brochure and distributing it in community centers and libraries as well as in computer stores. Consider teaching a one-night introductory course on how to get on-line at a local community center, high school, or other continuing education facility to give participants a taste of what is possible. Or give a seminar on the same topic but with a commerce focus to a local small business organization, such as a chamber of commerce.

If you are targeting craftspeople, for example, consider distributing your brochure directly to them at a craft show or at a seminar or conference put on by their association. Advertising your services in industry newsletters or other publications that directly target your potential clientele is another option.

Associated businesses: Computer setup and training, Web site design, Web site administration.

3. Telecommuting consulting

Description: A telecommuter is an employee who works from his or her home full time or for a few days per week. Telecommuting allows employers to offer some flexibility to skilled or talented employees who are considering quitting because of long commutes or obligations at home.

Often telecommuting employees are linked to the main office via fax, e-mail, or an intranet (internal corporate network). In some cases, they may be involved in videoconferences with the main office and/or clients.

This type of consulting work involves helping the home worker choose a suitable location for a home office (a space with good lighting and ventilation, and one that can be closed off to limit distractions), and setting up the computer system, software, and Internet (or other) connection to the office.

It can also involve helping assess which employees are good candidates for telecommuting, as it is not a suitable arrangement for every employee, nor for every task in a workplace. Assessments could include setting up trial periods for telecommuting hopefuls, or phasing it in gradually, for example, one day a week for the first month, to see how it works for both the employer and employee.

Skills: Training or experience in human resources, as well as familiarity with hardware, software, and Internet setup.

Equipment: Your computer is not that important, as the work will mostly take place in the client's environment.

Potential customers: Medium- to large-sized businesses with professional, executive, or creative staff whose work is suitable for telecommuting.

Promotion: Contact clients directly with a brochure describing your services. Advertise in a publication that targets business executives and human resources managers.

Consider offering a seminar describing the benefits and pitfalls of telecommuting to an association of business executives and human resource managers.

Associated businesses: Videoconferencing consulting, Computer setup and training, On-line setup and training.

4. Videoconferencing consulting

Description: Videoconferencing is an area of computer technology that is advancing every day. The graphical and audio capabilities of the World Wide Web have made it realistic, though not yet common, to transmit images, sound, and text in "real time." Videoconferencing transmits the voices and images of two or more participants via the Internet, or an intranet (internal corporate network). Some videoconferencing allows the participants to work on or edit the same file or document simultaneously.

Because this is a developing technology, standards are still emerging. Compatibility, therefore, is an issue when helping clients set up a videoconferencing system.

This type of consulting can involve helping clients assess their hardware and software needs, in compliance with the technology used by other participants (branch offices, remote workers, or clients). It can also involve helping set up streamlined, lightweight mobile systems for sales staff or executives who spend a lot of time on the road.

There are a few companies that are already offering videoconferencing bundles — software, cameras, and microphones — for consumer use. These packages may be suitable for setting up small offices or telecommuters.

Skills: Knowledge of the specialized software and hardware (e.g., video cameras that sit on top of or beside the monitor to transmit images) and the various Internet connections that are suitable for this type of work. Because of the pace of development in this field, you'll need to keep current with what's new and what standards are emerging.

Equipment: Because this consulting is done in the client's environment, your own equipment is less important.

Potential customers: Any businesses with professional, executive, or creative staff members who are in two or more remote locations but working on the same projects.

Promotion: Contact clients directly with a brochure describing your services. Advertise in a publication that targets business executives. Consider offering a seminar on videoconferencing to an association of business executives in your area.

Associated businesses: Telecommuting consulting, Computer setup and training, On-line setup and training.

5. Computer consulting for people with disabilities

Description: Getting used to working on a computer for the first time can be difficult for anyone who is unfamiliar with keyboards and pointing devices such as a mouse or trackball. Add to that a physical disability and the challenge is multiplied. Luckily, many hardware and software companies are hard at work creating tools that can help people with disabilities join the computer revolution.

This type of consulting can begin with assessing the type of hardware and software clients need, helping them select it, and then training them to use it.

Voice recognition software is one area that has had a lot of coverage recently because of its uses for the able-bodied computer user. This type of software technology is also highly useful to people with disabilities. In its various applications, it allows users to navigate around their computers by speaking to it, to dictate directly into their computers, and to have their dictation or other documents read back to them. Some voice recognition software is also able to adapt to an accent, whether regional, national, or related to some type of speech impediment. Voice recognition software has uses for people with either visual or physical impediments.

Hardware developments that aid people with disabilities include computer mice that move slowly (allowing people with shaky hands to better control them), keyboards with sticky keys for multikey commands (allowing users to press one key after the other, rather than two or more keys at one time), and keyboards with larger keys (giving people with less control of their hands a larger target to hit). Much of the hardware developed for children as young as two years old can be adapted for use by people with disabilities who, like the children, have less motor control.

Skills: Depending on the type of user you are targeting, some experience working with people with disabilities is beneficial, especially with those clients who have difficulty communicating because of their impairment. You will also need some knowledge of the physical limitations of various disabilities as well as the imagination to use existing software and hardware to work around those limitations.

You must be well versed in what hardware and software is currently available and be able to tap into what is being developed. Patience and an ability to communicate your thoughts, as in all types of training, is necessary when dealing with people who are less knowledgeable and, in this case, less physically able, than you.

Equipment: As with other types of consulting, your computer setup is not that important because the training takes place in the client's environment. If, however, you will be demonstrating your services to develop a client base, you will need a mobile computer with the audio and video power to accommodate the specialized software you plan to use with clients, as well as examples of the hardware you plan to use.

Potential customers: Your clients can include people with a range of temporary or permanent disabilities related to vision problems, motor skill impairment, or inability to use a traditional input device such as a keyboard. It can also extend to age-related vision and motor-skill impairment (e.g., developing a way for an elderly person with Parkinson's disease who can no longer write a letter to communicate through e-mail).

Promotion: Approach the associations of medical professionals or support groups for caregivers and offer to demonstrate your services. Advertise in the newsletters or on-line forums for these groups. The community of people with disabilities is also very active on-line, so you could promote your services through it, and take part in on-line discussions. This would also give you an idea of what needs are not being filled for those computer users.

Associated businesses: On-line training and consulting, Computer and on-line training for children.

6. Occupational therapy

Description: Occupational therapy involves physical or mental activities designed to assist recovery from a disease or injury. Computers can offer more options, in conjunction with traditional therapies.

A person who is having to relearn motor skills and can't pick up or control a pen, for example, could use an adapted keyboard or touch-screen monitor to successfully write letters or communicate. This type of incremental achievement helps build confidence as part of the bigger goal of recovery.

Specially developed computer games, journal exercises, or story writing can be used to help clients express their thoughts as well as rebuild their mental skills and confidence. You could also train or consult with occupational therapists who want to find out how computers and technology can benefit their clients.

Skills: A background in occupational therapy, or working under the guidance of, or in conjunction with, a trained occupational therapist. A knowledge of existing hardware and software and the imagination to tailor it to the particular needs of your clients.

Equipment: Ideally, clients will have their own systems, or access to computers at a clinic, community center, or caregiving facility so they can work independently as well as with a trainer. If not, you will need a portable computer with the requisite software, special keyboards, and input devices so you can work in your client's environment.

Potential customers: People with various mental or physical disabilities, and other occupational therapists.

Promotion: Contact occupational therapists, associations for people with physical and mental disabilities, and workers' compensation groups in your area. As with other training and consulting businesses, you can offer to demonstrate your services to these organizations as a way to promote your business or as an adjunct to your main business.

Associated businesses: Computer consulting for people with disabilities.

7. Ergonomics consulting

Description: Now that the use of computers is becoming more widespread on the job and at home, the toll of long hours spent in front of computers is starting to show. Computer-related injuries can be sustained from misuse or over use of nearly every component of a computer workstation: the monitor, keyboard, mouse, document holder, desk, chair, lighting, telephone, ventilation, and location of frequently used items such as printers, books, and files. And there are good and bad solutions, from simple posture adjustments to elaborate and expensive pieces of hardware or software, for all these problems.

Your role as an ergonomics consultant is to assess the problem or potential for problems of a computer workstation or office setup, and to tailor your solutions to your client's needs and budget. The consulting can include helping select and set up the hardware and software, then training the user in how to use it to avoid injuries. It can also involve assessing an existing office or workstation setup where repetitive strain or other computer-related injuries have already become a problem, and helping the client redesign the setup or invest in new equipment, and learn how to use it safely.

A selling point to this type of consulting is that though your services and the resulting changes to hardware and furniture will be an added expense, it should be weighed against the cost of employees working less efficiently or having to take time off because of avoidable injuries.

Skills: Like the consultant for people with disabilities, this field requires knowledge of specialized hardware, software, and computer furniture — and there is a lot of it on the market. Knowing what will legitimately prevent injuries and what is suitable to a particular task or individual will be what keeps you in business. You also need to know the basics of ergonomics, such as proper sitting posture, the correct angle of arms on the keyboard, and the correct distance to sit from the monitor.

Unless you are a medical professional, however, you should not be diagnosing a worker's computer-related injuries because these can be serious and permanently disabling if not properly treated. If you do recognize symptoms of a computer-related injury, recommend that your client see a doctor. Limit your advice and training to your area of expertise.

Equipment: Your own computer equipment is not that important, as your consulting will be done in the client's environment. If your business involves demonstrating your services, you will need a mobile computer capable of operating the required software.

Potential customers: Any business or institution where workers spend a lot of time in front of computers that does not have its own in-house consultant. This can include large businesses, schools, or organizations, as well as individual users or home-business operators.

Promotion: Publish a brochure promoting your services and directly target businesses in your area. Consider advertising in local business publications or the business section of a local newspaper. You could also teach a one-evening course at a high school, community college, or other continuing education facility to give potential clients a taste of the importance of proper office setup and of the services you provide. You could also give seminars to business or other professional associations to promote your business or as an adjunct to your consulting business.

Associated businesses: Computer consulting for people with disabilities.

8. On-line teaching and tutoring

Description: As people's lives get busier and Internet technology improves, people are beginning to do more and more from the comfort of their home computers. One of these things is to get training on-line or to supplement a more traditional education with on-line tutoring.

A businessperson, for example, may not want to leave home after a long day at work to sharpen skills in a second language needed for business or to get tutoring in a course that is a requirement to advance in a certain field.

High school, community college, or university students may need help in a particular field of study, and as the Internet is second nature for them, it is a logical place to look for tutoring.

The advantage to this type of tutoring or training is that it can be done at the student's own pace, at a time of day or night that suits his or her schedule, and for parents, it doesn't require setting up child care.

Teaching English to visiting students or to new immigrants is in much demand in many areas, urban and rural, and can easily be adapted to the Internet. With this type of business, your potential clientele is not limited by geography. Depending on the effort you want to make in promoting your services, and your payment methods, you can train or tutor people in another city or even another country.

Skills: Some existing expertise on a subject is required, and some training or teaching experience is an asset. This type of business is a good opportunity for teachers or retired teachers who want to supplement an existing income. If you are a professional writer or have excellent written writing skills in English or other language, this would also be a good business opportunity. As with other

57

training endeavors, patience and an ability to put your thoughts across clearly is a requirement.

Equipment: An e-mail program on a computer hooked up to the Internet via a basic telephone line is adequate for this type of business if you simply need to send e-mail back and forth to students. If you plan to spend more time and want to project a more professional image, you might want to use a more sophisticated e-mail program that allows you to attach files from another program that the client can download, amend, and then send back to you. Some e-mail programs also allow users to create chat rooms to communicate in real time with one or more clients.

If you have several students, you may want to develop a Web site from which they can download assignments, discuss projects with you or other students, and access a frequently asked questions (FAQ) page. A Web site will also help you promote your services to prospective students. For a Web site, you'll need Web site design software (which is getting easier to use; many programs include templates that simply need to have blanks filled in and links made) and a computer with the graphical capabilities (in the monitor and the computer's RAM) to run and view this type of software.

You can also contract an experienced Web site designer to set up your site and show you how to update it yourself, if you find your skills are not adequate in this area.

As you'll be logging a lot of time on-line, you should find a reliable ISP and arrange a rate based on your projected use of the service. You may want to consider some form of high-speed or dedicated connection.

If you plan to solicit customers in other geographical areas, you should find an ISP that can provide you with electronic commerce capabilities.

As videoconferencing equipment becomes more reasonably priced and more widely available, you may want to consider adding this feature to your training and tutoring tools.

Potential customers: Anybody who is trying to advance or gain knowledge in a subject area in which you have a degree of expertise.

Promotion: A Web site is a great tool for soliciting business from a wide group of potential clients. If you are targeting students who are seeking tutoring for school courses, you can post a brochure touting your services at educational institutions and libraries.

Associated businesses: On-line research training, Job hunting training.

9. Computer and on-line training for children

Description: Parents who know the benefits of familiarity with computers and the Internet want to make sure their children can take advantage of this technology, but they may not have the time or skills to teach their children themselves.

This type of training can be ongoing, one-to-one instruction of a single child in the child's home, or even specific training for a shorter period of time for a group of children — a week-long computer camp, for example.

You can begin by teaching basic skills, such as typing, or develop fun skill-building projects, such as creating a Web site, going on an Internet scavenger hunt, designing a newspaper or magazine, or even doing some basic programming.

Skills: In addition to the technical expertise required for the particular skills you are teaching, experience working with children is an asset. Before you jump in, you should know if you have the required patience and motivational skills for this eager and curious, yet easily distracted, clientele.

Equipment: If you are teaching children in their homes, the quality of your own equipment will be not that important.

If the training is taking place in your own home or office and involves several children, a small network of computers will be necessary. A network will allow the connected computers to share files and peripheral equipment, such as printers and scanners. Depending on the focus of your training, you may also need on-line access for one or more of these computers.

This will be a significant investment. If you do not have the money or want to start more slowly, check out the availability of the computer labs at schools or community colleges in the evenings, on weekends, spring breaks, or during summer vacation. These are times when such equipment may not be used and when parents are looking for extracurricular activities for their children.

Potential customers: Any family with a home computer. This is a great area for repeat business. You can develop new programs that grow in complexity as the skills of your students develop, and at the same time teach the basic courses to those students' younger siblings.

Promotion: Develop a brochure describing your services and distribute copies to public libraries, community centers, and computer stores. Consider advertising in your local paper if it has a parenting section, or ask if it is planning any special sections promoting activities for children for spring or summer break. There are also many parenting Web sites and on-line forums, but unless these are directly targeted to parents in your geographical area, this type of promotion may not be suitable.

Associated businesses: Computer setup and training, On-line setup and training.

10. On-line research training

Description: The Internet is one of the most powerful research tools available. Many of the on-line resources, including dictionaries, technical encyclopedias, and searchable collections of quotes, are free. There is also a wealth of other material, including databases and on-line reference books that can be mined for a one-time fee or on a monthly subscription basis.

There is a good market for teaching on-line neophytes how to harness this incredible resource. This training includes helping users locate the many on-line search engines and determine which are the best for their tasks. Training will also cover how to use a search engine. Failing to properly narrow your query, for example, can provide the new user with thousands of Web site possibilities.

You can help your client locate and participate in newsgroups and chat rooms tied to their particular area of research or interest.

This training can also focus on a particular area of research with wide appeal, such as genealogy or medical information.

Skills: Familiarity with Web browser software and the many on-line search engines.

Equipment: Web browser software, a high-speed Internet connection, and a fairly powerful computer with lots of RAM so that your trainee is not overly frustrated waiting for Web pages to download.

Potential customers: Students at every educational level, as well as professionals whose work involves research, such as journalists, educators, or academics.

Promotion: Create and distribute a brochure promoting your services at libraries in educational facilities. Advertise in a newsletter produced by associations for the particular professionals you are targeting. Consider offering seminars to the same associations promoting your skills or as an adjunct to your other services.

Associated businesses: On-line research training, Job hunting training, Employer on-line hiring training, Electronic clipping service, People tracing, Product and service tracing, On-line setup and training.

11. Job hunting training

Description: Recent studies of companies posting job opportunities on their Web sites have shown that these listings are no longer limited to high-technology companies or positions. There are more traditional businesses taking advantage of this nontraditional approach to finding skilled applicants in technical and nontechnical fields.

This type of training involves making clients aware of these opportunities and showing them how to find listings using the various search engines available on-line.

Many companies request résumés in an electronic form, so training can include helping your clients create documents in the format desired by the recipients (most prefer a plain text document containing the résumé and the cover letter within the body of a single e-mail message).

Some companies that receive a large volume of responses to job postings sift through résumés electronically, looking for key words and phrases. You can help clients prepare résumés including these key words. Clients can also learn how to locate on-line résumé banks where they can post their résumés for free.

Even if your clients are taking a more traditional approach to job hunting, you can provide them with the skills to research their prospective employers on-line, enabling them to write a more informed résumé or better prepare for an interview.

You may also consider focusing on a particular job area, such as business or engineering graduates, or overseas employment opportunities.

Skills: You must be well versed in on-line technology as well as on-line opportunities and resources.

Equipment: The basics for this type of training are e-mail and Web browser software, a fast modem connection, and a fairly powerful computer with lots of RAM (you don't want your job hunter to be overly frustrated waiting for Web pages to download). A high-speed Internet connection, such as ISDN or cable, may be worth considering. You will also need desktop publishing software and a printer for creating résumés.

Potential customers: Recent graduates or students about to graduate from university, community colleges, or vocational programs; professionals who are already employed but are eager to explore other opportunities. People who are unemployed and receiving government assistance have access to a variety of job search programs at no charge, so this would not be a lucrative market. However, you could approach a government job center about contracting your training services.

Promotion: Create and distribute brochures describing your skills to libraries, job centers, and service bureaus (photocopying and desktop publishing services) at educational institutions. Consider offering seminars through job centers to promote your services or as an adjunct to your business. Offer a one-evening course on the topic through the continuing education programs at local educational institutions or community centers.

Associated businesses: Employer on-line hiring training, On-line research training, Résumé writing.

12. Employer on-line hiring training

Description: As more job hunters turn to the Web, employers need guidance in reaching this group of candidates, which according to surveys is more educated and more technologically sophisticated than the general population.

Training will involve making employers aware of the tools on-line job hunters use, such as key word queries using on-line search engines.

It also involves training your clients to manage the résumés they receive, whether electronically or on paper. This can include installing and training your clients to use résumé scanning and searching software, such as ResTrac or Resumix. These types of programs sift through résumés that have been scanned in or received electronically, looking for those with the most key words in the document matching the requirements for the position.

There are also many on-line specialty recruiting sites that your client may consider linking to, on your advice.

Skills: You must be well versed in on-line technology as well as on-line opportunities and resources. As well, you should be fluent in the operating system of your clients, as résumé management software is available for many platforms, from the Windows environment to high-performance UNIX-based systems. Knowledge of scanners and OCR software is also an asset.

Equipment: As with other on-site training and consulting opportunities, your own equipment will be less important than your knowledge and skills, as most of your time will be spent in the client's environment.

Potential customers: Growing businesses with an inadequate or technologically unsophisticated human resources department.

Promotion: Advertise in publications targeting human resources and management professionals. Consider offering seminars to a professional association or other business organizations, such as a chamber of commerce or board of trade, to promote your services.

Associated businesses: Job hunting training, On-line research training, Résumé writing.

K. DATA BACKUP, ARCHIVING, AND SECURITY

1. Data backup service

Description: Backing up data is important because while it is easy enough (if properly insured) to replace the hardware and software lost because of theft, fire, or other type of damage, the data is often irreplaceable.

But it is an area where shortcuts are often taken. Backing up data involves a lot of time and, depending on the system, slows it down or shuts it down while this is done. So backing up data is left to the end of the day, when someone has to stay late to do it, or it is done only intermittently because of the inconvenience. As well, a copy of the backed-up data must be stored off site, which involves someone storing it at home or having to access a storage site, such as a safety deposit box in a bank.

Businesses with valuable data should be eager for a regular, dependable method of backing up data that can be done during their low-activity periods, such as evenings and early mornings. This data can then be stored in a safe place, such as a vault, at your business or at a bank.

This type of work can include doing the backup and/or simply setting up a system within the company. There are many backup options, including tape, CD-R, CDRW, and Zip and MO cartridges and drives.

Skills: Excellent knowledge of backup technologies, and reliability. As your clients are buying your services to protect their data, there will be little tolerance of mistakes that damage this valuable commodity.

Equipment: Companies you work for may have their own backup equipment. If not, a portable CD-R or CDRW drive is a good choice. Compact discs can hold a lot of data and can be read by CD-ROM drives, which are now very common. Unless your clients have their own Zip or MO drives or other less common technology, these are not good choices, as clients will not be able to easily access their own data.

Potential customers: Medium-sized businesses or institutions without an in-house systems administrator, and any business that highly values its data, such as dental and medical practices.

Promotion: Target businesses directly. Create and distribute a pamphlet to potential clients on the importance of backing up data, which includes a description of the various services you provide. Also consider offering seminars on backing up data to local business or professional associations, such as chambers of commerce or boards of trade.

Associated businesses: Data archiving, Data conversion, Data security consulting.

2. Data archiving

Description: Archiving data is similar to data backup services but involves more permanent or long-term forms of storage. Files that exist only electronically are constantly being developed and modified. Archiving this information is like taking a snapshot of it at a particular point in time.

Archiving involves much of the same technology as backing up data, but it is done less often and the media (e.g., CDs, tapes) is not updated as changes are made.

Like backing up data, it is important to keep a copy of the data off site in case of theft, fire, or other type of damage.

Skills: Excellent knowledge of various backup technologies and the durability of their medium (discs and cartridges that are magnetic, for example, are more susceptible to damage and are less durable over time). Because much of this technology is new, the jury is still out on their suitability for long-term storage. You will need to be on top of developments in this area and should regularly check that archived data is not deteriorating. As with backup services, reliability is an important quality in protecting this valuable commodity.

Equipment: A portable CD-R drive is a good choice for this type of business because the medium, CD-ROM, can hold a lot of data in a compact form. Because the discs are not going to be rewritten, size is an important factor. You have more storage options with smaller media. CD-ROMs are also durable, cheap, and very accessible for clients. There are many other storage and archiving technologies that have their own strengths and weaknesses.

Potential customers: Any small- to medium-sized company that needs to keep files or records for long periods of time and does not have an in-house systems administrator or information technology manager. This can include medical and dental practices, and other businesses with substantial accounting or billing records.

Promotion: Target businesses directly. Create and distribute a pamphlet to potential clients on archiving data, which includes a description of the various services you provide. Also consider offering a seminar on archiving to a local business or professional association, such as a chamber of commerce or board of trade.

Associated businesses: Data backup service, Data conversion, Data security consulting.

3. Data conversion

Description: When companies change software platforms or applications, documents and databases of all types must be changed. Although much of this can be done automatically, and there are various conversion programs, glitches are magnified when you are dealing with large amounts of data and some manual work is usually required.

This type of work can involve consulting with clients and recommending ways of converting their systems, what new systems may better suit their needs, the type of conversion software needed for the task, and training staff to do the conversions or to work with the new operating systems and software applications.

It could also involve doing the work yourself. The advantage to clients if you do the work is that you can do it quickly or over a weekend, evening, or series of evenings that will be the least disruptive to their businesses. Data conversion involves some follow up after the conversion.

Skills: Fluency in many operating systems and various categories of software, such as databases, word-processing or desktop publishing programs. Unlike backing up and archiving data, which involve working with the same clients on a regular basis, this will demand a steady stream of new customers, so some sales skills are required.

Equipment: Your equipment will be less important than the client's, as you are likely to do most of your work in the client's environment.

Potential customers: Any business changing its operating system or applications.

Promotion: Target businesses directly. Create and distribute brochures describing your services. Also consider offering seminars on your services to local business or professional associations, such as chambers of commerce or boards of trade.

Associated businesses: Data backup service, Data archiving, Data security consulting.

4. Data security consulting

Description: Computers for the most part are no longer standalone systems but rather are often part of intranets (internal networks) or are connected to the biggest network, the Internet. This connectivity provides more opportunity for corrupting valuable data, whether through carelessness or deliberately.

This type of business involves data backup and archiving in addition to other areas of data security, such as encryption (allowing data to be safely transmitted across public networks), and keeping applications safe from viruses (ensuring software can be downloaded safely from public networks).

Skills: Knowledge of encryption standards, such as DES (data encryption standard) which uses the same secret key for sender and receiver, and RSA (rivest-shamir-aelman), which uses a secret and public key, as well as knowledge of the software required to encode and decode the data. You will also need a knowledge of antivirus software. For both of these areas, you need to keep current on the rapid advancements in technology, since hackers and other cyber-menaces are a determined lot.

Equipment: Your equipment is not that important, as the work will be done in the client's environment.

Potential customers: Any small- to medium-sized business that values its data but has no in-house systems administrator or information technology manager.

Promotion: Like other areas of data security (backup and archiving), businesses can be targeted directly in person or with an information pamphlet on the various threats to data integrity, which also describes and promotes your services. Consider offering short courses or seminars on this topic to business and professional organizations or as part of a continuing education program. This could be an adjunct to your business in addition to being a way of promote your services. On-line promotion of your services, such as a Web site, gives clients another way to find you.

Associated businesses: Data backup service, Data archiving, Data conversion.

5. System security consulting

Description: Little can stop a thief determined to steal computer equipment, but steps can be taken to discourage the opportunist, including fastening hardware to desks, making sure equipment is not visible to passersby, and making it difficult to enter the business in the first place (e.g., by reinforcing doors,

barring windows, using motion detectors and other alarm devices).

Laptop computers are especially prone to theft because they are light, easy to conceal, and are often used in public places such as airports. There are devices, programs, and good advice that can help businesses lessen the chance that these expensive systems are stolen and can raise the likelihood that they are eventually retrieved if they are stolen.

This work can involve assessing the vulnerability of an office or business, suggesting changes to the setup and modes of operation, and installing security devices.

Skills: A knowledge of the wide range of security devices and software.

Equipment: Your computer equipment is not that important because your work will take place in the client's environment.

Potential customers: Any business with a significant investment in computer hardware and software, and/or valuable data.

Promotion: Produce a brochure with information on your services and directly target your prospective clients. On-line promotion of your services, such as a Web site, gives clients another way of finding you.

Associated businesses: Data backup service, Data archiving, Data security consulting.

L. DATABASE SERVICES

1. Database management

Description: Database management is a consulting service on an on-going basis. It involves helping a business that does not have an in-house database specialist operate a new or existing database. This can include making sure hardware (network servers or stand-alone computers) is not over burdened by a growing database, setting up a suitable backup system, and editing the database fields to adapt to the needs of a growing or changing business.

Database management could also involve setting up remote access, or a system to download information from handheld PCs or personal digital assistants (PDAs).

Skills: Knowledge of database technology and software, as well as experience or training in programming.

Equipment: As the work will likely take place in the client's environment, your equipment is not that important.

Potential customers: Any manufacturer, retailer or wholesaler, medical or legal practitioner, or a service provider needing a client, sales, or inventory database that does not have an in-house systems administrator or database specialist.

Promotion: Advertise in the business section of a local newspaper. List your service in the Yellow Pages or other business directory in your area. Join a local business association, such as a chamber of commerce, to network and learn about new business opportunities.

Associated businesses: Database creation, Database conversion.

2. Database creation

Description: Databases are much in demand, but it is difficult to create one that can be used by other people. Everyone has a way of organizing things that makes sense to them. A good database is not only intuitive to use, it is efficiently constructed and in many cases is integrated with the other software applications that a business uses, such as word processing. Databases are needed for inventory/ordering, reservations, sales and marketing, and billing.

There are many powerful and flexible database programs available, so database creation will involve adapting the software to the client's needs as well as importing information into the database.

Skills: Familiarity with database technology, various database applications, and programming experience or training.

Equipment: As the work will likely take place in the client's environment, your equipment is not that important.

Potential customers: Any manufacturer, retailer or wholesaler, medical or legal practitioner, or a service provider needing a client, sales, or inventory database.

Promotion: Advertise in the business section of a local newspaper. List your service in the Yellow Pages or other business directory in your area. Join a local business association, such as a chamber of commerce, to network and learn about new business opportunities.

Associated businesses: Database management, Database conversion.

3. Database conversion

Description: Database conversion is provided for businesses that are upgrading or changing their current database software to an application that is more suitable to their needs. This could involve consulting with clients to select the right programs and then helping them install the new programs and training staff to use it. It also involves making sure clients' hardware configurations meet the system requirements of the new database applications, and eliminating any conflicts with other software.

Skills: Familiarity with database technology, various database applications, and programming experience or training.

Equipment: As the work will likely take place in the client's environment, your equipment is not that important.

Potential customers: Any manufacturer, retailer or wholesaler, medical or legal practitioner, or a service provider that is upgrading a client, sales, or inventory database.

Promotion: Advertise in the business section of a local newspaper. List your service in the Yellow Pages or other business directory in your area. Join a local business association, such as a chamber of commerce, to network and learn about new business opportunities.

Associated businesses: Database creation, Database management.

M. E-MAIL SERVICES

1. Mailing list service

Description: A mailing list service offers private e-mail discussion groups for business or personal use. It might also be attractive to an electronically inclined, but geographically dispersed, family or group of friends that wishes to keep in touch. This service gives members their own mailing list, allowing the group to keep in touch without having to remember a long list of Internet addresses. To deliver a message to all members of the group, an individual simply need send his or her message to the single e-mail address of the discussion group. The service will then forward the message to all members registered with the mailing list.

This is an excellent adjunct to other e-mail services.

Skills: Knowledge of e-mail software and technology.

Equipment: A computer with a high-speed modem and e-mail software.

Potential customers: Clubs or organizations such as university or college alumni associations that are geographically dispersed but want to keep in touch with members as easily as possible.

Promotion: Contact potential clients directly with a brochure describing your mailing list service.

Associated businesses: Anonymous remailer service, Electronic mailbox service, Junk e-mail filter service.

2. Electronic mailbox service

Description: It is common for Internet users to switch service providers as they find the service wanting or cheaper prices from other providers. By using an electronic mailbox service, these people won't lose mail as they change ISPs.

Each time Internet users change providers, their e-mail address changes (unless they have their own domain name). An electronic mailbox service provides users with an e-mail address that remains constant regardless of the ISP. All mail that arrives at the electronic mailbox is automatically forwarded to the client at their new ISP e-mail address.

As a provider of this service, you give clients an e-mail account for a nominal monthly or annual fee.

Skills: Knowledge of e-mail software and technology.

Equipment: A computer with a high-speed modem and e-mail software.

Potential customers: Individual Internet users or small business operators.

Promotion: Advertise in a newspaper or other publication that has advertising for ISPs in your area. List your service in the Yellow Pages or other local directory of business services.

Associated businesses: Anonymous re-mailer service, junk e-mail filter service, mailing list service.

3. Anonymous re-mailer service

Description: Some e-mail users prefer that their on-line interactions remain anonymous but reachable by e-mail (e.g., if they are responding to personal advertisements).

With an anonymous re-mailer service, a client sends an advertisement or message to the re-mailer's computer system. The message contains the address of its final destination embedded in the body. The re-mailer forwards it to its intended destination, substituting an anonymous address for the user's real e-mail address. The re-mailer's computer retains the connection between the user's real e-mail address and the anonymous address. When e-mail is sent back to the user at the anonymous address, the re-mailer receives the e-mail and forwards it to the real address, keeping the user's address hidden from the sender.

Skills: System administration skills, familiarity with e-mail software and technology.

Equipment: A computer with high-speed modem and e-mail software.

Potential customers: Individuals who want to keep their identity and personal or professional on-line transactions anonymous for security or other reasons.

Promotion: Develop a Web site promoting your service and register it with several search engines so potential subscribers can find you. Advertise in a local newspaper or other publication that carries advertisements for ISPs and on-line personal advertisements.

Associated businesses: Junk e-mail filter service, Electronic mailbox service, Mailing list service.

4. Junk e-mail filter service

Description: This service, which involves electronically sifting through e-mail for messages, is attractive to Internet users who don't want junk e-mail (also known as spam). All incoming e-mail is electronically reviewed, which means a program looks for key words or phrases or messages that originate from specific people or Internet domains that are known as sources of spam. This does not involve a person opening and reading private e-mail.

Junk e-mail filtering is the equivalent of telephone call blocking that is available for voice-telephone service. This is an excellent adjunct to an electronic mailbox or anonymous re-mailer service.

Skills: System administration skills, familiarity with e-mail and filtering software.

Equipment: A computer with a high-speed modem, and e-mail and filtering software.

Potential customers: Individuals or small businesses that don't have the time or inclination to deal with junk e-mail.

Promotion: Advertise in a newspaper or other publication that has advertisements for ISPs in your area. List your service in the Yellow Pages or other local directory of business services.

Associated businesses: Electronic mailbox service, Anonymous re-mailer service, Mailing list service.

N. INTRANET AND NETWORK SERVICES

1. Network consulting

Description: The one-computer office, and even the one-computer home, is becoming less common. As businesses get more computers, they recognize the need to link those systems to share peripherals (such as printers) and data, as well as for simple e-mail communication within a business and access to the Internet.

Some larger businesses set up their own versions of the Internet, called intranets. These internal corporate networks offer e-mail communication, as well as graphical functions such as home pages and on-line databases that are accessible only to those within the network.

Network consulting involves helping a business select and set up the hardware and software needed for its network as well as training staff.

Skills: Knowledge of networking hardware and software. Experience and/or training in network administration.

Equipment: As the work will likely take place in the client's environment, your own equipment is not that important.

Potential customers: Businesses or organizations of any size that want to set up networks.

Promotion: Advertise in the business section of a local newspaper. List your service in the Yellow Pages or other local directory of business services.

Associated businesses: Network administration.

2. Intranet administration

Description: Once a business has its network up and running, it still needs attention since the intranet is the pipeline of all internal correspondence, and, in some cases, the site of databases of important information. The administration of the network can involve solving hardware or software conflicts, making sure the intranet has adequate and updated virus protection, as well as setting up connections for remote workers or telecommuters.

Skills: Familiarity with networking software and hardware, as well as some network administration training or experience.

Equipment: As the work will likely take place in the client's environment, your equipment is not that important.

Potential customers: Any business with an internal network but no in-house network administrator.

Promotion: Advertise in the business section of a local newspaper. List your service in the Yellow Pages or other local directory of business services. Join a local business association, such as a chamber of commerce or board of trade, to network and learn about new business opportunities.

Associated businesses: Network consulting.

O. WEB SITE DESIGN AND SERVICES

1. Web site design

Description: More and more people are accessing the World Wide Web and more and more businesses are developing an on-line presence. Web sites now play a real role in marketing a business or organization, so there is a growing need for designers who can provide technical knowledge and an eye for design to develop professional-looking, easily navigable Web sites that will hold a reader's attention.

If the sites you are designing and marketing include products or services that can be ordered on-line, your technical knowledge will need to encompass the various on-line payment methods.

Skills: Knowledge of on-line programming languages and standards, Web site design software and on-line payment setup and options.

Equipment: Web site design software and a computer with a powerful processor and enough RAM and storage capacity to run the application. As well, a high-speed Internet connection is required.

Potential customers: Businesses, institutions, and organizations that want to develop an on-line presence.

Promotion: Advertise in the business section of a local newspaper. List your service in the Yellow Pages or other local directory of business services. If you are new to this type of business, consider developing a Web site for a local charity or service organization as a way of gaining experience and references.

Associated businesses: Web site administration, On-line form design.

2. Web site administration

Description: Once a Web site is operating — especially one that includes frequent updates and changes, or access to databases or archives — there is a need for frequent attention to make sure links within the site or to other sites still exist and that on-line forms or payment interfaces are functioning.

Administering a client's Web site can be done remotely from your own office or home office.

Skills: Knowledge of on-line programming languages and standards, and familiarity with on-line payment systems, forms, and applications (if these are aspects of the site).

Equipment: A computer with a powerful processor and enough RAM and storage capacity to run the application. As well, a high-speed Internet connection is required.

Potential customers: Any business, institution, or organization with a Web site but no staff member skilled or responsible for administering it.

Promotion: Advertise in the business section of a local newspaper. List your service in the Yellow Pages or other local directory of business services. Develop a Web site promoting your service as your potential

clientele is already on-line. Register your Web site with several search engines, especially those that are regional or national, so clients can find you on-line.

Associated businesses: Web site design, On-line form design.

3. On-line form design

Description: On-line forms and applications are a very useful addition to a Web site. An on-line form can be used by students to apply for entrance to an educational institution, by members of an association to register for an upcoming conference in another city, for a customer to order a product, or for readership surveys by on-line magazines or newspapers.

While there *are* elements of design in this work, creating such forms is a more technical task than Web site design and involves working with databases and usually some form of data encryption.

Skills: Familiarity with on-line programming, database applications, and encryption standards.

Equipment: A computer with a powerful processor and enough RAM and storage capacity to run database software. As well, a high-speed Internet connection is required.

Potential customers: Businesses, institutions, or organizations with an on-line presence that want to make their Web sites more interactive.

Promotion: Advertise in the business section of a local newspaper. List your service in the Yellow Pages or other local directory of business services. Develop your own Web site with working examples of various on-line forms and applications.

Associated businesses: Web site design, Web site administration, Mail order sales (on-line).

4. On-line catalogue creation

Description: This is a niche area of Web site design. It involves helping a business create a virtual catalogue of products, including descriptions, images, pricing, and shipping or delivery information. The site will also include some form of on-line ordering and payment.

If the business has an existing, paper-based catalogue, the original images and copy can likely be used for the Web site. If not, your work might include writing or commissioning the copy and taking photographs of the products.

Skills: Familiarity with on-line programming languages, Web site design and database applications, encryption standards, and methods of on-line payment available from various financial institutions and ISPs.

Equipment: Web site design and database software and a computer with a powerful processor and enough RAM and storage capacity to run the application. As well, a high-speed Internet connection is required.

Potential customers: Any manufacturer, retailer, or wholesaler that sells products or services.

Promotion: Advertise in the business section of a local newspaper. List your service in the Yellow Pages or other local directory of business services. Develop your own Web site with a mock catalogue or links to sites of current or former clients.

Associated businesses: Web site design, Web site administration, On-line form design.

5. Electronic mall service

Description: An electronic mall is a series of catalogues for several businesses accessible through one Web site with a unified on-line ordering and payment system. This allows small businesses that do not have the time, expertise, or money to develop and administer their own site to have an on-line presence.

As with developing on-line catalogues, this service involves creating a virtual catalogue of products, including descriptions, images, pricing, and shipping information.

Skills: Familiarity with on-line programming languages, Web site design and database applications, encryption standards, and methods of on-line payment available from various financial institutions and ISPs.

Equipment: Web site design and database software and a computer with a powerful processor and enough RAM and storage capacity to run the application. As well, a high-speed Internet connection is required.

Potential customers: Small manufacturers, retailers, or wholesalers — including craftspeople and artisans — that want to expand the market for their products or services. Try to group together complementary, not competing, service providers and producers.

Promotion: Develop a brochure promoting your service and deliver it directly to potential clients. The brochure could include the address to your Web site, which could contain a mock up of an electronic mall or links to an example of your work for other clients. List your service in the Yellow Pages or other local directory of business services.

Associated businesses: Web site design, On-line catalogue creation.

6. Bulletin board service

Description: A bulletin board service (BBS) is a subscription-based on-line service provider with membership in the hundreds, thousands, or tens of thousands. BBSs tend to be local and generally don't have toll-free access. Typical services provided by a BBS to subscribers are discussion groups, conferencing, document search and retrieval, fax on demand, real-time chat, electronic entertainment, e-mail, computer files for downloading (e.g., games, applications, photographs), and even Internet access.

If you have a particular hobby or expertise, this is an excellent business opportunity as it will combine your area of interest with business.

Skills: Familiarity with BBS software and on-line technology.

Equipment: A computer with a modem and BBS software.

Potential customers: Members of the on-line community that share a particular interest, hobby, or occupation.

Promotion: Research current BBSs to see whether there is an area of interest that is not yet served by a BBS, or one that you could improve on. Register your BBS with on-line directories of BBSs in your area code so that potential subscribers can find you.

Associated businesses: Mail order sales (on-line), Mailing list service, Anonymous re-mailer service.

P. SALES AND MARKETING

1. Mail order sales

Description: This service involves setting up a mail order sales system for a client or running the system yourself. The first step is to develop and design an on-line, CD-ROM, or paper-based catalogue, then set up an order and payment system.

This type of service is especially appealing to craftspeople, artisans, or small producers who would like to spend more time at their craft or business and do not have the time or skills to market their products.

As with an electronic mall service, a mail order sales catalogue and ordering system can also be developed for a group of small businesses that cannot afford this service individually.

Skills: Training or experience in sales and marketing. Familiarity with on-line, CD-ROM, or desktop publishing technology, as well as with on-line ordering and payment systems and courier and mail services in your area.

Equipment: The type of system required depends on the type of technology used. The minimum requirement is a computer capable of running database software to track sales, delivery, and inventory. For design purposes — whether for desktop publishing, Web site, or multimedia design — a more powerful processor, more RAM, and storage capacity will be required, in addition to the requisite software and peripherals (e.g., printers, scanners, drawing tablets, and digital cameras). A modem and Internet connection is also required for on-line ordering and communicating with clients and their customers.

Potential customers: Small producers and service providers, artisans, and craftspeople.

Promotion: Contact clients directly with samples of your work: a paper-based catalogue, a CD-ROM, or an on-line catalogue (you could run a sample version, for which you wouldn't need an Internet connection, from a laptop computer). Offer to demonstrate your service to an association of craftspeople, artisans, or small producers in your area.

Associated businesses: On-line catalogue creation, Direct-mail marketing.

2. Direct-mail marketing

Description: Direct-mail marketing involves helping a client with a special promotion to target as directly as possible a particular type of buyer for the product or service, or even potential donors for a charity or nonprofit organization.

Developing this type of mailing list can include buying a list used in a recent campaign with a similar customer profile or researching existing surveys and databases. Statistics Canada, for example, will sell marketers census information by postal code (this federal agency does not sell information on individuals but rather will give percentages of individuals within a postal code area who fit a specific demographic, such as income, occupation, marital status, or number of children).

The skill in this type of work is making sure the information is as fresh and accurate as possible.

Skills: Excellent research skills. Training or experience in marketing. Knowledge of statistics, as well as sources of suitable, up-to-date mailing lists and postal code and other databases.

Equipment: A computer with a powerful processor (for searching and compiling databases), inkjet printer, modem, and Internet connection. You will also need database and word-processing software.

Potential customers: Any business or nonprofit agency that does not have staff specializing in direct marketing.

Promotion: Contact potential customers directly. Join an association of marketing professionals in your area to network and learn about business opportunities. If you have limited or no experience in this type of marketing, consider helping a charity or nonprofit organization with its direct-mail campaign on a volunteer basis as a way of developing skills and references.

Associated businesses: Fax-on-demand service, Mail order sales (on-line).

3. Computer accessory sales

Description: Selling computer accessories is an excellent sideline for an existing consulting business that focuses on a narrow area of technology where accessories may be unusual or hard to find. Areas suitable for this type of sales include ergonomic computing accessories and computing accessories for people with disabilities.

Specializing in this type of sales work involves researching technology to find new and unusual solutions for people with disabilities or injured computer users. Manufacturers of these types of limited distribution products often welcome an agreement for someone to represent their products outside their normal distribution channels.

If you are living in a small town or rural area without access to a computer store, you could sell more common computing accessories, such as keyboards, mice, and other input devices, and some software.

Skills: Some sales skills and knowledge of the particular field you are specializing in, for example, background in working with people with disabilities if this is your target market.

Equipment: If your work involves demonstrating the system in the client's environment, you will need a portable computer that is compatible with the accessories or software you are demonstrating. An Internet connection is advisable to communicate with manufacturers and to research new products and developments. It will also allow you to create a Web site to promote your service.

Potential customers: Individual buyers or businesses with special needs.

Promotion: Contact potential clients directly and distribute a brochure describing a few of the products you sell. This could include the address of your Web site, where you could have a more complete, up-to-date listing of the products.

If you are located in a remote area and are selling more common accessories, consider hosting an evening where you demonstrate the products you are selling. This is an excellent thing to do if you are selling educational software as it will give people a chance to try before they buy.

Associated businesses: Used PC sales, Ergonomics consulting, Consulting for people with disabilities, Computer setup and training.

4. Used PC sales

Description: Individuals and small businesses that upgrade their computer systems often have no need for their old computers. They would welcome some cash for systems they deem obsolete, but finding buyers may involve more time and energy than they are willing to devote to it.

But these machines — even 286 and 386 PCs — are still suitable for word processing, running simple DOS programs, and use as basic e-mail terminals. Older Pentium-based PCs or 486s have an even wider range of uses.

If you are willing to invest some money in this type of business, you could buy, recondition, then sell the used machines. Another option is to act as a broker and sell the computer systems on a consignment basis: you get a percentage of the final sale price, or the owner gets a flat amount once the computer is sold. The only investment in the latter is in advertising and any retail rent or storage.

While software also becomes obsolete, there is less money in used titles than in selling hardware. You may want to consider selling software as a sideline to selling hardware, however.

Skills: Knowledge of the going rate for computer hardware. In addition to finding sellers, you will also need to develop a good source of buyers, so sales and marketing skills are an asset for developing this business opportunity.

Equipment: While a basic computer is helpful for inventory and accounting purposes, a more powerful, Web-enabled computer system is necessary if you plan to market your service via a Web site or to communicate with buyers and sellers through e-mail.

Potential customers: On the selling side, any individuals or businesses that are upgrading their computer systems. On the buying side, any individual or business looking for a secondary system or an additional system that can perform limited tasks for a network.

Promotion: List your business in the Yellow Pages or other directory of business services in your area. Whether buying or selling, distribute to libraries, community centers, and educational institutions a brochure describing the types of systems you are interested in buying and selling. Distribute this brochure directly to potential buyers. Consider developing a Web site (which you can promote in the brochure) on which you could list your inventory and current rates for buying and selling systems. Through this site, you could communicate with potential buyers and sellers via e-mail.

Associated businesses: Computer accessory sales.

DEFINITIONS OF ABBREVIATIONS

CD: compact disc
CD-R: CD-recordable
CD-ROM: CD-read-only memory
CDRW: CD-rewriteable
EPS: encapsulated postscript
GIF: graphics interchange format
ISDN: integrated services digital network
ISP: Internet service provider

JPG: joint photographic experts group
Mb: megabyte
MO: magneto-optic
OCR: optical character recognition
PC: personal computer
RAM: random-access memory
TIFF: tagged image file format

Part II

GETTING

STARTED IN

YOUR SMALL

BUSINESS

2
SELF-ASSESSMENT

M any small business owners never do a thorough, honest appraisal of their strengths and weaknesses. If you haven't identified your skills, attributes, and talents, how can you determine your computer specialty areas and the target market? How are you able to package and sell your services and take advantage of opportunities? Without this awareness it is difficult to project the self-confidence necessary to operate your business and respond to questions a potential client might ask you.

Most people never go through the steps outlined in this chapter, and that gives you a distinct competitive advantage. To know yourself — your strengths and weaknesses — is to have power and a prescription for success.

A. ASSESSING YOURSELF AND YOUR MARKETABLE SKILLS

The following exercise is important to help you determine the direction you should take in your new business using your computer skills. For the maximum benefit, take all the time you need to complete each stage. Be honest and candid with yourself. The material you are preparing is for your information and benefit only.

After you have completed the exercise, you will have a comprehensive, detailed, and exhaustive guideline for your successful business. Review it, update it, and modify it on a regular basis. If you have taken the time to thoughtfully complete the exercise, you should feel confident that you have developed a realistic framework for the next important stages of your business development.

81

SELF-ASSESSMENT

1. Summarize your own autobiography. Review and detail all facets of your past, including work positions, projects you have done, education, credentials you have obtained, free-time activities including hobbies and sports, and family and personal relationships. Include all the work experiences performed during summers, weekends, or holidays. Start with the most current period and work backward.

2. List all areas of your special interest, achievement, knowledge, and personal satisfaction.

3. List all your skills, that is, things that you can do. Skills are developed or acquired abilities such as instructing, administering, researching, and problem-solving.

4. List all your talents. Talents are a natural endowment, often a unique "gift" or special, often creative, attribute. Frequently a talent is a combination of skills. Think of any evaluations that may have been made about you or comments made by your friends in which your talents were observed.

5. List all your attributes. Attributes are inherent characteristics such as an analytical or inquiring mind, intuition, or sensitivity. Various studies have found the following attributes essential to a successful business:
    *   Good physical and mental health
    *   Professional etiquette and courtesy
    *   Stability of behavior
    *   Self-confidence
    *   Personal effectiveness and drive; that is, responsibility, vigor, initiative, resourcefulness, and persistence
    *   Integrity; that is, the quality that engenders trust
    *   Independence; the successful business owner must be self-reliant and not conform to the opinions of others; must be able to form judgments in the areas of his or her competence and experience
    *   Intellectual competence
    *   Good judgment; the faculty of sound appraisal with complete objectivity
    *   Strong analytical or problem-solving ability; the ability to analyze, assemble, sort, balance, and evaluate the basic factors of challenging situations of different degrees of complexity

- Creative imagination; the ability to see the situation from a fresh perspective
- Ability to communicate and persuade, with above-average facility, in oral, written, and graphic formats
- Psychological maturity; the successful business owner is always ready to experience people, things, and events as they really are, with their unique individual characteristics; to view them in perspective and to take the action needed in a calm and objective manner without being diverted from a sound, logical, and ethical course by outside pressure
- Skill in interpersonal relationships, including an ability to gain the trust and respect of clients; a receptiveness to new information or points of view expressed by others; and an appreciation of the dynamics of interpersonal communication
- Technical knowledge, which means an all-encompassing knowledge of the business and also recognizing lack of skill where it exists and seeking to acquire that skill or employing people with that skill

6. List all the skills and attributes you lack that you believe are necessary for your specific type of business.

7. List the skills and attributes you lack related to being a business owner that you believe you can improve; write down how that will happen and how long it will take. Prioritize.

8. Of the skills and attributes that you believe you cannot improve, state how they will affect your business choices, if at all.

9. Speak to friends, relatives, or family members who know you well and whose judgment, candor, and goodwill you respect. Ask them to think about your strengths and weaknesses as they see them, and prepare a list. Also ask them to outline the skills, talents, and attributes they believe you possess and those you lack.

10. Update and modify the personal inventories you previously prepared.

11. Review your list of skills, talents, and attributes and provide specific examples where each trait was used that could have a marketing application in providing your business services.

12. Prioritize the ten activities that gave you the most pleasure and personal satisfaction. Outline how well you did these activities. Don't overestimate or underestimate your abilities.

13. List the top ten skills or talents, starting with the most important, that you feel are basic to your business.

14. Imagine the type of business projects that you would like to do. Write them down in detail as well as why you would like to do them. Then review your notes and identify the skills, talents, and attributes required to successfully complete these projects.

15. Imagine your personal life in the future. In what direction are you currently headed with your family and career, socially, financially, spiritually, and personally? What effect would a business have on your existing lifestyle? Would the long hours and pressure of the first 6 to 12 months create strains on the family? Are you interested in marketing your abilities locally, regionally, nationally, or internationally? What effect will these decisions have on you and the people in your life?

16. Think of all the business opportunities that might be available to you. Part I of this book should have stimulated your ideas further.

17. Increase your awareness of additional business opportunities by using the following resources.

    (a) *Magazines and newspapers.* You should attempt to read everything you can relating to your computer specialty and general awareness of current events. Subscribe to trade journals related to your area of interest. Get on all the free mailing lists that are of interest or relevance to your specialty area. Read your local daily newspaper and, in Canada, the *Globe and Mail* and the *Financial Post*; in the United States, the *New York Times,* the *Washington Post,* and the *Wall Street Journal.* There are other newspapers, of course, that you might prefer to read, but these provide a general indication of trends and interpretation of important events, all of which could have a bearing on opportunities for your business.

    There are numerous excellent business and computer magazines which can stimulate further ideas and sources of contacts and information. Browse through your local international news outlet for an indication of the publications available. Another alternative is your public library.

(b) *Professional associations.* Contact with professional associations will provide you with an opportunity to obtain information related specifically to your specialty from newsletters, publications, meetings, or other business contacts. Check with your local public library for directories and associations in the U.S. and Canada.

If there is a local association of business owners, either of a general or specialized nature relevant to your needs (for example, the chamber of commerce), try to attend a number of meetings and ask a lot of questions.

The Small Business Administration (SBA) in the United States sponsors SCORE (Service Corps of Retired Executives), an organization providing consulting without charge for beginning businesses. The Business Development Bank of Canada (BDC) sponsors Counselling Assistance to Small Enterprises (CASE), which is a program where consultants at a very normal rate provide expertise and research skills to beginning small businesses. You may wish to take advantage of their expertise to assist you with the business aspects of your business. (These organizations are discussed in more detail in chapter 5.)

(c) *Government agencies and publications.* Depending on the area of your interest, you may want to get on the mailing list of government organizations or departments that have regular publications distributed free or at a nominal charge to the public. The government could be a purchaser of your services.

(d) *Public and university libraries.* There is a vast amount of information that is current and accessible for you to research or to get general ideas at public and university libraries.

(e) *Continuing education courses and seminars.* School boards, colleges, and universities have continuing education courses pertaining to business and related services. The SBA (U.S.) and the BDC (Canada) have small business seminars and workshops on an ongoing basis, as well as numerous publications pertaining to successful small business management.

(f) *Competitors.* Attempt to identify the competitors in your specific field. Determine what their styles and methods of operation are, how long they have been in business, how they market themselves, what they charge, and who their clientele is. Try to ascertain why they are successful, if they are, and how you can best distinguish yourself and find your own niche in the market. You want to have your own unique style if comparisons are made between you and your other competitors by a prospective client.

18. Define the computer services you would like to provide.

19. Identify who you believe could be possible clients and why.

20. Project how you would like to operate your business. List the important stages and time frames of your business over the next year, three years, and five years.

21. List how you intend to market your services, that is, how you intend to create a demand for your service and make potential clients realize that you exist. This issue will be discussed in chapter 12, but it is helpful to go through the reflective exercise yourself.

3

SETTING UP YOUR BUSINESS

You have now assessed your skills, attributes, and abilities and have determined your area of interest and expertise. Various administrative matters have to be understood, considered, and dealt with before embarking on your road to success.

This chapter and the following chapters deal with the administrative fundamentals.

Before setting up your office and opening your doors to the public, many matters have to be considered. Your fee structures, marketing plan, and business plan, which includes your cash flow projections, will all determine how much revenue you must generate to pay your overhead. It is wise to be conservative when estimating anticipated revenue and the lead time it will take to reach a break-even point. Your legal, tax, accounting, and financial advisers will influence your initial decisions.

These important aspects are covered in other chapters.

This chapter discusses how to establish the basics of an office while controlling your expenses. With thorough review and comparison of the costs of the key overhead areas, you should require minimal capital investment and keep your overhead and risk at a safe level.

A. START-UP COSTS AND MONTHLY EXPENSES

There are many factors that determine what your costs and expenses are going to be, such as whether you are going to use your own home or rent an office, whether you are going to buy, finance, or lease new or used furniture and equipment, and whether you intend to hire staff or do the typing yourself. Your individual finances and needs and your shrewdness and negotiating ability will clearly affect your overhead.

1. Start-up costs

Start-up costs vary widely depending on your choices and circumstances. Sample #1 is a start-up expense checklist for estimating initial costs of your business. It is important to keep a record of your estimated and actual costs for overhead expenses as well as for your cash flow projections during the start-up and first year of operation. The date to pay column should assist you in scheduling your cash flow or other funds to meet the initial expenses. You should be able to fill in the estimated costs schedule after you have done your research thoroughly. Further details on aspects of start-up costs are covered later.

2. Monthly overhead expenses

Naturally, monthly expenses will vary widely depending on the type of service you are planning to operate. Sample #2 should assist you in planning and budgeting for your possible overhead expenses.

3. Personal expenses

Personal monthly overhead expenses obviously influence your cash flow needs and the amount of resources available to invest in your business. When you prepare your business plan (see chapter 6), you will take into account your personal needs. It will be helpful, though, to consider your personal cash flow needs while planning your

business expense outlay. See Sample #3 as a guide for detailing your personal expenses.

B. SELECTING A NAME

Selecting your name is an important decision, both from an image and from a legal perspective. It is essential to be aware of the implications of selecting your name from the outset.

1. General considerations

Many business owners prefer to use their own name because they are offering a personal service and promoting and selling themselves. The drawback of using your name is that it implies a one-person operation; this could cause a client to doubt your capacity to complete a project if you are ill or injured.

If you decide to incorporate your business, you must have the name approved by the responsible government department and the name must end in Ltd. or Limited, Inc. or Incorporation, or Corp. or Corporation. The pros and cons of forming a corporation are discussed in another chapter.

2. Fictitious name

If you are operating your proprietorship or partnership business under a name other than your own, you are required in most jurisdictions to register your fictitious name. Filing for fictitious names does not apply to corporations.

The procedures vary from area to area. The costs generally range from $10 to $75. Ask your lawyer about the requirements for your area. The procedure generally is to fill out

Expense	Date to pay	Estimated cost	Actual cost
Business licenses and permits	_____	$ _____	$ _____
Business announcement or other initial business development including brochures	_____	_____	_____
Supplies and stationery	_____	_____	_____
Equipment/furniture	_____	_____	_____
Rental deposit on office (if outside home: first, second, and last months)	_____	_____	_____
Telephone installation and deposits	_____	_____	_____
Utility deposits (if outside home)	_____	_____	_____
Insurance (health, life, liability, theft, etc.; unless paid monthly or quarterly)	_____	_____	_____
Legal and accounting	_____	_____	_____
Professional or business membership or expenses	_____	_____	_____
Answering service deposit (first and last months)	_____	_____	_____
Other	_____	_____	_____
Cushion for unexpected costs (contingency)	_____	_____	_____

Sample #1
Start-up
Expenses

89

Sample #2 Monthly Expenses

Expense	Date to pay	Estimated cost	Actual cost
Office rent (if outside home)	_____	$_____	$_____
Printing and supplies (not paid for by clients)	_____	_____	_____
Equipment (monthly payment and/or what you need to set aside for future cash purchases)	_____	_____	_____
Preparation of tax return and other accounting expenses	_____	_____	_____
Legal services (projected and prorated)	_____	_____	_____
Typing and secretarial services	_____	_____	_____
Telephone	_____	_____	_____
Utilities (if outside home)	_____	_____	_____
Insurance costs (prorated over 12 months)	_____	_____	_____
Retirement contribution if applicable (estimated costs prorated)	_____	_____	_____
Savings (for yourself and your business)	_____	_____	_____
Loan payment	_____	_____	_____
Taxes (including social security or pension plan prorated over 12 months)	_____	_____	_____
License renewal (prorated)	_____	_____	_____
Advertising	_____	_____	_____
Answering service	_____	_____	_____
Subscriptions	_____	_____	_____
Books and reference material	_____	_____	_____
Marketing	_____	_____	_____
Entertainment and promotion	_____	_____	_____
Automobile	_____	_____	_____
Travel (in town or out)	_____	_____	_____
Conventions, professional meetings, trade shows	_____	_____	_____
Professional development	_____	_____	_____
Salary (what you need to meet personal expenses)	_____	_____	_____
Miscellaneous	_____	_____	_____

Budget for the month of _____

Item	Budget	Actual	Deviation
Food	$ _____	$ _____	$ _____
Housing			
Monthly payment	_____	_____	_____
Taxes (if owned)	_____	_____	_____
Insurance	_____	_____	_____
Clothing	_____	_____	_____
Auto			
Payment	_____	_____	_____
Gasoline	_____	_____	_____
Repairs	_____	_____	_____
Insurance	_____	_____	_____
Utilities			
Electricity	_____	_____	_____
Heat (if not electric)	_____	_____	_____
Telephone	_____	_____	_____
Other (water, gas)	_____	_____	_____
Personal spending (gifts)	_____	_____	_____
Credit cards (not covered elsewhere)	_____	_____	_____
Installment and other loans	_____	_____	_____
Life insurance	_____	_____	_____
Taxes	_____	_____	_____
Recreation	_____	_____	_____
Travel	_____	_____	_____
Investment, including saving	_____	_____	_____
Donations	_____	_____	_____
Medical and dental	_____	_____	_____
Education (family)	_____	_____	_____
Miscellaneous	_____	_____	_____
Totals	$ _____	$ _____	$ _____

forms disclosing the people behind the name and, in some cases, to place an advertisement in the local newspaper or legal gazette outlining the information in the filing documents.

C. SELECTING AN OFFICE

Many start-up small business owners operate out of their homes. As the business grows, the decision might be made to move into outside office space.

Usually, you will go to the client's office, rather than the client coming to you.

1. Home office

There are several advantages to operating out of your home. You save money on gas and rent. The stress of commuting to work is reduced. You are able to deduct from income tax the portion of your home you are using for business purposes. (The tax deductions you can use when you have a home office are covered in chapter 8). Being close to family is also an important consideration for many people.

There are also disadvantages to having a home office. You may be distracted by your family members during the work day, or your presence may be distracting to family members. The mix of home and office dynamics could negatively affect your private life. You could turn into a workaholic because of the proximity of your office. Your home might be distant from your clients' offices, which would make it difficult for you to visit clients. If clients come to your home office on occasion, your home must present a positive impression and not detract from your professional image.

Because of the limitations of working out of your home, you may wish to consider a professional identity package provided by various office service businesses. This includes a mail-drop address and telephone answering service, as well as other features you may desire.

Using a mail drop means having an address that is recognizable as a business. The staff at this location are able to receive or send out courier packages for you and receive envelopes or messages from clients who may stop by "your" office.

These services can generally be found under "Secretarial Services" or "Stenographers — Public" in the Yellow Pages.

A post office box number has a negative effect in terms of your credibility and business reliability, and should be avoided if possible. However, there is a way to avoid this problem. One of the largest mail box rental franchise operations in North America and internationally is Mail Boxes, Etc. But look in the Yellow Pages under "Mail Box Rentals" and you will see a listing for many companies that provide a wide range of other services such as fax transmissions, e-mail, courier, word processing, desktop publishing, and photocopying. If you work out of your home, it may be an advantage to rent a mail box. Such boxes tend to have a three-digit number, so you could put a number symbol in front of the digits, for example, #220 - 500 Main Street, Anytown. For security and marketing reasons, you may prefer to keep your home address confidential.

Having a personalized telephone answering service connected to your telephone at home lets you know your telephone calls are being handled in a professional manner whether you are at home or out at meetings. By keeping the answering service informed of your schedule for the day, your callers will receive the appropriate response and know when their calls might be returned.

Generally, it's not a good idea to use an answering machine; it doesn't present a professional image, and callers get the impression that you are a one-person operation (which, of course, you may be).

2. Office outside of home

You may wish to get an office outside your home when circumstances and finances justify it.

When considering an office location, you should examine factors such as expense, image of business address, and your proximity to clients.

Try to look at your long-range goals over two years and imagine what your office needs might be. It is costly to pay for new office stationery and other start-up costs, and several moves may create an image of instability.

(a) Office sharing arrangement

You may wish to look for an office with complementary professional or business tenants and prospective business clients. In this kind of setup, you have your own office and generally supply your own personal office furniture, but the rent expenses of the office and the receptionist's salary are shared on a proportional basis by the tenants. Secretarial expenses are negotiated depending on use.

If you do seek out a pooling arrangement, try to have a minimal notice period to vacate. You may wish to leave because of expansion, inability to pay the rent, or personality conflicts. It is fairly common to have a three-month notice provision. Make sure that the terms of your rental relationship are in writing and signed by the necessary parties before you begin your relationship.

As a general caution, avoid sharing space with a client. You could have a falling out or the client could attempt to use your time for free or look on you as staff.

(b) Sharing same private office

Two or more people may use the same office space. The parties agree on the costs of furnishing the office, unless it is already furnished, and an agreement is worked out in terms of the hours and days of use. Costs of this arrangement are negotiated on a per-use basis.

(c) Office rental package

There are firms in the business of renting packaged office space. There can be anywhere from 5 to 50 tenants or more. Each tenant has a private office, and there is a common reception area.

The office package arrangement could be a good source of potential contacts for networking or prospective clients, depending on the mix of the tenants.

Telephone answering and office furniture are frequently included in the package price, as well as a nominal number of hours of secretarial time per month. The rental arrangement may be a minimum two- or three-month notice to vacate, or a six-month or one-year lease arrangement. Prices and terms of various office package arrangements may be negotiable if there is competition in that marketplace in your community.

There are several other advantages of an office package arrangement. Other services that might be available to save you considerable money on staff and equipment include:

(a) Street mailing address — not a post office box number

(b) Postage metered mail for prompt delivery and a professional appearance

(c) Typing and desktop publishing — a variety of typestyles available on computer for letters, reports, invoices, statements, etc.

(d) Dictaphone transcription

(e) Secretarial services, including letter composition and editing using correct business language and form

(f) Photocopying — a bond copier with various features including collating could be available to produce quality copies on your letterhead, transparencies, or address labels

(g) Word-processing services with the advantage of speed, efficiency, and storage and retrieval capacity

(h) Data management and bookkeeping

(d) Occasional office

You can rent a board room or an office for as short a time as an hour, a half day, or a day. The cost is negotiable. The occasional office space can be found through office rental package services described earlier. Some firms require that you have a telephone answering or professional identity package arrangement with them before you are able to rent occasional office space.

(e) Leased space

Leasing space has its advantages and disadvantages. The primary drawbacks are the risk that you can't afford the rent at some later point and that the space becomes unsuitable — either too big or too small. It is most important that you consult your accountant and a competent lawyer familiar with commercial leases before signing anything. You should shop around for space to make sure you have the best arrangement for your needs and to assist you in negotiating by knowing what else is out there.

Leases are generally for a period of one to five years. There are three basic types of lease-payment formulas. The terminology may vary, but the concepts are the same. In the first type, called a net lease, the base rent is the total rent. In other words, the flat, negotiated rate is the only monthly payment you need to make.

The second type of rent, *double net*, is similar to the first except you have to pay a pro rata share of any tax increases over the base tax period outlined in your lease. If the taxes increase substantially, you could have extra overhead you had not anticipated.

The third type, *triple net* rent, can be very expensive. The base rent is just the beginning. All other landlord costs, such as taxes, insurance, maintenance, repair, improvements, management, and administration fees, are passed on proportionately to the tenants. This could increase your monthly rent by 50% to 100%. The other problem with this type of rent structure is the uncertainty you face when you try to budget for your rental overhead expenses.

A variation of the triple net rent formula involves paying the landlord a percentage of your gross revenue. For most professionals, this is an unacceptable arrangement.

Some of the clauses to be wary of when you are considering a lease include ones that restrict your ability to sublet or assign your lease, that restrict the use you intend for the premises, or that limit alterations or improvements to the premises; clauses setting out liabilities and duties of the landlord and tenant; acceleration clauses in case of a default; and clauses requiring your personal guarantee if you are doing business as a corporation.

If you are still interested in signing a lease, attempt to negotiate as many attractive features as possible. All leases are negotiable and there are no standard clauses. Your lawyer can properly advise you and possibly negotiate the lease on your behalf. If you plan to negotiate your lease yourself, you may want to read *Negotiate Your Commercial Lease*, another title in the Self-Counsel Series. The following tips will help when you are negotiating your lease:

(a) Rather than negotiating a three-year lease, for example, try to negotiate a one-year lease with two additional one-year options. This way you minimize the risk if you later cannot afford the lease, if you need to expand, or if the premises are otherwise unsuitable for your needs.

(b) Consider offering the last two or three months' rent as a deposit. If you default on the lease and leave before the end of the term, the deposit monies go to the landlord and you are free of any further liability.

(c) State in the lease that alterations or improvements you intend to make will be at the landlord's expense.

(d) Attempt to get the first few months free of rent as an incentive for you to lease the premises.

(e) Try to get out of paying the last month's security deposit rent. If this is not possible, try to negotiate with the landlord to pay you interest at a fixed rate on the security deposit money.

Another factor in leasing space is the additional expense for furniture and equipment for your office and reception area, plus the additional costs of a secretary or receptionist. All these additional costs have to be carefully factored out to ensure there is sufficient cash flow to justify the commitment.

3. Equipping an office

Equipping an office is not too expensive if you buy secondhand furniture. You can obtain good used business furniture from bankruptcy sales, auction sales, or through the classified section in the newspaper. The type and quality of furniture that you select naturally will relate to your type of clientele and the image you want to project.

Refer to Part III of this book for a discussion of office equipment and setup.

4. Office supplies

The basic supplies you need include business cards, letterhead, stationery and printed envelopes, brochures, records for bookkeeping, invoices, filing folders, and various types of calendars.

(a) Business stationery, cards, envelopes

Your business stationery is very important, as it represents you, your image, and your business. It should present a professional image. It should state your name, your business name, the type of business, address, postal/zip code, and telephone number with area code.

All your stationery should correspond with the format and image of your business card. Choose a good quality paper stock. Purchase blank pages of your letter stock so that your second page will match the color of the first. Neutral shades such as beige, ivory, or white create a professional impression. You have a choice between litho (flat) or thermo (raised) ink. The raised, glossy appearance of thermo creates a richer effect. The cost of raised letter

is not much more than flat, but extra time is required for printing and you can't use thermo ink letterhead with a laser printer. The printing business is very competitive, so be sure to compare rates.

Some people prefer to have a logo on their business cards. Have a graphic artist or desktop publisher design and prepare the logo and other customized material.

(b) Brochures

Depending on the type of business you have and the nature of the clientele you wish to attract, brochures may be part of your marketing plan. You may choose to have a promotional writer assist you in preparing the text for a brochure that will effectively outline the services you provide for your specific clientele or market.

Consider having your brochure designed on a desktop publishing program. Often writers provide desktop layout and design services as well as writing and editing. Such services can be found under the "Sales Promotion Services" section of the Yellow Pages.

For printing, check for competitive rates and allow yourself considerable lead time to obtain the best rate. One color ink on colored stock is less expensive than two inks and can be just as effective. Naturally, brochures are less expensive by quantity.

(c) Record-keeping documents, invoices, and file folders

Record-keeping documents, invoices, and file folders are necessary for the orderly maintenance of projects, systems, and good business management.

(d) Calendars

For recording appointments, telephone calls, and deadlines, you should have a desk calendar, a wall calendar, and a daily diary that you carry with you. The time that you spend on client files must be recorded in detail for proper billing and for your protection if there is dispute.

5. Personnel

(a) Secretarial staff

Most beginning business owners do not have the workload or cash flow to justify hiring a secretary. It is far more cost efficient and practical to "rent" a secretary. Often, the typing costs related to a client file can be billed directly to the client, in addition to your fees. You then have verification from the typing service if there is any question on your account.

Find a professional typing service that offers temporary or one-time service. Ask how much lead time is required, what the turnaround time is, and what other services it offers. Interview personnel from several professional typing services and ask to see sample copies of their reports, newsletters, and correspondence so that you can judge the professional quality of the work.

A professional secretarial service can also look after all your correspondence and document needs, including preparing invoices and reminder letters for your account receivables. Ask the secretarial service if one staff member only can work on your file so that person will become familiar with your style.

(b) Retaining other specialized experts

Employing another computer expert as an independent contractor is a common technique to reduce overhead and increase your resource base and efficiency. There are times when you might need specialized skills or additional help to be able to satisfy a potential client contract. Try to develop a subcontracting network of experts you can call on when needed. Many people take on projects they could not complete themselves and subcontract portions to someone else.

It is important to maintain your position with your client as the main source of information and communication. In many cases, your client need not know that you have subcontracted out a part of the job.

D. SELECTING A TELEPHONE SYSTEM

Your telephone is, in many ways, a critical lifeline to a successful business. Many small business people start out using their home telephone number and a telephone answering device, but there are problems with this. Inexpensive alternatives exist. The important consideration is the impression your telephone system gives your clients or prospective clients and how effectively you receive incoming messages.

1. Separate telephone at home

Many business owners operating out of their homes prefer to have a line for their businesses separate from their personal lines. This saves the frustration caused by children answering the telephone or family members tying up the telephone with personal calls.

2. Business line terminating at answering service

You may wish to have an office number that does not go to your home but terminates at your answering service. Your answering service can then telephone you at home (if those were your instructions) and advise you of a telephone message.

Alternatively, you could telephone the answering service from time to time to pick up messages. You could then return calls on your personal line. The advantage of this system is that you save on the monthly line charge for a business telephone installed in your home, but you still have a telephone answering capacity.

When selecting an answering service, it is very important to consider the personal aspect of the service. An answering service that has only 40 to 60 lines will generally be more attentive, know your business better, and personalize the responses so that the caller is unaware it is an answering service. Compare various answering services and ask for references from their clients.

The quality of your answering service is vital to the reputation and goodwill of your business. Often, the person answering the telephone will be the first representative of your business to the caller. A drawback of large answering service companies with trunk lines and hundreds of customers is that the switchboard operators are frequently very busy and therefore unable to personalize your telephone messages. Another drawback is the high turnover that can occur in personnel. With the larger answering services, it is very difficult to hide the fact that it is an answering service.

3. Business line terminating at home and answering service

Your business line can pass through an answering service's switchboard. All calls may be intercepted by the answering service if those are your instructions, or you can decide to answer the telephone yourself for certain periods of the day. The answering service staff can be told the appropriate procedures for incoming telephone calls. There are additional monthly line charges for this system.

4. Overline

An overline feature allows an incoming telephone call to come through on a second line while you are on the first line. This is an appropriate feature if you have only one telephone. Too many busy signals give a negative impression and may result in the loss of a prospective client. Another technique is to give out your business telephone number for incoming calls and use your personal telephone for outgoing calls.

5. Measured business line

A measured business line can reduce your monthly telephone charges for service by half. The reduced business rate has a limit of a maximum number of outgoing telephone calls per month. No limit is placed on the number of incoming calls. If you make more than the maximum outgoing calls in a month, you are charged an additional fee per telephone call (usually about 11¢ but it varies).

If you make many outgoing telephone calls, this system is not economical. Some people use the measured line system for incoming calls and their personal telephone for outgoing calls.

6. Shared line

A number of people may agree to share a common telephone number. This is usually a feature offered by a telephone answering service for one of its unused lines. Telephone expenses can be reduced considerably using a shared line. The telephone is answered "4444," "Suite 100," or some such nondescriptive phrase, or it can be answered with a generic business name if there are two or more people receiving calls on the same line.

There are many invaluable telephone feature options available to create an impressive and positive professional business image. They will also save you time and money while improving your efficiency. Ask your telephone company for a current list and details.

E. OTHER COMMUNICATION OPTIONS

1. Telephone answering devices

The purpose of a telephone answering device (TAD) is to help you avoid losing critical calls if you are away from your office. It also acts as an efficient office screening agent. The TAD answers the telephone, gives a message, and accepts a message from the caller on your behalf. After you have dictated your message into the machine, dial your own number so you can critique your message.

There are five basic kinds of answering machines. Because of the intense competition in this market area, comparative pricing is recommended if you are in the market for a TAD.

(a) *Announce only* answers the telephone with one or more prerecorded announcements up to several minutes long.

(b) *Announce/record* gives a prerecorded message and allows the caller to leave a message.

(c) *Call screening* helps you avoid unwanted calls. By turning the volume higher, you can listen to a caller's message without his or her knowledge. If you wish, you can pick up the telephone, interrupt the regular answering cycle, and talk to the caller.

(d) *Record* can record a conversation. This is useful if you need proof that you have communicated important information to another party. In many jurisdictions you are obliged to notify the other party that the call is being recorded. For this reason, some of these machines may emit a tone at intervals to remind both parties that the conversation continues to be recorded.

(e) *Remote control* allows you to transmit a signal from any other telephone by means of a remote device. The machine will automatically respond and play back over the telephone any messages that have been recorded. This is convenient if you are out of town but expect calls at your office.

As mentioned earlier, telephone answering devices have their limitations. They can create an impression that you are very much a beginner in business and still struggling. Some callers find it very annoying to talk to an answering machine; others refuse to leave a message or they leave a message that is unclear. Therefore, you may prefer to consider other options, such as voice mail or an answering service.

2. Voice mail

Voice mail is an effective means of communicating for many businesses. It is similar to a telephone answering machine in various aspects but is far more versatile.

Most telephone companies offer this feature, although generally with just a few menu options for the person phoning. Each menu option involves a separate voice mailbox that is interconnected. There are voice mail companies that can customize features and create new options for you (e.g., pushing a specific number on the telephone to be connected to your associate, to receive a fax, or to have you paged).

You can also buy your own computer software voice mail system. Many professional plans offered through a packaged office service also provide this option. The following are some of the key benefits of voice mail:

- Operates all the time, 24 hours a day, seven days a week.

- You can call-forward your regular telephone number to the voice mail number so that it connects automatically. The advantage of this is that you won't have your sleep interrupted by someone phoning you in the middle of the night (for example, international clients who live in different time zones), as you would if you had a regular answering machine.

- Reduces frustrating games of "telephone tag" because it gives the caller the opportunity to leave a message.

- If you are out of town, you can telephone your voice mail in the evening to benefit from lower long distance rates when you retrieve messages.

- Voice mail can be connected to your pager or cellular, or be programmed to telephone you at your regular telephone number or at another telephone number if a message is left.

3. Toll-free number

You may want to consider obtaining a toll-free telephone number if the nature of your business involves existing or potential clients phoning you long distance. For example, if you offer public seminars across the country, people prefer to telephone a toll-free number rather than incurring long-distance charges. You could have the number directed to a 24-hour, seven-day answering service that will take the registration details and charge card information.

Often, telephone companies charge a nominal basic monthly fee of about $10 for the number, and in addition you pay only actual usage charges with no minimum charge. Basic long-distance rates could be from 30¢ to 40¢ a minute, depending on where the caller is phoning from. However, you are also entitled to time-of-day discounts as well as volume usage discounts. The net effect could be affordable, efficient, and profitable, depending on your needs.

When you obtain a toll-free number, it is reserved for you and accessible throughout the United States and Canada. However, you can limit access to certain area codes if you prefer, depending on your marketing objectives.

4. Generic telephone number

Some business cards have more numbers than a lottery ticket. The caller may not know which is the best number to reach you at: are you available at your office telephone number, pager, voice mail, or cellular telephone number?

Many telephone and other companies offer a single telephone number that can direct calls anywhere you want, for example, to your office, home, car, cellular, voice mailbox, out-of-town hotel number — anywhere in the world. If you are busy or unable to take a call, your caller can leave a message.

Other features are also available, such as call screening (you receive only the calls you want), call connection (caller waits on the line while you are paged to any touch-tone telephone), and call director (gives your caller a number of options).

Some generic numbers also have a fax mail feature that can automatically recognize a fax transmission and store it for future confidential retrieval from any fax machine.

5. Fax on demand

This feature allows you to program an option onto your outgoing voice mail message that lets the caller activate an immediate fax transmission. The caller inputs his or her fax number on a touch-tone telephone and your fax message is sent to the caller's fax machine. You can store any number of pages for transmission on your computer. If you have a business that gives seminars, for example, you can save time by sending out current information for routine enquiries. To save money, check to make sure you are billed on the basis of 6-second transmission increments minimum, not 30 or 60 seconds.

6. Pager

Pagers can be an ideal way to be notified when someone is attempting to reach you by telephone. You can buy, rent, or lease pager units. They are small, light, easily attached to your belt or your pocket, and can notify you with an audio tone or a beep or with a visual or vibrating alert that you have a message. Pager services are available through telephone or private pager companies. There are different types of pagers, so be sure to ask about your options.

7. Cellular telephone

You may want to consider a cellular telephone for your business needs. Because of intense competition in this industry, prices have gone down as the number of features available have gone up. There are also many air-time volume discount packages available. To save money, make sure you are billed based on a minimum of 6-second usage intervals, not 30 or 60 seconds.

Rather than giving a client direct access to your cellular number, you may want to have a pager that records messages left on your cellular or telephone voice mail and then notifies you. This is effective for urgent messages or time-sensitive calls. Alternatively, you could call up your voice mail from time to time to retrieve messages from your cellular. That way you control cellular time use and costs more effectively. For example, you may decide to return a client's call from a regular telephone or pay telephone. You can also minimize unexpected or unwanted interruptions.

You can also buy cellular telephones that can support two-way data and fax communications. Such a cellular telephone could be connected to a portable fax machine or computer with a fax and/or computer modem to send and receive data.

Cellular telephones have many features; check with the supplier for the ones that best suit your needs.

8. Electronic mail (e-mail)

With your computer, you can transmit messages over the telephone lines to someone else's computer through electronic mail (e-mail). You need to know the recipient's e-mail address or password to access his or her computer. The message you send remains stored in computer memory until he or she retrieves it. Many people have their e-mail address printed on their business cards. Communicating via e-mail can be appropriate in certain situations because it is speedier than letters, faxes, couriers, or telephone.

4

LEGAL FORMS OF BUSINESS STRUCTURE

There are three basic forms of legal structure: proprietorship, partnership, and limited company. You should seek competent legal and accounting advice before deciding on your business structure, as there could be distinct advantages or disadvantages to each depending on your situation.

When determining which business structure is best for your business, it is important to consider your risk of being sued (e.g., for an outstanding debt, breach of contract, or negligence). You need to do a potential risk assessment. For example, if you are a computer programmer and your software is ineffective or full of viruses, you could be sued for negligence. A corporate business structure could be your first line of "insurance" protection from being named personally in the law suit.

Many people start out as a sole proprietor, as that is the easiest way to start a business. If additional skills or personnel are required on a specific project, independent contractors could be subcontracted by the proprietor.

Going into business with one or more people in a partnership is another option.

Forming a corporation is a third option. The corporation can be owned by just one person (similar to a proprietorship) or by two or more people (similar to a partnership).

This chapter discusses the factors that you and your professional advisers should examine when making a decision about your business structure.

A. SOLE PROPRIETORSHIP

A sole proprietorship is a business owned and operated by one person. To establish a sole proprietorship, you need only obtain whatever local licenses you require to operate a business and then open your business. It is the simplest form of business structure and operation.

1. Advantages

Ease of formation: There is less formality and few legal restrictions associated with establishing a sole proprietorship. You can start almost immediately. There are no complex forms to complete and no documentation required between you and any other party. In most jurisdictions, all that is legally necessary to operate as a sole proprietorship is to register the business and obtain the proper licenses. Licenses can be required by various levels of government.

Cost: Registering the business and obtaining licenses involves minimal costs. There are no partnership or corporate agreements required by you because you are the sole owner. Legal fees are reduced accordingly.

Lack of complexity: A sole proprietorship is straightforward. Unlike other forms of business, there is little government control and, accordingly, fewer reports are required to be filed with government agencies and departments. The owner and the business are taxed as one.

Decision-making process: Decisions are made exclusively by the sole owner, who has complete authority and freedom to move. The owner does not have to obtain approval from partners or shareholders or a board of directors.

Sole ownership of profits: The proprietor does not have to share the profits with anyone. The profits generated by the business belong to one person. The sole owner decides how and when the money will come out of the business.

Ease of terminating/sale of business: Apart from legal responsibilities to employees, creditors, and perhaps clients, you can sell the business or close it down at your will.

Flexibility: You are able to respond quickly to business needs in day-to-day management decisions as governed by various laws and common sense.

2. Disadvantages

Unlimited liability: The sole owner's personal assets, such as house, property, car, and investments, are liable to be seized if necessary to pay for outstanding debts or liabilities. As mentioned earlier, the proprietor and the business are deemed to be one and the same in law.

Less financing capacity: It is more difficult for a proprietor to borrow money than for a partnership with various partners or a corporation with a number of major shareholders. A lender, when looking for security and evidence of outside resources, can turn to other people connected with the business rather than just the one person in a proprietorship. A partnership or corporation can give an investor some form of equity position, which is not available in a proprietorship.

Unstable duration of business: The business might be crippled or terminated upon the illness or death of the owner. If there is no one appropriate to take over the business, it may have to be sold or liquidated. Such an unplanned action may result in a loss.

Sole decision-making: In a partnership or a corporation, there is generally shared decision-making or at least input. In a proprietorship, just one person is involved; if that person lacks business ability or experience, poor decision-making can cause the business to suffer.

Taxation: At a certain level of profit there are tax disadvantages for the sole proprietor.

B. PARTNERSHIP

A partnership is usually defined as an association of two or more persons to carry on a business in common with a view to making a profit. The partnership is created by a contract, either verbal or written, between the individual parties.

1. Advantages

Ease of formation: Legal formalities and expenses in forming a partnership are few compared to incorporating.

Pride of ownership and direct rewards: Pride of ownership generates personal motivation and identification with the business. The profit motive could be reinforced with more people having a vested interest.

Availability of more capital: A partnership can pool the funds of a number of people compared to a sole owner who has only his or her own resources to draw on, unless loans are obtained.

Combination of expertise and talent: Two or more partners, by combining their energies and talents, can often be successful where one person alone would fail. This is particularly true if the business demands a variety of talents such as technical knowledge, sales ability, and financial skills. It is important that working partners bring complementary skills to the business, thereby reducing the workload of each partner.

Flexibility: A partnership may be relatively more flexible in the decision-making process than a corporation, but less so than a sole proprietorship.

Relative freedom of government control and special taxation: Compared to a corporation, a partnership is relatively free from many restrictions and bureaucratic red tape.

2. Disadvantages

Unlimited liability: The major disadvantage of a partnership is the unlimited liability. This unlimited liability is much more serious than in a proprietorship because all the partners are individually and collectively liable for all the debts and liabilities of the partnership. Each partner's personal assets are liable to be seized if necessary to pay for outstanding business debts.

Unstable duration of business: Any change in the partnership automatically ends the legal entity. Changes could include the death of a partner, or the admission or withdrawal of a partner. In each case, if the business is to continue, a new partnership agreement must be made.

Management of difficulties: As mentioned, when more than one owner assumes responsibility for business management, there is a possibility that differences of style, priorities, personalities, philosophy, and other factors will arise. If these differences become serious disputes and are unresolved, the partnership may have to be terminated, with all the financial and personal trauma involved. It is difficult for future partners to foresee whether personalities and methods of operating will clash.

Relative difficulty in obtaining large sums of capital: This is particularly true of long-term financing when compared to a corporation.

Partnership agreement problems: The larger a partnership becomes, the more complex the written agreement has to be to protect the rights and identify the responsibilities of each partner. This can result in additional administration and legal costs.

Difficulty of disposing of partnership interest: To withdraw capital from the business requires approval from all other partners. This takes time and involves legal and administrative expenses.

3. Partnership agreement

A partnership agreement, sometimes called articles of partnership, is absolutely necessary in a partnership relationship. The agreement normally outlines the contribution of each partner in the business, whether financial, material, or managerial. In general, it defines the roles of the partners in the business relationship.

Some of the typical articles contained in a partnership agreement are shown in Table #1.

If you are considering a partnership relationship, complete the checklist headings and then see your lawyer and accountant. By the time you have completed the checklist with your prospective business mate, the engagement could be off.

C. CORPORATION

A corporation is a legal entity, with or without share capital, which can be established by one or more individuals or other legal entities. It exists separate and distinct from these individuals or other legal entities. A corporation has all the rights and responsibilities of a person with the exception of those rights that can be exercised only by a natural person.

1. Advantages

Limited liability of shareholders: Shareholders' personal assets are separate from the business and cannot be seized to pay for outstanding business debts incurred by the corporation. There are exceptions, dealing primarily with the issue of fraud.

Flexibility for tax planning: Various tax advantages are available to corporations that are not available to partnerships or proprietorships. Tax planning must be undertaken with the help of a professional accountant.

Corporate management flexibility: The owner or owners can be active in the management of the business to any desired degree.

ARTICLES IN A PARTNERSHIP AGREEMENT

*Table #1
Articles in a
Partnership
Agreement*

1. Name, purpose, and location of partnership

2. Duration of agreement

3. Names and character of partners (general or limited, active or silent)

4. Financial contribution by partners (at inception, at later date)

5. Role of individual partners in business management

6. Authority (authority of partner in conduct of business)

7. Nature and degree of each partner's contribution to firm's consulting services

8. Business expenses (how handled)

9. Separate debts

10. Signing of checks

11. Division of profits and losses

12. Books, records, and method of accounting

13. Draws or salaries

14. Absence and disability

15. Death of a partner (dissolution and winding up)

16. Rights of continuing partner

17. Employee management

18. Sale of partnership interest

19. Release of debts

20. Settlement of disputes; arbitration

21. Additions, alternations, or modifications to partnership agreement

22. Noncompetition in the event of departure

Agents, officers, and directors with specified authority can be appointed to manage the business. Employees can be given stock options to share in the ownership, which can increase incentive and interest.

Financing more readily available: Investors find it more attractive to invest in a corporation with its limited liability than to invest in a business whose unlimited liability could involve them to an extent greater than the amount of the investment. Long-term financing from lending institutions is more readily available since lenders may use both corporate assets and personal guarantees as security.

Continual existence of corporation: A corporation continues to exist and operate regardless of the changes in the shareholders. Death of a shareholder does not discontinue the life of the corporation. Continual existence is also an effective device for building and retaining goodwill.

Ownership is readily transferable: It is a relatively simple procedure to transfer ownership by share transfer unless there are corporate restrictions to the contrary.

Draw on expertise and skills of more than one individual: This feature is the same concept as in a partnership, where more partners (shareholders) contribute diverse talents. However, a corporation is not required to have more than one shareholder.

2. Disadvantages

Extensive government regulations: There are more regulations affecting a corporation than a sole proprietorship or partnership.

Corporations must report to all levels of government.

Manipulation: Minority shareholders are potentially in a position to be exploited by the decisions of the majority of the company.

Expense: It is more expensive to establish and operate a corporation because of the additional documents and forms that are required compared to a proprietorship or partnership.

3. Corporate purposes

Some jurisdictions require that the articles of incorporation include a statement of the purposes of the corporation. When you provide a list of the purposes of the corporation, make sure that you define them expansively. Do not restrict the activity of your corporation. A general clause should be included allowing the corporation to expand into any business activity permitted by law. A competent lawyer can assist you in preparing this document to enable you to maximize your corporate options.

4. Shareholders' agreement

A shareholders' agreement involves the same concepts of protection as a partnership agreement. Many of the provisions outlined in the partnership agreement are also included in the shareholders' agreement. There are additional provisions frequently covered in the shareholders' agreement, including:

(a) A restriction on transfer of shares

(b) A buy-sell provision that sets out the formula for buying and selling shares in the company

(c) A provision on personal guarantees of corporate obligations

(d) A provision on payback by corporation of shareholders' loans

(e) A provision giving all shareholders the entitlement to sit as a director or nominate a director as their representative. This protects minority shareholders from lack of managerial information and provides them with a directorship vote or veto on corporate decisions. If you intend to be a majority shareholder, you may not wish to volunteer this provision.

Many shareholders believe that corporate bylaws set out the recipe for resolving problems within the corporation and between the shareholders, directors, and officers in some magical fashion. In most cases, the bylaws only cover formulas for resolving disputes in a few circumstances. It is the shareholders' agreement that expands the protections to resolve fairly any disputes between shareholders.

If you intend to incorporate and have one or more additional shareholders in your corporation, it would be wise to obtain your lawyer's advice on a shareholders' agreement to protect your interests.

D. S CORPORATION (SUB-CHAPTER OR SUB-S) (UNITED STATES)

You may wish to consider the advantages of structuring your business as an S corporation in the United States. The purpose is to permit a small business corporation to treat its net income as though it were a partnership. One objective is to overcome the double-tax feature of taxing corporate income and shareholder dividends. Another purpose is to permit the shareholders to have the benefit of offsetting business losses incurred for the corporation against their income.

Only closely held corporations, that is with 75 or fewer shareholders, may make the S election. All shareholders must consent to the S election, and only one class of outstanding stock is allowed. A specific portion of the corporation's income must be derived from active business rather than passive investments. No limit is placed on the size of the corporation's income and assets.

At some future point you may wish to revert to a full corporation for tax advantage reasons. This is permitted, but the corporation may not be able to reelect the S vehicle for several years once the S election is reversed. This is to eliminate small corporations from changing frequently to maximize tax advantages. Since S forms of incorporation are not recognized in all states, you should obtain further information from your professional advisers.

E. LIMITED LIABILITY CORPORATION (LLC) (UNITED STATES)

A limited liability corporation (LLC) is a form of doing business that combines the limited liability for loans and lawsuits of a corporation with the "pass-through" tax benefits of a partnership. Pass-through taxation means that the business is taxed only once — at the member/shareholder level — rather than at both the member/shareholder and LLC/corporate level.

S corporations are also eligible for pass-through taxation, so why form an LLC instead of an S corporation? Because certain limitations are placed on S corporations that do not affect LLCs. For instance, an S corporation must not have more than 35 shareholders, and the shareholders must be individuals, estates, or certain types of trusts. Corporations, partnerships, LLCs, and nonresidents may not be shareholders in an S corporation. All these entities, however, can be members in an LLC. Another limitation placed on S corporations is that they may have only one class of stock. As a result, the financing options are limited.

S corporations are not good tax shelters because deductions for losses are limited to the shareholder's basis in the corporate stock.

LLCs have an advantage over S corporations when it comes to foreign investors. Because an S corporation cannot take on nonresidents as shareholders, it is unable to have much interaction in the fast-growing international business market. Also, LLCs, unlike S corporations, are not subject to additional partnership tax status qualification requirements. LLCs must simply meet partnership tax requirements. LLCs need not elect partnership tax status and then be continually vigilant in order to retain such status as S corporations must.

For more information, refer to the Self-Counsel book *How to Form and Operate a Limited Liability Company.*

5

SELECTING BUSINESS AND PROFESSIONAL ADVISERS

Since you may be operating on your own, or with a few associates, you will need an extended management team to advise you in specialized areas where you lack knowledge, ability, or interest. Your advisers are, in effect, your employees and associates and should be considered an integral part of management decision-making.

Every business decision involves a legal decision or implication. Every business decision involves accounting, legal, and at times, tax considerations. The fatality rate of small businesses is enormously high. Statistically, the odds are practically ten to one that your small business will not be in business three years after you begin.

This chapter discusses the benefits of the effective use of business and professional advisers, with sections on how to selectively evaluate them and how to use their skills to your advantage.

A. GENERAL CRITERIA FOR ADVISER SELECTION

How well you select your professional and business advisers will have a direct bearing on your business success. Poor advisers or no advisers will almost certainly lead to your business downfall. Your main advisers are your lawyer and accountant, followed by your banker. You should see at least three different people from each of these three areas before you make your selection. It is important to have the comparative assessment.

111

The following general guidelines should assist you in the careful search and selection of your advisers.

1. Recommendations

One of the most reliable methods of finding an adviser is a personal recommendation from your existing advisers or friends in business whose judgment and business sense you trust. Bankers and business advisers who deal on a regular basis with professional advisers are in a good position to pass judgment based on their business dealings. When lawyers, accountants, or bankers refer to each other, it implies a good working relationship and mutual trust.

Don't rely completely on any referral; make your own cautious assessment. You might also want to try the lawyer referral service in your area. For a nominal fee you can see a business or corporate lawyer for an initial consultation.

2. Credentials

In Canada, all lawyers have an LL.B. designation. In the United States, lawyers have either an LL.B. or J.D. designation.

Accountants in Canada have a professional designation such as C.A. or C.G.A. In the United States, look for the designation C.P.A. The training requirements and public practice background of C.A.s and C.P.A.s are similar if not identical.

Certification and credentials ensure only that the individual has passed minimum standards of education. They do not ensure that the person is a dynamic, innovative, or creative business adviser with a specific amount of experience relevant to your needs.

3. Clientele

Most professional advisers have a homogeneous client base. Some advisers have many small business clients, others emphasize personal clients, while others go after corporate business. An adviser with a good base of small- to medium-sized commercial clients will probably be the most appropriate for your business needs.

4. Fees

Fees will often vary by the size of the community in which the professional practice is operated, the size of the practice, and the volume of business. You may find that advisers who charge fees in the middle range, edging toward the higher end of the scale, are often quality practitioners in high demand who are still aggressive and innovative in their business practice.

Advisers who are at the low end of the fee scale can be entrepreneurial types, but cut-rate pricing may also indicate a cut-rate, high-volume approach to business which will not suit your objectives. Low prices are sometimes an indicator of low quality, low esteem, or little experience.

Very high-priced advisers tend to be more conservative, less aggressive, and less willing to spend the necessary time with small business clients because their priorities lie with the big firms. Fees vary and many professionals will negotiate them.

It is important to be very open when discussing fees and payment expectations.

5. Technical competence and industry knowledge

You must satisfy yourself that your advisers are competent in the areas of your greatest need. Ask them how much experience they have had, and how comfortable they are with your field.

A specific understanding of the problems, needs, and issues of your type of business can enable your advisers to provide the exact assistance you require. This is different from technical skill competence. It has more to do with experience in a particular type of industry. If the adviser has provided guidance to other small business owners in similar situations, there is an increased possibility that the adviser will be able to provide you with more reliable assistance.

6. Style and personality

A critical factor in the selection of advisers, beyond simple compatibility, is style. You can have greater confidence in the aggressive adviser who takes the initiative and offers advice before you request it. This style indicates an initiator rather than a reactor, a person who anticipates and performs before matters become serious. It also indicates a creator, an entrepreneur, and a person who can empathize with your problems and concerns. This kind of adviser is more likely to come up with creative solutions to problems and be a complement to your planning function. This type of adviser will not only be a sounding board but a true part of the management team.

7. Confidence

You should feel a sense of confidence when relating to your adviser, whether it be in the general sense or in dealing with a specific problem or issue. You should have a certain amount of personal compatibility with your adviser. If you don't, you will probably end up rejecting a fair amount of advice. In other words, if you do not feel that good chemistry exists with an adviser, seek a replacement as soon as possible. If you do not relate well to the adviser, you may hesitate to ask for advice, which could result in some poor management decisions.

Never allow your advisers to treat you in a condescending or paternalistic manner. You should consider them as equals with special knowledge offering a service in the same manner that you are offering a service to your clients.

8. Communication

You should select an adviser who communicates well, openly, and free of jargon. Your adviser should explain the necessary concepts to you so that you understand the issues involved and the decisions that have to be made. Effective communication also means that your advisers forward to you any correspondence sent or received through their offices relating to your business.

9. Commitment

It is important to sense that your adviser is committed to your best interests and your success. An adviser who is involved with clients who are larger, more important, or higher paying than you are may become indifferent to your needs. You should be alert to this.

10. Availability

It is important for your advisers to be available when you need them. You are spending time and resources to develop a relationship that will enhance your business decisions. If your adviser is frequently out of town or, in the case of a lawyer, in court on a regular basis, you may not have the immediate access you need. Of course, if the adviser is of exceptional quality and ideally suited to your type of practice, some allowances should be made.

11. Length of time in practice

There is naturally a correlation between the degree of expertise and length of time in practice. You should therefore ask directly how many years of experience your adviser has in the area of your needs.

12. Ability to aid growth

A good professional adviser will have a history of assisting growth in other clients. The adviser should be able to anticipate growth problems in advance and provide guidance to deal with them.

13. Small firm versus large firm

Choosing a small or large firm is in many ways a matter of your own personal style and the type of firm you relate to most comfortably. Larger firms tend to be in the central area of the city, which may involve parking problems. Their fees are higher. Generally, the larger firms do not have a small business orientation in their marketing and service priorities. The larger firms do have highly specialized advisers and a resource base of associate personnel. This degree of depth may or may not be necessary in your situation. It is not uncommon in larger firms to have small business clients passed over to junior associates or students in training as the more senior advisers handle larger clients.

Smaller firms generally deal with and relate to small business entrepreneurs. Selecting an adviser in a small- or medium-sized firm of three to ten people provides you with a resource base if you need it. An adviser who is a sole practitioner may be very busy, too generalized in his or her areas of practice, and lacking a referral resource base within the firm.

14. Comparison

Make sure you check out at least three advisers before making a final decision. The more selective you are in comparing the personalities, styles, competence, and attitudes of prospective advisers, the more likely it is that you will find someone with whom you can establish a good relationship.

Prepare questions for your potential advisers and compare their answers. Assess the quality of answers to your questions, then decide who will be the most benefit to you.

Most initial consultations are free; be sure to confirm this when you set up the meeting. The more interviews you conduct, the greater your knowledge base and the greater your confidence that you will choose the right person or firm.

B. LAWYER

There are basically two types of lawyers that you should consider as your advisers. The same lawyer might be able to assume both roles.

You need a lawyer who specializes in small business. A lawyer who cares about small business clients assumes the same role and attitude toward your business health and survival as your does physician toward your personal health.

The other type of lawyer you need is one who specializes in contract law. You will need to have several boilerplate contracts prepared depending on the type and style of service you are providing. There are times you will need to have a specialized contract made up by a lawyer or have the lawyer review and advise you on a contract that has been prepared by the client.

If your business lawyer does not have the expertise in contract law, request that you be referred to someone within the firm or outside who does. For continuity and efficiency, you want to maintain your business lawyer for all matters that don't require additional expertise. You should be able to telephone your lawyer as your needs arise and feel confident that the unique aspects of your business are known and understood.

For your protection, you should retain a lawyer before you start up your business, as there are many legal pitfalls that can be encountered. There is a temptation to save money on legal fees in the beginning stages of the business when cash flow is minimal. Some people do their own incorporation to save on initial start-up expenses, but then continue the saving by never obtaining legal or accounting advise, an unfortunate example of false economy and bad judgment.

C. ACCOUNTANT

An accountant is the other essential business adviser on your management team. It is very important that you retain a qualified accountant with the designations described earlier. A bookkeeper is not an accountant but, in most jurisdictions in Canada and the United States, there is no restriction on anyone's using the name "accountant" and purporting to provide accounting services without any qualifications or training.

There are many essential services that an accountant can provide. An accountant can advise on all start-up steps of a new business, including the tax and accounting considerations of various types of business organization. Most often, an accountant will communicate with or coordinate work with your lawyer. The accountant considers important matters such as when your fiscal year-end should be and whether you should use a cash or accrual method in keeping your books.

An accountant can advise on preparing a business plan for a loan application. This includes recommending the type of loan you should consider and how it is to be paid. Documents such as a profit and loss statement, a balance sheet, and a financial statement can be prepared by the accountant. He or she may refer you to a banker, which can have a positive effect on your loan application if the banker knows and respects the accountant.

An accountant can advise on all aspects of tax planning and tax-related business decisions which occur from time to time, as well as file your tax returns.

An accountant can advise how to set up your office bookkeeping system, including a computerized system. The accountant can have the bookkeeping done by someone in his or her firm at a negotiated fee or you can hire an independent bookkeeper. Your accountant should be able to recommend some bookkeepers.

An accountant can analyze and interpret your financial information, point out areas that need control, and recommend ways of implementing the necessary change.

An accountant can coordinate your personal and business affairs and advise you on investments, tax shelters, income splitting, and other matters. An accountant also may be aware of various government grant programs that could be of interest to you.

An accountant can advise and assist you if you want to change your proprietorship or partnership into a limited company at some point. If the transfer is done correctly, you can minimize any negative tax consequences.

D. BANKER

Your relationship with your bank and banker is your financial lifeline. The process of selecting a bank and banker is a critical one, and substantial comparative shopping is necessary to obtain the optimal combination of personality and knowledge.

The qualifications of the banker should be considered along with his or her specific experience with your type of business, specific reputation for taking risk, and the demands that are made for security and for reporting results.

Find out the amount of the banker's loan approval limit. If your needs are less than the limit, the loan can be approved by that individual without further review by another loans officer. This means you have to convince only one person to approve your loan request, not additional anonymous people behind the scene.

There are specific danger areas that can affect your banker's relationship with you. When the bank's manager changes, there is always a period of risk and uncertainty. The new manager does not want to have any medium- or high-risk loans on the books to taint his or her record. During the first three or four months after a new manager takes

116

over, outstanding loans are reviewed and categorized within the criteria set by him or her. This is the time when loans can be called or additional security requested or interest rates increased. You should develop a personal relationship with the manager when you take out a loan. If you hear that a new manager has taken over, make a point of quickly introducing yourself and briefly discussing your business in a positive way.

Ask your accountant and lawyer which bank and banker they recommend. This is probably one of the most effective introductions. If the banker has an ongoing relationship with a professional who is advising you as a client, a less impersonal relationship will exist and there is a better chance that decisions affecting your loans and your business will be made more carefully.

E. INSURANCE

It is important to select a professional insurance broker with experience and knowledge in the areas of insurance you require. An insurance broker can have various professional qualifications, and you may wish to find out what those credentials are. Insurance is covered in detail in chapter 9.

F. CONSULTANTS

1. Private consultants

You may wish to approach a practicing consultant for advice to assist you in your business. Consultants are not restrictively licensed like other professionals. To protect yourself, you should inquire about their expertise, qualifications, and length of experience in your field. Obtain references and contact them. Apply the general criteria for adviser selection. You will want to satisfy yourself that the consultant is personally successful. If the consultant has not been successful, how can he or she possibly offer advice that will help you? Consultant fees may range between $50 to $150 per hour or more, depending on many variables.

2. Consultants subsidized by the government

Both the Canadian and U.S. governments have consulting services available for small business.

(a) CASE (Counselling Assistance to Small Enterprises)

In Canada, the federal government, through the Business Development Bank of Canada (BDC), sponsors consultants in CASE. The counselors are retired and active business experts who wish to be mentors or provide other assistance. They are able to identify areas of opportunity, solve problems, and help people manage more effectively. Businesses starting up, expanding, closing, or just not making the kind of profit expected can benefit from the help of an experienced businessperson.

The requirements of the clients are matched with the background and expertise of available counselors. The CASE coordinator selects the appropriate counselor, reviews reports outlining recommendations submitted by the counselor, and follows up on assignments.

The hourly fee for the counselor's time is modest compared to the fees charged by private consultants, and includes meeting with the client, doing necessary research, and outlining recommendations in a written report to the client. Further information can be obtained from a local BDC office.

The BDC also sponsors small business management seminars and workshops, strategic planning, and other services, as well as various forms of financing. Contact your local branch to obtain further information and to place your name on the mailing list.

(b) Service Corps of Retired Executives (SCORE)

This U.S. program is similar to the Canadian program, and is sponsored by the United States Small Business Administration (SBA). SCORE is composed of retired and active executives who share their knowledge, experience, and business counseling for a modest fee. Further information can be obtained from a local SBA office.

The SBA also sponsors small business management seminars and workshops. Contact your local branch to obtain further information and to place your name on the mailing list.

6
PREPARING YOUR BUSINESS PLAN

A. WHY PREPARE A PLAN?

Planning and good management skills are vital to business success. Those who do not plan run a very high risk of failure. If you do not know where you are going in your personal or business life, there is little prospect that you will arrive. A business plan is a written summary of what you hope to accomplish by being in business and how you intend to organize your resources to meet your goals. It is an essential guide for operating your business successfully and measuring progress along the way.

Planning forces you to think ahead and visualize; it encourages realistic thinking instead of overoptimism. It helps you identify your customers, your market area, your pricing strategy, and the competitive conditions under which you must operate. This process often leads to the discovery of new opportunities as well as deficiencies in your plan.

Having clear goals and a well-written plan aid in decision-making. You can always change your goals, but at least with a business plan you have some basis and a standard comparison to use in evaluating alternatives presented to you.

A business plan establishes the amount of financing or outside investment required and when it is needed. It makes it much easier for a lender or investor to assess your financing proposal and to assess you as a business manager. It inspires confidence in lenders and self-confidence in yourself to know every aspect of the business when you are negotiating your financing. If you have a realistic, comprehensive, and well-documented plan, it will assist you greatly in convincing a lender.

Having well-established objectives helps you analyze your progress. If you have not attained your objectives by a certain period, you will be aware of that fact and can make appropriate adjustments at an early stage.

Spending three or four hours each month updating your plan will save considerable time and money in the long run and may even save your business. It is essential to develop a habit of planning and reassessing on an ongoing basis as an integral part of your management style.

There are many excellent business plan software programs available.

B. FORMAT

The business plan format shown in Sample #4 is a starting point for organizing your own plan. The comments following the subheadings should help you decide which sections are relevant to your business situations.

The business plan format normally consists of four parts: the introduction, the business concept, the financial plan, and the appendix.

The plan starts with an introductory page highlighting the business plan. Even though your entire business is described later, a crisp one- or two-page introduction helps capture the immediate attention of the potential investor or lender.

The business concept, which begins with a description of the industry, identifies your market potential within your industry and outlines your action plan for the coming year. Make sure your stated business goals are compatible with your personal goals and financial goals, your management ability, and family considerations. The heart of the business concept is your monthly sales forecast for the coming year. As your statement of confidence in your marketing strategy, it forms the basis for your cash flow forecast and projected income statement. This section also contains an assessment of business risks and a contingency plan. Being honest about your business risks and how you plan to deal with them is evidence of sound management.

The financial plan outlines the level of present financing and identifies the financing sought. This section should be brief. The financial plan contains pro forma (projected) financial forecasts. These forecasts are a projection into the future based on current information and assumptions. In carrying out your action plan for the coming year, these operating forecasts are an essential guide to business survival and profitability. It is important to refer to them often and, if circumstances dictate, rework them. Samples #5, #6, and #7 show forms you might want to include in your business plan.

The appendix section of your business plan contains all the items that do not naturally fall elsewhere in the document, or which expand further on the summaries in the document. These might include a personal net worth statement (Sample #8) and a statement of accounts receivable (Sample #9).

C. ESTIMATING YOUR START-UP FUNDS

1. Assessment of personal monthly financial needs

Personal expenses will continue in spite of the business and have to be taken into account when determining monthly cash flow needs. It is important to calculate personal expenses accurately so that appropriate decisions can be made in terms of funding and the nature of the start-up practice — whether it should start out on a part-time or full-time basis, using the home as an office or renting an outside office. Refer back to Samples #2 and #3 to review this important information.

2. Estimated business start-up cash needs

During your first few months you will probably not have enough sales revenue to finance your short-term costs. This usually occurs for one of three reasons: your sales are below projection, your costs rise unexpectedly, or you have not yet been paid for work already performed (overdue accounts receivable). Your conservative cash flow

analysis prepares you for this situation and enables you to plan your cash needs.

D. SUMMARY

Before presenting your business plan to a lender or investor, have two or three impartial outsiders review the finished plan in detail. There may be something you overlooked or underemphasized. After your plan has been reviewed by others, take it and your financial statements to your accountant for review. You should also discuss with your accountant all the personal and business tax considerations that might be involved. You may wish to have your accountant come with you to the bank when you discuss your loan proposal. This is not uncommon and can create a very positive impression.

Discuss with your lawyer the security you are proposing. Your lawyer should explain fully before the plan is submitted the effect of your pledging collateral security and what the lender could do if you default. You should also seriously evaluate whether the security pledged is too excessive for the loan or risk involved and whether the risk is too great to pledge your personal assets.

Your familiarity with your business plan will increase your credibility and at the same time provide you with a good understanding of what the financial statements reveal about the viability of your business.

BUSINESS PLAN FORMAT

1. Introductory page

(a) Company name
 – Include address and telephone number

(b) Contact person
 – Business owner's name and telephone number

(c) Paragraph about company
 – Nature of business and market area

(d) Securities offered to investors or lenders
 – Outline securities such as preferred shares, common shares, debentures (if investors) or assignment of accounts receivable or personal guarantee (if lender)

(e) Business loans sought
 – For example, term loan, operating line of credit, mortgage

(f) Summary of proposed use of funds

2. Summary

(a) Highlights of business plan
 – Preferably one page maximum
 – Include your project, competitive advantage, and bottom-line needs

3. Table of contents

(a) Section titles and page numbers should be given for easy reference

4. Description of the industry

(a) Industry outlook and growth potential
 – Outline industry trends — past, present, and future — and new developments
 – State your sources of information

(b) Markets and customers
 – Estimated size of total market share and sales, new requirements, and market trends

(c) Competitive companies
 – Market share, strengths and weaknesses, profitability, trends

(d) National and economic trends
 – Population shifts, consumer trends, relevant economic indicators

5. Description of business venture

(a) Nature of business
- Characteristics, method of operation, whether performed locally, regionally, nationally, or internationally

(b) Target market
- Typical clients identified by groups, present patterns and average earnings, wants and needs

(c) Competitive advantage of your business concept
- Your market niche, uniqueness, estimated market share

(d) Business location and size
- Location relative to market, size of premises, home or office use

(e) Staff and equipment needed
- Overall requirement, capacity, home or office use, part- or full-time staff or as required

(f) Brief history
- Principals involved in the business or proposed business, development work done, résumés and background experience of principals, résumés of key associates if applicable

6. Business goals

(a) One year
- Specific goals, such as gross sales, profit margin, share of market, opening new office, introducing new service

(b) Over the longer term
- Return on investment, business net worth, sale of business

7. Marketing plan

(a) Sales strategy
- Commission sales staff, agents, subcontractors
- Sales objectives, sales tools, sales support
- Target clients

(b) Sales approach
- Style of operation and techniques

(c) Pricing
- Costing, mark-ups, margins, break-even

(d) Promotion
- Media advertising, promotions, publicity appropriate to reach target market
- Techniques of developing exposure, credibility, and contacts

(e) Service policies
- Policies that your business will adopt for credit and collection, nature of clients, etc.

(f) Guarantees
- Service performance guarantees or other assurances will vary depending on nature of business and type of contract or client

(g) Tracking methods
- Method for confirming who your clients are and how they heard about you

8. Sales forecast

The sales forecast is the starting point for your projected income statement and cash flow forecast.

(a) Assumptions
- One never has all the necessary information, so state all the assumptions made in developing the forecast

(b) Monthly forecast for the coming year
- Sales volume, projected in dollars

(c) Annual forecast for the following two to four years
- Sales volume, projected in dollars

9. Costing plan

(a) Cost of facilities, equipment, and materials (as applicable)
- Estimates and quotations

(b) Capital estimates
- One time start-up or expansion capital required

10. Operations

(a) Purchasing plans
- Volume discounts, multiple sources, quality, price

(b) Inventory system
- Seasonal variation, turnover rate, method of control

(c) Space required
- Floor and office space, improvements required, expansion capability

(d) Staff and equipment required
- Personnel by skill level
- Fixtures, office equipment

(e) Operations strategy

11. Corporate structure

(a) Legal form
  - Proprietorship, partnership, or incorporation

(b) Share distribution
  - List of principal shareholders

(c) Contracts and agreements
  - List of contracts and agreements in force
  - Management contract, shareholder or partnership agreement, service contract, leases

(d) Directors and officers
  - Names and addresses, role in company

(e) Background of key management personnel
  - Brief résumés of active owners and key employees

(f) Organizational chart
  - Identify reporting relationships

(g) Duties and responsibilities of key personnel
  - Brief job descriptions — who is responsible for what

12. Supporting professional assistance

(a) Would include lawyer, accountant, banker, insurance agent

13. Research and development program

(a) Service improvements, process improvements, costs and risks

14. Risk assessment

(a) Competitors' reaction
  - Will competitors try to squeeze you out? What form do you anticipate any reaction will take?

(b) List of critical external factors that might occur
  - Identify effects of strikes, recession, new technology, weather, new competition, supplier problems, shifts in consumer demand, costs of delays and overruns, unfavorable industry trends

(c) List of critical internal factors that might occur
  - Income projections not realized, client dispute or litigation, receivables difficulties, demand for service increases very quickly, key employee or associate quits

(d) Dealing with risks
  - Contingency plan to handle the most significant risks

15. Overall schedule

(a) Interrelationship and timing of all major events important to starting and developing your business

16. Action plan

(a) Steps to accomplish this year's goals
- Flow chart by month or by quarter of specific action to be taken and by whom

(b) Checkpoint for measuring results
- Identify significant dates, sales levels as decision points

17. Financial forecast

If a business has been in operation for a period of time, the previous two or three years' balance sheets and income statements are required.

(a) Opening balance sheet
- The balance sheet is a position statement, not a historical record; it shows what is owned and owed at a given date. There are three sections to a balance sheet: assets, liabilities, and owner's equity. You determine your firm's net worth by subtracting the liabilities from the assets.
- Your balance sheet will indicate how your investment has grown over a period of time — investors and lenders typically examine balance sheets to determine if the company is within acceptable assets to liability limits
- See Sample #5

(b) Cash flow forecast
- A cash flow budget measures the flow of money in and out of the business. It is critical to you and your banker.
- Many business operate on a seasonal basis, as there are slow months and busy months. The cash flow budget projection will provide an indication of the times of a cash flow shortage to assist in properly planning and financing your operation. It will tell you in advance if you have enough cash to get by.
- A cash flow budget should be prepared a year in advance and contain monthly breakdowns
- See Sample #6

(c) Income and expense forecast statement (profit and loss)
- The income and expense forecast can be described as the operating statement you would expect to see for your business at the end of the period for which the forecast is being prepared

- For a new business, the forecast would show what revenue and expenses you expect the business to have in its first year of operation
- It is very useful, of course, to prepare a forecast for a period longer than one year, so you might want to prepare a detailed forecast for the next year of operation and a less detailed forecast for the following two years
- Preparing an income and expense forecast for a new business is more difficult than preparing one for an existing business, simply because in a new business there is no historical record to go by. For this reason, the preparation of the forecast is an even more essential, interesting, and rewarding experience than doing it for an existing business, despite the time and effort required. This analysis exercise will answer the question of whether a profit will be made.
- The income statement (sales) is the most difficult because it is the most uncertain at the commencement of business; it is essential that a figure be projected on a conservative estimate
- The main concern is to account for expenses accurately and in as much detail as possible; this will then provide a target or break-even figure toward which to work
- Some headings may not be appropriate for your type of business; other headings should be added
- See Sample #7

(d) Cash flow assumptions

When reviewing the cash flow plan, certain assumptions should be made:
- Sales: monthly sales that are expected to materialize
- Receipts: cash sales represent cash actually received; receivables collected represents the collection of amounts due for goods sold on credit; rental income is rent that will be collected in advance at the beginning of each month
- Disbursements: accounts payable to be paid in month following month of purchase
- Accounting and legal: to be paid on receipt of bill, expected to be in the spring or after your fiscal year end financial statements have been completed
- Advertising: anticipated to be the same amount each month and paid for in the month the expense is incurred
- Automobile: anticipated to be the same amount each month and paid for in the month the expense is incurred
- Bank charges and interest: anticipated to be the same amount each month and monthly paid for in same month the expense is incurred
- Equipment rental: to be paid for in monthly payments

– Income taxes: amount for taxes of the prior year and to be paid in the spring
– Insurance: annual premium to be paid quarterly, semiannually, or annually in installments of equal amounts
– Loan repayment: amount is the same each month and paid in accordance with the monthly schedule furnished by the lending institution
– Office supplies and expenses: to be paid in month following receipt of invoice and supplies to be purchased on a quarterly basis
– Taxes and licenses: to be paid for on receipt of invoice, expected to be in January and July
– Telephone: to be paid for in month following the month the expense is incurred; amount expected to be the same each month except in the last quarter when rates are expected to increase
– Utilities: expected to fluctuate with weather conditions and to be paid for in the month following the month the expense is incurred
– Wages and benefits: wages to increase at the beginning of the year; amount considered to be the same each month and paid for in the month the expense is incurred
– Miscellaneous: expected to be the same each month and paid for in the same month the expense is incurred
– Bad debts: varies

(e) Break-even analysis
– The break-even analysis is a critical calculation for every business. Rather than calculating how much your business would make if it attained an estimated sales volume, a more meaningful analysis determines at what sales volume your firm will break even. An estimated sales volume could be very unreliable as there are many factors that could affect revenue. Above the break-even sales volume, it is only a matter of how much money your business can generate; below the break-even level of sales, it is only a matter of how many days a business can operate before bankruptcy.
– A break-even analysis provides a very real and meaningful figure to work toward; you may need to update it every few months to reflect your business growth
– The break-even point is where total costs are equal to total revenues
– The calculation of total costs is determined by adding variable costs onto the fixed costs
– Total costs are all costs of operating the business over a specified time period

    – Variable costs are those that vary directly with the number of services provided or marketing and promotion activities undertaken. These typically include automobile expenses, business travel expenses, supplies, and brochures. Variable costs are not direct costs which are passed on to the client in the billing.

    – Fixed costs are costs that do not generally vary with the number of clients serviced. Also known as indirect costs, these costs typically include salaries, rent, secretarial service, insurance, telephone, accounting and legal services.

18. Financing and capitalization

(a) Term loan applied for
    – The amount, terms, and when required

(b) Purpose of term loan
    – Attach a detailed description of the aspects of the business to be financed

(c) Owner's equity
    – The amount of your financial commitment to the business

(d) Summary of term loan requirements
    – For a particular project or for the business as a whole

19. Operating loan

(a) Line of credit applied for
    – A new line of credit or an increase, and security offered

(b) Maximum operating cash required
    – Amount required, timing of need (refer to cash flow forecast, section **16.c.**)

20. Present financing (if applicable)

(a) Term loans outstanding
    – The balance owing, repayment terms, purpose, security, and status

(b) Current operating line of credit
    – The amount and security held

21. References

(a) Name of present lending institution
    – Branch and type of accounts

(b) Lawyer's name, address, and contact numbers

(c) Accountant's name, address, and contact numbers

22. Appendix

The nature of the contents of the appendixes attached, if any, depends on the circumstances and requirements of the lender or investor, or the desire to enhance the loan proposal. It is recommended that the appendixes be prepared for your own benefit and reference to assist your business analysis, and to be available if the information is required. The following list is a guide only. Some of the headings described may be unavailable or unnecessary.

(a) Personal net worth statement
  - Includes personal property values, investments, cash, bank loans, charge accounts, mortgages, and other liabilities. This will substantiate the value of your personal guarantee if required for security.
  - See Sample #8

(b) Letter of intent
  - Potential orders for client commitments

(c) Description of personal and business insurance coverage
  - Include insurance policies and amount of coverage

(d) Accounts receivable summary
  - Include aging schedule of 30-, 60-, and 90-day periods
  - See Sample #9

(e) Accounts payable summary
  - Include a schedule of payments and total amounts owing

(f) Legal agreements
  - Include a copy of contracts, leases, and other documents

(g) Appraisals
  - Fair market value of business property and equipment

(h) Financial statements for associated companies
  - Where appropriate, a lender may require this information

(i) Copies of your brochure

(j) Testimonial letters from clients

(k) References

(l) Sales forecast and market surveys

(m) List of investors

(n) Credit status information

(o) News articles about you and your business

DATE:_____ NAME OF COMPANY:_____

Sample #5
Opening
Balance
Sheet
(New
Business)

ASSETS

Current assets
   Cash and bank accounts $ _____
   Accounts receivable   _____
   Inventory   _____
   Prepaid rent   _____
   Other current assets   _____
    Total current assets   (A) $ _____
Fixed assets
   Land and buildings $ _____
   Furniture, fixtures, and equipment   _____
   Automobiles   _____
   Leasehold improvements   _____
Other assets   _____
    Total fixed and other assets   (B) $ _____
     Total assets (A + B = C)   (C) $ _____

LIABILITIES

Current liabilities (debt due within next 12 months)
   Bank loans $ _____
   Loans — other   _____
   Accounts payable   _____
   Current portion of long-term debt   _____
   Other current liabilities   _____
    Total current liabilities   (D) $ _____
Long-term debt
   Mortgages and liens payable (attach details) $ _____
   Less: current portion   _____
   Loans from partners or stockholders (owner's equity)   _____
   Other loans of long-term nature   _____
    Total long-term debt   (E) $ _____
     Total liabilities (D + E = F)   (F) $ _____
Net worth (C - F = G)   (G) $ _____
   Total net worth and liabilities (F + G = H)   (H) $ _____

Sample #6
Cash Flow
Budget

	JANUARY		FEBRUARY		MARCH	
	Estimated	Actual	Estimated	Actual	Estimated	Actual
Cash at beginning of month						
In bank and on hand	$_____	$_____	$_____	$_____	$_____	$_____
In investments	_____	_____	_____	_____	_____	_____
Total cash	$_____	$_____	$_____	$_____	$_____	$_____
Plus income during month						
Cash sales (include credit cards)	_____	_____	_____	_____	_____	_____
Credit sales payments	_____	_____	_____	_____	_____	_____
Investment income	_____	_____	_____	_____	_____	_____
Receivables collected	_____	_____	_____	_____	_____	_____
Loans	_____	_____	_____	_____	_____	_____
Personal investment	_____	_____	_____	_____	_____	_____
Other cash income	_____	_____	_____	_____	_____	_____
Total cash and income	$_____	$_____	$_____	$_____	$_____	$_____
Expenses during the month						
Rent (if applicable)	_____	_____	_____	_____	_____	_____
Utilities	_____	_____	_____	_____	_____	_____
Phone	_____	_____	_____	_____	_____	_____
Postage	_____	_____	_____	_____	_____	_____
Office equipment and furniture	_____	_____	_____	_____	_____	_____
Stationery and business cards	_____	_____	_____	_____	_____	_____
Insurance (health, fire, liability, theft, etc.)	_____	_____	_____	_____	_____	_____
Answering service	_____	_____	_____	_____	_____	_____
Printing and supplies	_____	_____	_____	_____	_____	_____
Typing/secretarial service	_____	_____	_____	_____	_____	_____
Accounting and legal services	_____	_____	_____	_____	_____	_____
Advertising and promotion	_____	_____	_____	_____	_____	_____
Carried forward	$_____	$_____	$_____	$_____	$_____	$_____

	JANUARY		FEBRUARY		MARCH	
	Estimated	Actual	Estimated	Actual	Estimated	Actual
Expenses during the month						
Brought forward	$____	$____	$____	$____	$____	$____
Business licenses and permits	____	____	____	____	____	____
Dues and subscriptions	____	____	____	____	____	____
Books and reference materials	____	____	____	____	____	____
Travel: in town	____	____	____	____	____	____
Travel: out of town	____	____	____	____	____	____
Conventions, professional meetings, trade shows	____	____	____	____	____	____
Continuing education	____	____	____	____	____	____
Entertainment	____	____	____	____	____	____
Contributions	____	____	____	____	____	____
Gifts	____	____	____	____	____	____
Salaries	____	____	____	____	____	____
Employment insurance	____	____	____	____	____	____
Pensions	____	____	____	____	____	____
Miscellaneous	____	____	____	____	____	____
Loan repayment	____	____	____	____	____	____
Other cash expenses	____	____	____	____	____	____
Total expenses	$____	$____	$____	$____	$____	$____
Cash flow excess (deficit) at end of month	$____	$____	$____	$____	$____	$____
Cash flow cumulative (monthly)	$____	$____	$____	$____	$____	$____

Sample #7
Income
and
Expense
Statement
Forecast
(New
Business)

(Name of business)

For the period:_____ months ending _____ , 19____

PROJECTED INCOME

Sales

_____ $ _____

_____   _____

    Total sales $ _____

Other income   _____

       Total income   (A) $ _____

PROJECTED EXPENSES

Sales expenses

    Commissions and salaries $ _____

    Travel   _____

    Advertising   _____

    Automotive   _____

    Other   _____

       Total selling expenses   (B) $ _____

Administrative and financial expenses

    Management salaries (or proprietor/partner draws) $ _____

    Office salaries   _____

    Professional fees   _____

    Office expense and supplies   _____

    Telephone   _____

    Rent   _____

    Interest and bank charges   _____

    Inventory   _____

    Bad debt   _____

    Other   _____

       Total administrative and financial expenses   (C) $ _____

       Total expenses (B + C = D)   (D) $ _____

Operating profit (loss) (A - D) $ _____

Add: Other income

Less: Provisions for income taxes $ _____

Net profit (loss) $ _____

Date: _____

Name: _____

Address: _____

GENERAL INFORMATION

Telephone: Home _____ Business _____

Age _____ Marital Status _____

Dependents including spouse _____

Present employer _____

Position occupied _____

How long with this employer _____

Previous employer _____ How long _____

Landlord _____

Address _____

Monthly rental $ _____

Salary, wages, or commission per annum $ _____

Other income per annum $ _____

Source _____

Guarantees on debts of others:

Name _____ Amount $_____

Name _____ Amount $_____

ASSETS

Bank accounts $ _____

Stocks at cost (market value _____)   _____

Bonds at cost (market value _____)   _____

Life insurance (cash surrender value)   _____

   Beneficiary _____

Automobile: year _____ make _____   _____

Home: registered
      building size _____ lot size _____   _____

Other assets   _____

     Total $ _____

LIABILITIES

Bank loan $ _____

Charge accounts   _____

Policy loans on life insurance   _____

Other loans   _____

Installment purchases   _____

Mortgages: Interest rate _____
         Term _____ Payments _____   _____

Taxes   _____

Other liabilities   _____

     Subtotal $ _____

Net worth   _____

     Total $ _____

(Name of company)

AS AT _____ 199-

Date: _____

_____
(Name of company)

Name of debtors	Total	Current	31–60 days	61–90 days	Over 90 days & holdbacks	Remarks

1. Subtotals $ _____

2. Aggregate of accounts
   under $_____ $_____

3. Number of
   accounts_____ No._____ No._____ No._____ No._____ No._____

4. Totals $ _____

Percentage   _____100%_____ %_____ %_____ %_____ %

7

HOW TO OBTAIN FINANCING

Having completed your business plan and financial projections, you should now have a clear idea of what your short- and medium-term financial needs are. You will want to be familiar with the types of financing available, the various sources, how to approach financial lending institutions, and the type of security that may be required. You should also be aware of the reasons why lending institutions or investors may turn down a request for funding. These matters and other issues are covered in this chapter.

A. TYPES OF FINANCING

There are two basic types of financing: equity and debt.

1. Equity

The money that you put into a company or business is equity. Initially, all money must come from your own resources such as savings or personal borrowing from financial institutions, friends, relatives, or business associates. As time progresses, retained earnings in the business will increase your equity.

If you have formed a corporation, you can "buy" one or more shares and lend the rest of the money to the corporation as a "shareholder's loan." The advantages of a shareholder's loan include:

(a) Lenders consider these loans as equity as long as the money is left in the company.

(b) It is easier to repay the loan than sell shares back to the company or to other investors.

(c) Interest may be paid. For example, if you or your friends would like to earn a return on your investment, an interest rate may be established. The alternative is to pay dividends on shares when funds are available.

(d) Interest is tax deductible to the company.

2. Debt

A debt is a loan. It must be repaid, and the lender will charge interest on the money you have borrowed. With borrowed money, the principal with interest usually is paid back on a fixed monthly payment. You therefore have to include the principal and interest payments in a current business plan. Various forms of debt financing are discussed below.

(a) Short-term or operating loan (demand loan)

Short-term or operating loans are used for financing inventory, accounts receivable, special purchases or promotions, and other items requiring working capital during peak periods.

The main sources of short-term loans are commercial banks or similar financial institutions. Using a short-term loan is a good way to establish credit with a bank. This type of loan can be unsecured or secured by your personal or business assets.

Short-term loans are usually negotiated for specific periods of time, for example, 30, 60, or 90 days, and frequently for periods up to a year or more. They may be repayable in a lump sum at the end of the period or in periodic installments, such as monthly.

Other characteristics of a demand loan include:

- The interest rate at time of signing may be lower than for a term loan.

- There is a fluctuating interest rate.

- Repayment of the loan can be demanded at any time by the lender; this usually occurs only when the account does not perform satisfactorily or when there is serious deterioration in the affairs of the business.

- A short-term loan can often be obtained more quickly than a term loan.

(b) Line of credit

A line of credit is an agreement between you and the lender (a bank or similar financial institution) specifying the maximum amount of credit (overdraft) the bank will allow you at any one time for general operating purposes.

Credit lines are usually established for one-year periods, subject to annual renegotiation and renewal. Other characteristics of a line of credit include:

- Loan funds increase and decrease as you use the money or make deposits. This is referred to as a revolving line of credit.

- They are available from most banks.

- There is a fluctuating interest rate.

- The interest rate at time of signing may be lower than for a term loan.

- The lender uses accounts receivable (the money owed to you by customers) and inventory as the security. For accounts receivable, the lender may lend between 50% and 75% of the value, not including amounts over 90 days. For inventory, a lender may lend up to 50%.

- A line of credit can often be obtained more quickly than a term loan.

- Repayment of the loan can be demanded at any time by the lender or the line of credit can be reduced; usually this occurs only when the account does not perform satisfactorily or when there is serious deterioration in the affairs of the business, or reduction in the value of the security provided.

- The amount of credit granted is based on the lender's assessment of the credit-worthiness of the company, its principals, and the credit requested, among other factors.

(c) Term loans

A term loan is generally money borrowed for a term of from 1 to 15 years. A term loan is usually amortized. In other words, the regular loan payments include principal and interest and are for a fixed aggregate amount over the life or term of the loan agreement.

Term loans are commonly used to provide funds for the purchase of an existing business, to help finance expansions or capital expenditures, and to provide additional working capital for a growing business.

While the majority of term loans are secured by collateral such as fixed assets or other chattels (e.g., cars, building, land, and equipment), the lender places great importance on the ability of the borrower to repay his or her indebtedness out of the business's earnings over the life of the loan.

Here are the main characteristics of a term loan:

- It may be repaid over a period of time generally related to the useful "life" of the assets; for example, car — three to five years; land and building — after three years.

- The lender will give you only a percentage of the value; for example, car — 80%; building — 75%. The other 20% or 25% of the cost of the asset must come from the equity you have in the company or new funds from shareholders or yourself.

- The company must be able to show the lender that future sales will generate enough cash to repay the loan.

- There are different lenders for different types of term loans. One consideration in the approval of your proposal is *leverage* or *debt to equity ratio*. This is the ratio of the money you owe to the money you put in the business. Generally, the lender's assessment of this ratio is discretionary, but if you are a new business, or just building up a reputation, it is unlikely that the lender will want to go beyond 2:1 or even 1:1. Consequently, this may place an additional restriction on the amount that you can borrow.

- Interest rate at time of signing is slightly higher than for a demand loan.

- Your payments, principal plus interest, are all the same.

- Repayment period of loan is specified and agreed on in advance.

- It could take a longer time to obtain a loan approval than a demand loan.

(d) Trade credit or supplier financing

Trade credit (supplier financing) is the most often used form of short-term financing. With this type of financing, the supplier will not insist on immediate payment for purchase of merchandise. Terms of payment — generally 30 to 90 days — can be arranged between both parties.

(e) Renting or leasing

Renting or leasing assets is an alternative form of financing. Leasing companies will consider arranging a lease with an option to purchase on virtually any tangible asset. Renting premises, as opposed to buying a building, is also a financing alternative. Typewriters, office furniture, computers, automobiles, and telephone equipment are examples of assets that can be leased or rented. The advantages of leasing include:

- It frees up equity capital for investment in areas of greater return.

- It frees up borrowing power for the more critical areas of the business.

- There is no down payment requirement with leasing.

- Rates are usually fixed for a set term.

- The full payment is an allowable expense.

- Purchase options can be exercised at a later date at a predetermined price.

There are also disadvantages. You should discuss the tax and financial considerations with your accountant before you make your decision.

B. SOURCES OF FINANCING

1. Equity

The most common source of equity capital is personal funds from savings. In exchange for the funds provided to the company, the owner obtains all the shares of the corporation or ownership of the business.

Equity can be further increased from the savings of friends willing to invest, or even from relatives. However, many small businesspeople have created problems by bringing in friends or relatives as investors.

Conflicts generally occur if the business is not doing as well as everyone initially imagined, or if the terms and conditions of such loans are not clearly spelled out, or if the lenders or investors insist on becoming involved in day-to-day operations.

Any agreement should be documented in writing between the parties and signed in advance to eliminate any misunderstanding.

Agreement should be reached on the rate of interest to be paid, when the loans will be repaid, any options you have to pay them back early, and the procedures that all parties will follow if the loans become delinquent. Consult competent legal counsel in advance to protect your interests.

An equity investment can be in the form of stockholder loans, or common stock or shares in the company, or a combination of loans and shares. The investment structure will vary in each situation.

Generally, the advantage of money being invested as shareholder loans is that it can be paid back to lenders without tax, other than personal tax and interest you receive before the loan is paid off.

If the money is in the form of shares, it is much more difficult to withdraw since shares must be sold to someone else and may be subject to capital gains tax.

Long-term debt investors may therefore place restrictions or conditions on when and how the company can pay off shareholder loans, redeem shares, or possibly even pay dividends on shares. These restrictions or conditions are imposed to protect the long-term debt invested.

The advice of a tax accountant is recommended since your personal tax situation and that of other potential equity investors could have a bearing on whether the shareholder investment should be in the form of loans or purchase of shares.

2. Debt

Commercial banks are a major source of capital for new and continuing small ventures. Additional organizations that provide financing include insurance companies, pension companies, real estate investment, trust, commercial, and mortgage banks, and even trust companies and credit unions.

(a) Small Business Administration (United States)

You may wish to consider the Small Business Administration (SBA) in the United States. The SBA was created by the federal government to assist entrepreneurs. Since 1953, the SBA has expanded to include many activities including finance and training.

The SBA is organized in ten regions and each region is subdivided, providing branch offices in many areas. SBA guidelines defining who qualifies for small business assistance vary, depending on the general classification of the enterprise. As the lender of final resort, the SBA tries not to compete with or replace the private banking system but to supplement it. There are various types of loans available from the SBA, the most common one being guaranteed loans.

Since the SBA's loan regulations do change from time to time, you should verify current conditions by contacting your nearest branch of the SBA (listed in the telephone directory under U.S. Government) or write to: Small Business Administration, Washington, DC 20416.

(b) Business Development Bank of Canada (Canada)

In Canada, the Business Development Bank of Canada (BDC) was established by the federal government especially to help those companies that could have difficulty obtaining financing. To obtain BDC financing, the amount of your investment in the business must generally be sufficient to ensure that you are committed to it and that the business may reasonably be expected to be successful.

BDC financing is available as loans, loan guarantees, equity financing, export receivables financing, or any combination of these methods in whatever way best suits the particular needs of your business. The BDC also assists with financial packaging; for a fee, the BDC can make arrangements with other institutions or investors on your behalf. If loans are involved, the interest rates are usually at higher rates than those offered by chartered banks.

If you wish to obtain further information, contact your local branch of the BDC or write to Business Development Bank of Canada, 800 Victoria Square, Montreal, QC H2Z 1C8

C. COMPETITION BETWEEN LENDERS

There is considerable competition among banks and other financial institutions. Compare at least three different financial institutions to assess the most favorable loan package available.

All aspects of financial dealings are negotiable. Obtain the lending terms in writing before you sign. Have your outside advisers, such as your accountant or lawyer, review the terms. In addition, you may want to obtain the advice of your associates. Don't rush into a relationship with a financial institution without reasonably exploring all the other alternatives.

D. TIPS ON APPROACHING YOUR LENDER

When you approach a financial institution, you must sell the merits of your business proposal. As in all sales presentations, consider the needs and expectations of the other party — in this case, the loans officer. A loans officer will be interested in the following:

(a) Your familiarity with the business concept and the realities of the marketplace as reflected in your detailed business plan.

(b) Your ability to service the debt with sufficient surplus to cover contingencies, including carrying interest charges, and eventually repay the debt in full as demonstrated in your cash flow forecast and projected income statement.

(c) Your level of commitment as shown by your equity in the business or cash investment in the particular asset being purchased.

(d) Your secondary source of repayment, including security in the event of default, and other sources of income.

(e) Your track record and integrity as shown in your personal credit history, your business plan, and business results or past business experience.

(f) Your approach. During the loan interview, remember you're doing business just as you do when you're with a client. Don't be subservient, overly familiar, or too aggressive. Keep in mind that a lender is in business for the same reason you are — to make a profit. Keep the profit motive in mind during the interview. Don't try to appeal to a lender's social conscience. It won't work, since loans aren't granted for their social impact.

(g) Your judgment in supplying information. Be sensible about the number of documents you provide at the outset. You do not want to overwhelm the loans officer with too much material. For example, the introductory page, summary, and financial plan sections of your business plan provide a good basic loan submission if the amount requested is small. You should have all other documents prepared and available if requested.

(h) Your personal appearance. You should present yourself in a manner that projects self-confidence and success.

(i) Your mental alertness. What time during the day are you at your mental peak? This should be the time that you arrange for an interview with the loans officer.

(j) Your consideration in allowing sufficient lead time for approval. The lender needs a reasonable time to assess your proposal. Also, the loan may have to be referred to another level within the financial institution for review.

(k) Your credit rating. It's a good idea to review your credit rating periodically, as there may be errors to correct in your file. Note your positive and negative points so you can discuss them when raised by the lender.

If your request for financing is approved, find out everything you need to know about the conditions, terms, payment methods, interest rates, security requirements, and any other fees to be paid. No commitment to accept the financing should be made until all this information is provided and understood and its impact on the proposed business analyzed. Ask your accountant and lawyer to assist you in the loan application in advance and review the bank's approval. Make certain you get the approval particulars in writing.

E. WHY LOANS ARE TURNED DOWN

If a request for financing is not approved, find out why. Use the lender's experience to your advantage. Lenders handle many requests for financing and have experience in the financial aspects of many businesses, even if they do not have direct management experience.

If there is something specifically wrong with the financing proposal, see if it can be corrected and then reapply. If not, use this knowledge when approaching other potential lenders or on future occasions when seeking funds.

A loan could be rejected for the following reasons:

(a) The business idea was considered unsound or too risky. A lender's judgment is generally based on past performance of other businesses similar to the one you are proposing.

(b) Insufficient collateral. A lender must be satisfied that there are sufficient assets pledged to meet the outstanding debt if your business does not succeed financially. If you are just starting a business, a lender generally requires you to pledge personal assets, such as your home, car, and other securities, against the loan. If you are borrowing funds under a corporate name, your personal guarantee will generally be requested and in some cases your spouse's guarantee as well, depending on the circumstances. You may therefore not have sufficient security required for the amount of loan you are requesting or for the degree of risk, in the lender's opinion, that might be involved.

(c) Lack of financial commitment on your part. A lender will be reluctant to approve loan financing for business ventures if you are not fully committed.

The lender does not want to foreclose or repossess and then have to sell assets to collect your money. The lender will therefore want to know how much personal financial capital you have made available to the business venture in order to assess your commitment to repay the loan. If you have not made any financial commitment and yet have security that you wish to pledge, the security alone may not be sufficient.

(d) Lack of a business plan or a poor business plan. A lender could reject your loan application if you have not prepared a detailed business plan or do not understand its significance.

(e) The purpose of the loan is not explained or is not acceptable. It is important that the specific use of the funds being borrowed be outlined in detail. It is also important that the purpose and amount of funds being requested be reasonable and appropriate. For example, it could be considered unreasonable for you to calculate a large draw or salary from your business in the first six months. If you intend to use the loan to pay off past debts or financial obligations, it may not be approved since the funds would not be directly generating cash flow for your new business venture.

(f) Your character, personality, or stability can affect a lender's decision. It is important to appear confident, enthusiastic, well informed, and realistic. If your personality is not consistent with the personality required for your type of business in the eyes of the lender, it could have a negative effect. If you are going through a separation or divorce proceedings or have declared personal bankruptcy or had business failures in the past, these factors could have an adverse impact on your loan application.

F. TYPES OF SECURITY A LENDER MAY REQUIRE

Lenders primarily lend money to businesses that exhibit a strong potential to repay the loan. Nevertheless, they want to be covered in case of a default. Sometimes your signature is the only security the lender needs when making a loan. The kind and amount of security depends on the lender and on the borrower's situation.

The most common types of security or collateral are endorser, co-maker, guarantor, promissory note, demand loan, realty mortgage, chattel mortgage, assignment of accounts receivable, postponement of claim, pledge of stocks and bonds, and assignment of life insurance.

Never agree to signing any security unless you understand the implications fully, speak to your lawyer and accountant about the implications and options, and attempt to negotiate a better deal from the lender.

1. Endorser

A borrower often gets another person to sign a note in order to bolster his or her own credit. This endorser is contingently liable for the note he or she signs. If the borrower fails to pay off the loan, the lender expects the endorser to make the note good. Sometimes, the endorser may be asked to pledge assets or securities as well.

2. Co-maker

A co-maker is a person who takes on an obligation jointly with the borrower. In such cases, the lender can collect directly from either the maker or the co-maker.

3. Guarantor

A guarantor is a person who guarantees the payment of a note by signing a guarantee commitment. Both private and government lenders commonly require a personal guarantor from officers of corporations as security for loans advanced to the corporation. If the corporation defaults in its financial obligations, the lender has a choice of suing the guarantor or the corporation or both for the monies outstanding. Try to negotiate a limited guarantee to cover the shortfall in the security if other securities have been pledged. Be very careful not to sign a personal guarantee for the full amount of the loan if at all possible. Recover your guarantee as soon as the business has paid off its obligation or can carry the debt on its own security. Resist having your spouse sign a personal guarantee of your debts. Your personal guarantee is often all you have left to negotiate with on another occasion.

4. Promissory note

A promissory note is a written promise to pay a specified sum of money to the lender, either on demand or at a specified future time.

5. Demand loan

A demand loan involves a written promise to pay the amount of monies outstanding to the lender on demand.

6. Realty mortgage

A lender may require a mortgage against your property for the advancement of funds. It could be a first, second, or third mortgage against your property, or a collateral mortgage to a guarantee or demand note.

7. Chattel mortgage

A chattel mortgage is on specific property, such as a car or boat, other than land and buildings. The title of the chattel remains in the name of the borrower, but a lien against the chattel is placed in favor of the lender.

8. Assignment of accounts receivable

A borrower may have to assign the business receivables to the lender to secure an operating line of credit or other loan. The borrower still collects the receivables, but in a default, the lender will assume collection. The assignment is supported by submitting a list of the business receivables each month.

9. Postponement of claim

If there are any loans from shareholders, the lender may ask for an agreement that the company will not repay the shareholders until the lender has been repaid in full.

10. Pledge of stocks or bonds

The possession of stocks and bonds may be transferred to the lender, but title remains with the borrower. The security must be marketable. As a protection against market declines and possible expenses of liquidation, banks usually lend no more than 75% of the market value of blue chip stock. On federal government or municipal bonds, they may be willing to lend 90% or more of their market value.

The lender may ask the borrower for additional security or payment whenever the market value of the stocks or bonds drops below the lender's required margin.

11. Assignment of life insurance

A lender may request that the borrower assign the proceeds of a life insurance policy to the lender up to the amount outstanding at the time of death of the borrower. Another form of assignment is against the cash surrender value of a life insurance policy. Banks generally lend up to the cash value of a life insurance policy.

8
HOW TO LEGALLY MINIMIZE PAYING TAX

It is very important to obtain professional advice on tax planning. An accountant who specializes in tax should be retained before you start your business to advise you on all the various considerations. Because tax legislation changes constantly and varies by jurisdiction, it is highly recommended that you ask an accountant to obtain current tax advice in your specific situation. It is essential that advance tax and administrative planning be done to minimize frustration and expense. If you are based in the United States but intend to provide services in Canada, or vice versa, make sure that you obtain tax compliance advice from your accountant.

This chapter gives an overview of some of the key areas to consider when discussing your new business with your professional advisers. Your advisers will review the business plan you have prepared, your personal financial circumstances, and your anticipated profit, and then recommend the correct approach for your needs.

A. TAX AVOIDANCE AND TAX EVASION

The distinction between tax avoidance and tax evasion should be made clear. Tax avoidance is the principle by which the businessperson plans his or her transactions within the law using all available tax planning benefits to minimize the liability for paying income taxes.

Tax evasion is an action that is outside the law and normally implies the receipt of monies without declaring them as income. Tax evasion is criminal and can result in serious consequences, including jail.

B. CASH OR ACCRUAL METHOD

You have a choice about the method of accounting for financial transactions. Based on your individual situation, one method may be more attractive than the other. The cash basis of accounting is a method of recording transactions in which revenues and expenditures are entered in the accounts during the period in which the related cash receipts or disbursements occur.

The accrual basis of accounting is a method of recording transactions in which revenues and expenses are entered in the accounts during the period in which they have been earned and incurred, whether or not such transactions have been finally settled.

Tax planning is challenging for cash-based businesses because expenses are generally deductible in the period paid, and income is generally taxable as it is received. For accrual basis businesses, the problem is simplified in that cash does not need to exchange hands for the recognition of income, at least not within the tax period. For either type of method, the intent is that income and expenses be matched within like periods.

An example of tax planning for the business which reports on a cash basis is found in the timing of bill payment. Toward the end of the year, the cash basis business should maximize allowable deductions by paying all

bills applying to that tax year before the year closes. Accordingly, it is not wise to request advance payments from current clients before the year is closed.

C. FISCAL YEAR-END

The choice of fiscal year may depend on consideration of financial savings for accounting fees, tax deferral in the first year, government regulations, and administrative convenience.

It is prudent to select a fiscal year distinct from the calendar year if you intend to retain accountants for annual audit or tax purposes. January through April is the busiest time for accountants, and you are likely to have better service and more attention paid to your financial affairs if your corporate fiscal year ends, for example, in July rather than in February.

If you experience seasonal changes in business volume, it may be wise to tailor a fiscal year-end along seasonal lines. Ask yourself if you are particularly busy at a certain time of the year. For example, if you are a business owner who specializes in education, you will likely be busiest in the winter and relatively free during the summer months. If you have a retail business, you may be busiest during the period of time leading up to the holidays.

In these cases, you might benefit from structuring the fiscal year-end so that the highest concentration of income occurs in the beginning of the fiscal year. By doing this, you have the remainder of the year to plan for taxes, take care of business development for the next fiscal year, and regulate cash flow effectively.

D. CORPORATIONS, PROPRIETORSHIPS, OR PARTNERSHIPS

The tax implications of a proprietorship and a partnership are the same. The net income or net loss from the proprietorship or your share of the partnership are declared on your personal income tax filings. Depending on your level of taxation, you could be paying more tax than if you were incorporated.

Your particular situation will determine whether or not it is best to incorporate for tax reasons. Factors to consider include your salary draw level, value of benefits a corporation would absorb, tax bracket, and projected growth patterns. The immediate and long-range tax liability of the individual is a governing factor.

Remember, in the United States, an exception to the normal corporation exists that allows many business owners to have the advantages of a proprietorship and a corporation. The features of an S corporation are briefly discussed in chapter 4. Your accountant can better advise you in detail.

E. MAXIMIZING DEDUCTIBLE EXPENSES

It is very important to have a record-keeping system that keeps track of all expenses relating to your overhead as well as expenses that are directly payable by the client. For a specific project, you may have given a fixed price contract incorporating the expenses that otherwise would be passed on to the client for separate payment.

Expenses are allowed if they are related to the operation of the business, are reasonable, are "ordinary" and "necessary," and if they are for items to be used within a period of one year. Your accountant can advise you regarding your situation.

If you are going to incur expenses on items that would be useful for more than one year, generally that expense cannot be fully deducted within the year the money is spent. The depreciation formula for expenses such as computers, desks, and automobiles may be claimed for the useful life of the asset.

To ensure that you account for all expenses, keep all payment stubs, receipts, and vouchers, and maintain a record of entertainment and automobile expenses. The tax department can disallow claims for expenses if there is no verification that the expense was indeed incurred and that it was related to your business and the generation of income.

Some of the areas you should discuss with your accountant to obtain advice and guidelines are discussed below. The examples given are general guidelines only. It is critical that you receive expert tax advice in advance on these and other expense deductions related to your business. As mentioned earlier, tax regulations and interpretations are constantly changing and tax court decisions alter the law on an ongoing basis. Only a tax accountant can properly advise you on the appropriate deductions in your individual situation.

1. Home office

It is quite common for many business owners to operate out of their homes to keep overhead costs down. An office in the home is deductible, but the guidelines are very strict.

(a) The office must be necessary to the conduct of the business.

(b) A room or area must be used 100% of the time exclusively for the business.

(c) Deductions are allowed on a square foot percentage or other reasonable basis.

(d) Any deductions that are being claimed for an office in the home must be disclosed on the business owner's tax return.

It is important to keep an accurate account of home office expenses, as the potential for abuse in this area is well known. Deductible expenses are made on a percentage basis. For example, if 15% of the home's living space is used exclusively for the conduct of business, 15% of the following expenses are deductible:

(a) Interest paid on home mortgage

(b) Rent of home or apartment

(c) Home owner's or tenant's fire insurance

(d) Property taxes

(e) Reasonable expenses such as maintenance

(f) A portion of the telephone charges might also be deductible. Expenses related to the telephone should be itemized as applicable to business use rather than estimated as a percentage of the total. An alternative is for the business owner to install a business telephone line in the home office.

Your tax consultant can advise you about home office expense deductibility. It is necessary to maintain careful documentation of home office expenses to support deductions claimed on an income tax return.

2. Automobile

Claiming automobile expenses can be a problem if the same car is being used for both business and pleasure. A full deduction for business use is difficult to claim if you are using it personally at any time. A ledger record of business use is essential.

A complete log should be kept of all mileage pertaining to business with a description of the purpose of each trip. In addition, a record of all tolls and parking expenses, repairs, purchases, and insurance payments should be kept. In some cases, an estimate of business use for a jointly used car may be allowable if it seems reasonable in the circumstances. Because an estimation may be disallowed, good management requires accurate record-keeping.

If you have two cars, one for business use and one for personal use, it is easier to establish a case for full deduction of all expenses related to one car.

3. Entertainment

It is difficult to claim a deduction for entertainment unless an accurate record is kept showing the date, amount, location of entertainment, who attended, connection to business, and the purpose of the meeting. As this area is one of potential abuse, it is looked at very carefully on an audit and may be disallowed. It is important, therefore, to mark on the back of the receipt the necessary information immediately after the entertainment function, before you forget.

4. Travel

This is another area in which potential abuse occurs, and it is therefore scrutinized very carefully. Travel that is strictly for business is deductible. This usually includes the cost of transportation; lodging of a reasonable nature; portion of meals; transportation while away (e.g., taxis, rental cars, and buses); personal services such as laundry; and telephone costs.

A careful distinction must be maintained when business expenses and personal expenses are combined. For example, your spouse may accompany you on a business trip. All expenses pertaining to the spouse's share of travel, lodging, or meals are not deductible unless he or she has some involvement in your business.

Get tax advice in advance. You may deduct only the portion of the expenses that relate directly to business. The primary purpose of the trip must be for business, not pleasure.

There are limits on the number of business conferences and conventions outside the country that can be attended and deducted each year. Be sure to obtain specific advice on these points.

5. Bad debts

Income is recognized only as the cash is collected. Therefore, cash basis taxpayers cannot deduct bad debts for uncollected income. However, the business can deduct returned checks as bad debts. If you are an accrual basis taxpayer and want to deduct bad debts, two important tests are required to determine if the debt can be declared "uncollectible." The criteria are the record of your attempt to collect the debt and the length of time the debt has been outstanding.

6. Insurance

Insurance premiums for all business-related insurance policies are fully deductible. If coverage extends to both personal and business protection, only the business portion can be deducted.

7. Education and professional development

All expenses related to professional development are deductible if they are directly related to your business and generating income and if they are reasonable. Again, detailed documentation is required to support the deduction. Keep receipts for all expenses for conventions, conferences, seminars, books, magazines, periodicals, newspapers, and newsletters.

8. Salaries

You many wish to use the services of your spouse, children, or others to assist you in your business. Bookkeeping, record-keeping, word processing, desktop publishing, research, marketing, and administration are just some of the areas that can be delegated to staff. All these expenses should be deductible. Make sure you receive professional tax planning advice in advance. You may wish to structure the terms of employment so that any staff are self-employed rather than employees of your company.

9. Equipment

All your equipment costs can be depreciated over time, depending on the percentage permitted each year for the particular equipment. Your computer, printer, software, fax machine, photocopier, modem, and cellular telephone may all be depreciable. If you already personally own some or all of the above before starting your business, you can have your corporate business structure buy them from you personally to make the equipment an asset of your corporate business.

10. Furnishings

You will require various office furnishings such as desk, chairs, storage areas, and filing cabinets. These are all legitimate office expenses. They must be depreciated over time, however. If you already own furnishings for your business, you can have your business buy them from you so that they become an asset of your business.

9
INSURANCE

Proper risk management means planning for potential problems and attempting to insure against them. You should be familiar with the numerous types of insurance available, the method of obtaining the insurance, the best way to reduce premiums, and the pitfalls to avoid.

A. OBTAINING INSURANCE

Insurance companies market their services chiefly through the methods discussed below.

1. Agencies

Agencies are the small, individualized operations that place home, car, or other common types of insurance with several insurance companies to which they are contracted. Sometimes, small agencies, to earn their commission, are under an obligation to place a certain volume of insurance with each company they deal with. Therefore, it is possible that you might be sold policies offered by companies that may not suit your needs and may not necessarily be priced competitively.

2. Insurance brokers

Insurance brokers claim to have complete independence from any insurance company and more flexibility than the common agencies. In comparison with agencies in general, brokers from the larger companies are more knowledgeable about and flexible in the types of coverage and policies they offer, and they specialize in certain areas. Also, a broker should have no vested interest in placing insurance with any particular company and will therefore attempt to get you the best price and the best coverage to meet your needs. You should make specific inquiries to satisfy yourself.

As in all matters of obtaining professional advice or assistance, you should have a minimum of three competitive quotes and an opportunity to evaluate the relative strengths and weaknesses of each. If the brokers are using the same insurance base for the best coverage and premiums, all three brokers should recommend to you, in theory, the same insurance companies for the different forms of coverage you are requesting.

3. Clubs and associations

Ask your local Better Business Bureau and chamber of commerce about their group rates for insurance. These two organizations frequently have various types of insurance coverage available at a reduced group rate.

B. PLANNING YOUR INSURANCE PROGRAM

It is important to consider all criteria to determine the best type of insurance for you and your business. Your major goal should be adequate coverage, avoiding both over- and underinsurance. This is done by periodically reviewing risk and keeping your agent informed of any changes in your business that could potentially affect your coverage.

The following principles will help you plan an insurance program:

(a) Identify the risk to which your business is exposed.

(b) Cover your largest risk first.

(c) Determine the magnitude of loss the business can bear without financial difficulty, and use your premium dollar where the protection need is greatest.

(d) Decide what kind of protection will work best for each risk:
   • Absorbing risks,
   • Minimizing risks, and
   • Insuring against risks with commercial insurance.

(e) Insure the correct risk.

(f) Use every means possible to reduce costs of insurance:
   • Negotiate for lower premiums if loss experience is low.
   • Use deductibles where applicable.
   • Shop around for comparable rates and analyze insurance terms and provisions offered by different insurance companies.

(g) Risk exposure changes, so a periodic review will save you from insuring matters that are no longer exposed to the same degree of risk. Conversely, you may need to increase limits of liability. Review can help avoid overlaps and gaps in coverage and thereby keep your risk and premiums lower.

(h) It is preferable to be selective and have just one broker company. An advantage of the larger broker firms is that they have a pool of insurance professionals, expert in various areas, who you can call on as resource people.

(i) Attempt to keep your losses down in every way. Although your business may have adequate coverage, losses could be uninsurable, exempt from coverage, or have a large deductible. Problems with insurance coverage could seriously affect the survival of your business.

C. TYPES OF BUSINESS AND PERSONAL INSURANCE

The types of insurance you might need will vary widely according to the type of business you have. The following overview of insurance policies is provided to make you aware of what exists and of what might be appropriate in your situation. As mentioned earlier, these types of insurance are not necessarily recommended. Only you can make that decision after an objective assessment of your needs following comparative research in a competitive insurance market.

1. General liability

Most liability insurance policies encompass losses such as:

(a) Money you must legally pay because of bodily injury or damage to the property of others.

(b) All emergency, medical, and surgical expenses incurred from the accident.

(c) Expenses for investigation, your defense, settlements, and a trial.

A general liability policy covers negligence causing injury to clients, employees, and the general public. The policy is normally written up as a comprehensive liability policy.

2. Products or completed operations liability

This policy offers protection against a lawsuit by a customer or client who used your product or service and, as a result, sustained bodily injury or property damage from it.

3. Errors and omissions liability

This coverage protects you against litigation arising from losses incurred by your clients as a result of an error or omission in your advice to them.

4. Malpractice liability

This insurance protects you from claims arising from any losses incurred by your clients as a result of negligence or failure on your part to exercise an acceptable degree of professional skill.

5. Automobile liability

This coverage includes other people's property, other automobiles, persons in other vehicles, and persons in the insured automobile.

If you are using your car for business purposes, exclusively or occasionally, it is important that you have your premium cover business use. It is possible that your current motor vehicle insurance policy has a premium based on personal use only. Problems could occur if there were an accident and it was discovered that your car was indeed used for business purposes.

6. Home office insurance

The fine print of your home policy says only personal (nonbusiness) use of your home is covered. If you are operating out of your home, make sure you obtain extended coverage for home office use. Otherwise, the insurance company will void your claim coverage for fire, theft, and injury if the claim has any business-use connection.

7. Fire and theft liability

You probably already have fire and theft insurance if you are working out of your home. If you are working in an office or an apartment, it is important to make sure that you have satisfactory coverage.

8. Business interruption insurance

The indirect loss from a fire or theft can be greater than the loss itself. If your premises or files are destroyed, you can lose revenue. Certain expenses must still be met. Such a situation could put a severe strain on working capital and seriously affect the survival of the business.

Business interruption insurance is designed to cover the period between the time of the loss and the return to normal operating conditions. The insurance policy could also include the costs of temporarily renting other premises.

9. Overhead expense insurance

If your business income would cease if you were temporarily disabled by illness or accident, you may take out insurance to cover the cost of fixed business expenses or overhead which have to be met even when you are unable to earn income.

10. Personal disability insurance

You could possibly be disabled for a short or long period of time. This insurance pays you a certain monthly amount if you are permanently disabled, or a portion of that amount if you are partially disabled but capable of generating some income.

11. Key person insurance

The death of a key person could seriously affect the earning power of your business. For example, if you have an associate or partner who is critical to a particularly large project or your business as a whole, life insurance should be considered.

If the key person dies, the loss may result in a decrease of confidence by your existing or potential clients, leading to a loss of future contracts, competitive position, and revenue, and the expense of finding and/or training a replacement. The amount and type of insurance will depend on many factors, as designing an evaluation formula for a key person is difficult.

Proceeds of the key person policy are not subject to income tax generally, but premiums are not a deductible business expense.

12. Shareholders' or partners' insurance

If it is your intention to have a partner in your business or a shareholder in your corporation, you may wish to consider shareholder or partnership insurance. This type of insurance is usually part of a buy-sell agreement that allows for a deceased shareholder's or partner's interest to be purchased by the surviving partners or shareholders of the corporation.

In the absence of a buy-sell agreement funded by life insurance, the death of a partner could cause the immediate dissolution of the partnership in law. Unless there is an explicit agreement to the contrary, the surviving partner's duty is to liquidate the business, collect all outstanding accounts, pay off all debts, and account as trustee to the personal representative of the deceased partner for the value of the deceased's interest in the business.

In the case of a corporation, the deceased shareholder's interest is considered an asset and goes to the beneficiary outlined in the will, if a will exists. Naturally, the introduction of a new shareholder who owns an interest in the company, especially a majority interest, can have a very traumatic effect on the shareholders and the company's continued operation.

In summary, the procedure is that each partner shareholder applies for a life insurance policy on the life of the other. The applicant is the beneficiary and pays the premiums on his or her partner's life insurance policy. When a partner dies, the funds from the insurance are received tax free by the beneficiary (the partner). These funds are then used to purchase the deceased partner's share of the business. The surviving partner retains control of the business, and the heirs of the deceased get cash for their interest.

13. Business loan insurance

Your lender may be able to provide you with insurance coverage for the outstanding amount of your loan and will then incorporate the premium payments into the loan. If you die, the outstanding balance of the loan is paid off.

14. Term life insurance

This type of insurance insures a person for a specific period of time and then terminates. The most common period is five years. If the insured dies within the term of the policy, the insurance company pays the full face amount to the heirs. The costs of premiums are based on life expectancy for the person's age during the five-year period. Term life does not have a cash or loan value.

Because term life insurance can be written for various time periods, and because of inexpensive premiums, it is valuable to the businessperson. Such term policies are often used to provide collateral security for loans to the firm or for personal obligations.

It is wise to have term insurance in the amount of at least your personal and business financial obligations for which you have a direct or contingent liability. This area is frequently overlooked.

15. Medical insurance

It is important to take out sufficient medical coverage for your needs. If you are doing any work outside the country, you should have extended medical coverage that pays for medical bills that may be incurred by injury or illness outside the country.

16. Group insurance

You may be eligible for group insurance rates even if you have just one employee, that is, yourself. The policies of insurance companies vary, but medical and dental plans are available for small groups. Check with your local chamber of commerce or professional association.

17. Workers' compensation insurance

If you have a number of employees, you should make certain that you are covered by workers' compensation insurance if you are eligible. With this coverage, the insurer pays all costs that the employer is required to pay for any injury to the employee. The insurer also covers the employees for all benefits and compensations required by the appropriate laws.

If you have failed to pay your employer's portion of the insurance coverage, or have failed to meet your responsibilities adequately to your employees in terms of safety, it is possible that you as the employer could be held liable for any injury to the employee as determined by the common law as well as under workers' compensation laws. Employee coverage and the extent of the employer's liability vary considerably.

10
CREDIT, BILLING, AND COLLECTION

Many business owners starting out are more interested in performing their skilled service than developing a clear credit, billing, and collection policy. Often, a business owner has had no previous business experience and does not realize the pitfalls that can occur.

A system rigidly followed is essential to your survival. It does not take many bad debts to completely eliminate the profit of the business for the whole year. You could even go out of business if a substantial debt owing by a client is not paid.

A number of common mistakes occur with new business owners. First, the business owner, wanting to build a clientele and reputation as quickly as possible, takes on many clients, performs the service, and incurs expenses, but allows the client to defer payment. Second, the new business owner may be too busy or too inexperienced to monitor receivables carefully. Third, unpaid bills are not followed up quickly with appropriate steps to collect funds. The effect of this sloppy approach can be disastrous.

This chapter outlines the pitfalls to be aware of and the procedures to adopt when reviewing your collection policy. If you develop the correct system for your needs, it will enhance your cash flow and profit and minimize stress, client problems, and bad debts.

A. DISADVANTAGES OF EXTENDING CREDIT

When you extend credit, the understanding is that the client intends to pay, is capable of paying, and that nothing will occur to prevent the client from paying. You assume that most clients are honest and acting with goodwill and in good faith. Many of these assumptions may not be accurate.

There are a number of potential disadvantages to extending credit.

Extending credit may take a great deal of your time, and the administrative paperwork — checking references, monitoring and following up on slow-paying clients — may be tedious.

The expense of credit checking and collection could be more than you wish or are able to pay. Expenses could consist of credit reporting agency fees and memberships, collection costs, legal fees, and time lost that you could otherwise spend generating revenue.

You will need to increase your working capital requirements to keep your business in operation because receivables from your clients may or may not be paid when you expect or need them. You will be paying interest on additional working capital that you may have to borrow to offset your decreased working capital.

B. ASSESSING THE CLIENT

It is important to be very careful about extending credit. Apply the following general guidelines to your business.

(a) Develop a clear credit policy for your business after consultation with your accountant and lawyer. Experienced professional advice is essential before you extend credit.

(b) Develop a credit application information sheet that has all the necessary information for your files.

(c) Consider joining a credit bureau as well as a credit reporting agency such as Dun and Bradstreet. Check into the past debt payment profile of your potential client in advance.

(d) Check references from your client if appropriate. Ask about the client's length of time in business.

(e) Consider carefully the amount of credit being extended. The greater the amount of money unpaid, the greater the risk for you.

(f) If the work you do is highly specialized and you have very little competition, you have a lot of leverage in the nature of credit that you are extending.

(g) If the client is a large institution or government, ask about the customary length of time for accounts rendered to be paid. Specify in your contract the exact terms of payment; government payments in particular can be delayed by bureaucracy for two or three months or longer.

(h) If the client requests deferred fees, you run the risk of default or other problems. Sometimes clients request a deferment of fees or payment because it is a large project or the client is suffering cash flow difficulties. If you are faced with a decision about deferral of fees, you should consider charging interest on the total amount, charging higher fees, requesting a sizable retainer fee before you start the project, or obtaining collateral to protect yourself if your total fees are substantial.

(i) Consider the future benefit of a relationship with the prospective client. If there is a possibility of future contracts or contacts with other prospective clients, you may wish to weigh the benefits against the risks. However, this can be a risky adventure. Adopt a policy that you won't extend any more credit to a client than you can afford to lose.

C. AVOIDING CLIENT MISUNDERSTANDINGS ON FEES

Communication is vital to minimize client misunderstandings about fees. Many people feel uncomfortable discussing money matters during the first interview with the client. Or sometimes people become so involved in the project that the fee is not discussed. It is important that the amount of money you expect is understood and agreed on by the client before you begin work.

Three ways to eliminate misunderstanding on the issue of services performed for fees are through communication, written contract, and invoice.

1. Communication

Communication is a critical element to a satisfactory client relationship. It is important that the subject of fees is discussed openly at the time of the initial interview and resolved so that the client feels satisfied with the final bargain.

The interview should be followed by a letter of confirmation outlining the essence of the discussion about fees, among other matters. Progress reports should be sent to the client from time to time if the circumstances warrant it; copies of correspondence concerning the client should be sent to the client.

2. Written contract

A written contract must be signed before work begins. Basically, a letter of agreement or formal contract explains the nature of fees involved and the method of payment — whether it is payment on receipt, net ten days, or net 30 days.

Be very wary about financing a client; if at all possible, have payment on receipt terms. This should assist your cash flow and minimize risk of late payments. The contract should also state the interest that will be added to the outstanding debt if it is not paid within the terms of the contract. The contract should spell out in detail the exact services that you will be performing for the fee.

In certain circumstances, a stop work clause could be inserted in the agreement to the effect that if payment is not made within the terms of the contract, at the option of the business owner all work will stop.

Finally, the contract must be signed by the client's decision-maker in authority. It is preferable that this individual be the same person with whom you negotiated the contract.

3. Invoice

To minimize misunderstanding on invoiced amounts, it is advisable to provide a detailed breakdown of the charges for services and expenses for the particular phase of the contract. If appropriate, reference should be made on the invoice to the contract agreement on fee structure and method of payment.

D. MINIMIZING RISK OF BAD DEBTS

There are several effective techniques to minimize the risk of bad debts. As discussed previously, most business owners cannot afford to have one or two major nonpaying clients without seriously affecting the viability of the business. The following general guidelines may not all be appropriate in a given client situation; your judgment in each individual situation must dictate the appropriate approach.

1. Advance retainer

A client can be asked to pay a retainer or deposit of 10% to 25% or more of the total contract amount before the work begins. This can be justified on the basis that you are very busy and if you are going to schedule in a commitment to that client, it is your policy to require an advance commitment retainer.

This is an effective technique for a potentially high-risk client who has a reputation for nonpayment or late payment, or who constantly argues about bills. This approach can also be considered when dealing with a new client with whom you are unfamiliar.

2. Prepaid disbursements

Depending on the length of the job and the type of client, you may wish to request prepaid disbursements if they are going to be sizable. You do not want to carry the client for out-of-pocket expenses at the risk of your own cash flow. You also do not want to run the risk of nonpayment or dispute of the overall account. As mentioned earlier, it is one thing to lose your time; it is another thing to also be out-of-pocket your own funds.

3. Progress payments

It is common for business owners to request funds by means of invoicing at specific points in the project. Outline in the contract the stages at which progress payments are to be paid.

4. Regular billing

Statements can be sent out on a weekly or monthly basis, depending on the circumstances. It is important to outline in the contract, if appropriate, your policy on the timing of billings. That way the client will not be taken by surprise. This also provides you with the advantage of knowing at an early stage in the project if the client is going to dispute your fees, and at this point you can either resolve the problem or discontinue your services. It can be very risky to allow substantial work to be performed, or to wait until the end of the project, before rendering an account.

5. Billing on time

Generally a client's appreciation for the value of your services diminishes over time. This is a common problem. It is important, therefore, to send your bill while the client can see the benefit of the service you have provided. Present your final bill at the completion of the project.

6. Accelerated billing

If you sense that the client may have problems paying the bill, or if other factors cause you concern, accelerate your normal billing pattern. You want to receive payment on your account before difficulties can appear.

The risk of rendering an account that states "net 30 days" is that the client is not legally overdue in payment to you until after 30 days. If you become aware of client financial problems, it is difficult to begin legal action or garnishee before the 30-day period has expired.

7. Monitor payment trends of clients

Record and monitor the payment patterns of clients so you can watch for trends that may place your fees at risk.

8. Follow-up of late payments

If you see an invoice is more than a week or ten days overdue, begin the various steps of your collection system immediately.

9. Accepting credit card payments

To minimize bad debts and facilitate cash flow, you may wish to obtain a merchant number to accept client payment by means of Visa, MasterCard, and possibly American Express. Check into the commission fee structure for use of each.

E. BILLING FOR SERVICES

Billing requires a system that is carefully designed and effective. It is important to have a third party review your billing procedures before you open your business. Examine your billing procedures on an ongoing basis, especially during the first year, to make sure they are effective. Doing so also gives you an opportunity to review your fee arrangements to make sure you are bringing in the appropriate cash flow for the time you are spending. As mentioned previously, it is important to monitor each client's file to see general trends in your client billing patterns.

Proper records must be maintained that detail the time and expenses incurred so that the bill can be prepared at the appropriate time. You should have an established procedure for regular billing so outstanding accounts are rendered on a regular basis, thereby minimizing collection disputes or bad debts.

F. WHY CLIENTS PAY LATE

If you have established appropriate precautionary measures and a credit and billing policy, you should have very few overdue accounts. However, overdue accounts will occur in any practice, and understanding your options should minimize your problems in this area.

There are several common reasons why a client might be late in paying for your services. The client could be indifferent to your deadlines. Some clients have a sloppy attitude about paying accounts due and are accustomed to being pressured or reminded frequently before they finally meet their obligations.

Institutional or government payment procedures sometimes involve a two- or three-month wait for accounts to be paid. This type of information is easily available by asking the right questions before you begin. Your account may be lost in the maze and require personal attention.

A client may deliberately delay payment in order to save money at your expense. You save the client interest on working capital if he or she can use your money for free. This is why you should have an interest factor for overdue accounts built into your initial contract as well as showing on the statement. If the overdue interest is high enough, that should act as an incentive for the client to pay on time. If this is in the contract, the client cannot argue that there was no agreement on overdue interest. Rendering a statement with the interest factor noted on it is not in itself evidence of an agreement between the parties on the amount of interest on overdue accounts.

A client may prefer to give priority to other creditors, where pressure to pay is greater.

The client may not have the money. This does not necessarily mean that the client is going out of business, but just that he or she is cash poor at the moment. The technique for handling this problem is discussed in the next section.

G. COLLECTING LATE PAYMENTS WITHOUT LEGAL ACTION

Because of the expense, time wasted, stress, and uncertainty of legal action, it is preferable to collect as much as you can from clients yourself. Here are some steps that you may wish to consider:

(a) Send out a reminder invoice with a courteous comment that the invoice is "overdue and that perhaps it was an oversight or the check is already in the mail."

(b) The alternative to the above is to telephone the accounts payable department or the client directly to ask when the payment can be expected. Courteously ask if there was possibly a misunderstanding, or if they need further information or clarification on any matter. Make sure that you note in the client file the date and time, the person you spoke to at the client's office, a summary of the conversation, and when payment can be expected.

(c) If you have not received payment within a week of the preceding step, send a letter stating that the account is in arrears and that it is to be paid on the terms of the contract. The alternative is to again telephone the client and ask about the reason for the delay.

(d) Another technique is to ask when the check will be ready. Say that you will be around to pick up the check or will arrange for a courier service to pick it up as soon as the client telephones your office to advise that it is ready.

(e) If the client has still not paid, stopping work on the project is another option.

(f) If the client refuses to pay, legal steps may be required immediately, depending on the size of the bill, the importance of the client, the reasons for nonpayment, and the cost of legal action. Alternatively, you may decide to compromise with a client and settle for a reduced payment.

(g) If the client is unable to pay because of cash flow problems or other financial difficulties, you have to assess your options. If the client is not disputing the bill and wishes to have credit, there are basically three options:

   (i) Installment payment plan: the client would agree on definite dates for payment and would send you the amounts owing on receipt of statements from you.

   (ii) Postdated checks: you would receive postdated checks from the client for the agreed period and amount.

   (iii) Promissory note: the client would sign a promissory note agreeing to the total amount of the debt and the date on which the debt would be paid. The note should be signed by the principals if the client is a corporation. Interest on the full amount of the debt should be built into the promissory note. It is negotiable whether or not interest is added onto the other two payment plans.

For more ideas and information on debt collection, see *Collect Those Debts!*, another title in the Self-Counsel Series.

H. LEGAL STEPS IF ACCOUNT REMAINS UNPAID

If it is apparent that the client has no intention of paying you, is objecting to your bill, or is unable to pay you, you must consider legal action. It is critical that you begin legal action as quickly as possible after it becomes apparent that you will not be paid by other arrangements. At this stage you are not interested in keeping the client for present or potential future business. You just want to salvage the best of a bad situation. There are basically three legal options available.

1. Collection agency

You may wish to assign the debt to a collection agency. You will be charged between 25% and 50% of the amount collected. This is better than writing the account off as a total loss. Different agencies have different styles of collection, and one agency may achieve better results with your bad debts than another. If your client pays you directly during the period of the contract with the collection agency, you are obliged to pay the commission to the collection agency. Collection agencies are listed in the Yellow Pages.

2. Small claims court

Small claims court is a relatively quick, informal, and inexpensive method of taking your client to court. If you are successful and obtain a judgment against your client, that does not necessarily mean you are going to collect on the judgment. There are additional steps you will have to take, such as garnisheeing the client or filing a judgment against the title of any properties owned by your client. Your client could turn out to be judgment proof.

3. Lawyers

Lawyers can be very effective in the collection of debts if you act promptly and select a lawyer who is experienced in the law and tactics of collecting. Lawyers generally bill on an hourly basis, and the more time expended on attempting to collect a debt, the more money it will cost you without any assurance that you will be successful at trial. If you are successful and do obtain a judgment, your client could be bankrupt or judgment proof in terms of assets. As mentioned previously, the litigation process can be very protracted, uncertain, stressful, and expensive.

I. BAD DEBTS AND TAXES

Keep accurate records of any bad debt accounts and the procedures you went through to attempt to collect. Generally, you will be allowed to deduct bad debts from your other income, but this is a matter that should be discussed with your accountant as the laws and circumstances can vary.

11
DETERMINING MARKET OPPORTUNITIES

Before determining market opportunities and identifying clients with accuracy and success, you need to consider various matters.

You need to be very certain in your own mind of your area or areas of specialization. It is impossible to target your market without this basic information. Review the self-assessment exercises in chapter 2 to determine your specific skills, talents, and attributes, and attempt to visualize the market that is suited to your abilities. It is important to avoid the tendency to be too restrictive in your view of the market for your services. Look for a wide spectrum of opportunities to apply your services in vertical and horizontal markets and in both the public and private sector. Identify common themes and processes. Know why there is a demand for your services so you can aim your marketing at those concerns when targeting prospective clients.

Thorough research is required to educate yourself and stimulate your mind on the wide range of possibilities. Read selected newspapers, magazines, and trade journals on a regular basis, and look for opportunities created by political and economic changes affecting your area of expertise and interest.

The next chapter discusses marketing techniques in more detail. This chapter is intended to provide a brief overview of the private and public sector and the possibility of market opportunities.

A. PRIVATE SECTOR

There are numerous opportunities in the private sector. By being aware of the issues and problems and solutions in your service area, it will be easier for you to identify and think of opportunities every time you are exposed to information through personal communication, television, radio, newspapers, magazines, trade journals, or books. The habit of training yourself to be aware of marketing opportunities at all times is essential.

It is important to understand the motivating factors that will cause a potential client to want your services. You might be very aware of the needs of your service within your specialty area, but a client who does not recognize that your services are needed will not be receptive to your offer of assistance.

There are many reasons a client may be motivated to retain your services, but three of the basic reasons are to obtain information, to save time, and to save money. If you can visualize the ways you can save a client time and money, and provide the most current and accurate information in the client's area of interest and need, market opportunities in the private sector will be considerable.

1. Individuals

Individuals provide an excellent client base. There are many services individuals may buy, for example, computer tutoring.

2. Small businesses

Small businesses are another excellent client base. The failure rate of small businesses is very high. The small business owner/operator's lack of knowledge in important areas of small business management is often a factor. This would include technical knowledge, efficient operation, and systems and marketing techniques.

3. Medium-sized businesses

There is a high demand for services in medium-sized businesses. Companies often hire experts as required instead of hiring staff. Hiring staff involves the related costs of training, benefit packages, and long-term commitments for possibly short-term needs. Businesses are vulnerable to economic changes, and their survival is based on keeping overheads low and making a profit. Any areas of need you can identify to increase efficiency and productivity and sales and to decrease overhead and losses will create a demand for your services.

Medium-sized businesses, as well, are constantly going through various stages of growth with all the predictable problems involved.

The advantage of dealing with a medium-sized business is that projects tend to be more lucrative. There is also a greater chance of repeat business. Another advantage is that the decision-makers are generally more sophisticated than small business owners.

4. Large companies

There is a high demand for services in large companies. Large companies often hire experts as required instead of hiring staff. Hiring staff involves the related costs of training, benefit packages, and long-term commitments for possibly short-term needs. Businesses are vulnerable to economic changes, and their survival is based on keeping overheads low and making a profit. Any areas of need you can identify to increase efficiency and productivity and sales and to decrease overhead and losses will create a demand for your services.

Large companies, as well, are constantly going through various stages of growth with all the predictable problems involved.

The advantage of dealing with a large company is that projects tend to be more lucrative. There is also a greater chance of repeat business.

B. PUBLIC SECTOR

Government is a major user of computer-related services. Marketing opportunities are available in various forms in the public sector. You can submit a solicited or unsolicited proposal and attempt to get the contract directly. You can indirectly benefit from government by subcontracting with other companies who have been awarded the main contract.

If you are considering government as a source of business, you should be aware of the various ways of obtaining contacts or information to assist you. You should also understand the way the government approval system operates.

1. Making contacts and obtaining information

There are various steps you can take to obtain the necessary information and make the necessary contacts to assist you in your government dealings.

(a) Read government advertisements and publications pertaining to your areas of interest.

(b) Place your name on the government mailing list. There are numerous government departments and you can request that your name be placed on each list to receive all relevant information, including proposed procurements and contracts awarded relating to your field.

(c) Attempt to have your name placed on the government sourcing list as a consultant in various specialty areas. When the government is looking, your name should come to their attention. There are various computerized sourcing lists throughout the departments of government; make sure that your name is on all the ones that relate to your areas of interest.

(d) Contact government contract officers. Most government contracts are awarded at the department or agency level where the specific needs are best known and money has been allocated. The telephone book has listings for various branches of government. The public library has updated lists of all the key government departments, individuals, their titles, and telephone numbers. Once you have obtained the correct department, ask to speak to the contract officer who can provide you with further background.

(e) Visit government departments and agencies. After you have submitted your résumé to various government departments, you may wish to introduce yourself to the person in charge of approving contracts. This may or may not be appropriate or possible, depending on your geographic location and government policy. Maintaining contact with the key person who could award a contract shows your interest in keeping your name current. It also demonstrates initiative and confidence. On the other hand, it could cause irritation or you could discover you have a personality conflict. (In which case you may decide that you don't want to pursue contracts with this person.)

(f) Contact large consulting firms that are the recipients of government contracts and might require additional assistance for those contracts.

(g) Contact other companies that have recently received a government contract. You can discover the names of these companies by obtaining copies of government award publications or viewing them in the public library. These are published weekly and announce all the contracts that have been awarded, who received the contract, and the amount and nature of the services to be performed. With this information, you can determine what subcontracting opportunities might be available in your area of specialty and immediately contact the companies concerned.

(h) If you have friends or acquaintances who work in government, tell them you are looking for contract work in your field. You should also provide them with your résumé and brochure if possible. They might be in a position to inform you if they hear of an agency in need of your services. You might therefore hear of a need before the department has advertised for services or made a selection. You can then submit an unsolicited proposal.

2. Understanding the government approval system

The government approval system is very formal and bureaucratic in its operation. Most government contracts are awarded only after a call for proposals, whereas in the private sector, submitting an unsolicited proposal is the most common method for obtaining work. The general procedure for government approval is given below. The procedure is the same for any level of government (i.e., municipal, state/provincial, or federal).

(a) A government department head or agency requiring consulting service assigns personnel to an internal search to see if the service can be performed in-house.

(b) If no civil service employee is available to perform the work, a request for proposal is advertised, proposals are received, and the contractor is eventually selected. It is quite common that the contractor is preselected before the closing date of the advertisement. This is because the contractor may already be on the source list and be known as best suited for the project. The advertisement is a required government formality.

(c) The government department drafts a contract and submits it to the contractor for review and signature.

(d) The signed contract is reviewed and approved again by the government's legal department.

(e) A contract is forwarded to the chief administrative officer of the division for approval.

(f) The contract and specifications are forwarded to the government purchaser for approval.

(g) The contract and fee schedule are forwarded to the government controller to verify that funds are available and have been set aside to honor the payment commitment.

(h) Notification of formal approval is sent to the contractor to begin the contract services within the terms of the contract.

(i) Work begins and is completed.

(j) Payment is received at the end of the project or throughout the project, depending on the terms of the contract. Many government departments are slow to pay because of the bureaucratic nature and requirements within the system for approval before payment. As this may cause cash flow difficulties for you, you should try to make arrangements for progress payments. If necessary, you can get a bank loan for your cash flow needs based on the strength of a government contract.

12

MARKETING YOUR SERVICE OR PRODUCT

A. WHY YOU NEED TO MARKET YOUR SERVICE OR PRODUCT

Marketing, the stimulus that creates an awareness of and demand for your services, is essential for success in business. This process involves a wide spectrum of activities, ultimately directed at convincing prospective clients that their needs can be met and their problems can be solved by your specific services. Selling is one part of the marketing program that is intended to result in a contract.

The dynamics of the marketing/selling stages have to be clearly understood and cultivated. For example, when you are marketing yourself, you have to calculate the image that you want to project when you are packaging your product — that is, yourself and your services. You and your marketing efforts must project authority, confidence, friendliness, candor, expertise, competence, and leadership.

Many business owners fail, or maintain a marginal income, because of poor marketing. Many frequently do not appreciate the necessity of marketing, do not know how to market, do not like to market, do not want to market, or do not take the time to market.

This chapter will help you understand the various techniques required to build your image as an expert in your area, thereby creating a demand for your services or products.

For more information, refer to my book (with coauthor Donald Cyr) *Marketing Your*

Product, published by Self-Counsel Press and the Self-Counsel Press book *Marketing Your Service.*

B. MARKETING PLAN

A summary of the factors that go into your marketing plan follows:

(a) Define your skills and services. This is covered in chapter 2. You should have a clear idea now of the nature of services you will be offering potential clients. You may have decided on just one particular area of interest and specialty, or you may have decided on several areas that you will promote either to the same client or to different categories of clients.

(b) Target prospective clients. Identifying possible client opportunities is the next step in the marketing plan. This was covered in the last chapter.

(c) Make potential clients and the general public aware of your services, and create a demand. The various techniques required for this step are covered in the next section.

(d) Respond to inquiries with direct client meetings. Naturally, once interest has been shown by a prospective client due to your effective marketing, your next step is to follow up on the lead quickly, see the client personally if possible, attempt to ascertain the client's precise needs, and determine how to remedy the problem.

(e) Prepare a proposal. This step follows the preceding one, confirms the client meeting, and outlines what you intend to do, how, for how much, and when. You can write a convincing proposal only after you have had an opportunity to ascertain the client's needs and the benefits that you can provide.

(f) Perform the project. This is the purpose of the whole marketing exercise — to end up with the client so you can provide your service, generate revenue, and make a profit.

(g) Follow-up is the final step in the marketing plan. If you did not obtain a contract after your previous attempts to market, you should maintain some follow-up procedure in case the client needs your services in the future. Possibly there were budget restraints the first time.

If you were able to obtain a contract and provide a service, you should have a follow-up routine in place to encourage repeat business with that client. Open communication with the client is important to ensure goodwill and possible referral business.

C. MARKETING TECHNIQUES

The following suggestions describe traditional as well as creative ways of marketing services. Many of the techniques cost little or nothing except for your time. Whether you use just a few of the techniques or all of them depends on your style, your priorities, the nature of your service, and your type of clientele. Not all these suggestions are necessarily appropriate to or will be effective in your situation.

1. Newspaper

If you specialize in small business cash flow or management problems, and if there are small businesses with problems in your region, you might put a tasteful, professional advertisement in the display advertisements in the business section or in the classified section of your local newpaper to stimulate interest. You could be offering to assist in business plan creation, or design a customized software program, or recommend existing hardware or software to meet the perceived need.

2. Advertising in trade or professional journals

The advantage of advertising in these publications is the very specialized market you reach — the readers could all be potential prospects. Therefore, the cost/benefit feature of this form of advertising can be low. You should attempt to get all the trade and professional journals related to your area of skill and services and familiarize yourself with the format and the nature of the journal ads.

3. Directories

There are many excellent reference guides listing technical, professional, and trade organizations and associations. Your public library might have the *Encyclopedia of Associations* and the *National Trade and Professional Associations and Labour Unions of the United States and Canada.* Many of the organizations listed in the directories publish annual directories of their members.

Of the organizations that have directories, approximately half of them will include your name in their directory free of charge as an expert in that area of interest. Most of the other organizations have paid advertising available, which could be of benefit if the directory is read by a prime segment of your market.

4. Brochures

Brochures can be a very important part of marketing your business. There are many ways to use a brochure.

(a) Leave the brochure with a prospective client after a face-to-face meeting.

(b) Mail the brochure after a written or formal request for further information.

(c) Send the brochure in a direct-mail campaign targeted to prospective clients.

(d) Distribute the brochure at a seminar or presentation you are giving.

(e) The day after a seminar or presentation, send the brochure out to those attending as a form of follow-up communication.

Keep in mind that your brochure is probably the first contact a prospective client has with you and the services you offer. The reaction to the brochure may be positive or negative, depending on its format, content, and quality.

5. Direct mail

Direct mail can be a very effective means of making potential clients aware of and interested in your services. There are several advantages to direct mail: the cost is flexible, the sales message can be personalized to the needs of that particular target group, and with a word-processing program, letters can be individually addressed to specific persons. An important cost/benefit aspect is the controlled circulation to a very select audience.

An integral part of direct-mail marketing is the development or rental of a mailing list. There are many sources of rental lists for the United States and Canada. The lists include names, addresses, and postal/zip codes broken down into specific categories and regions. For further information, look under "Direct Mail" in the Yellow Pages.

The various directories of organizations related to your specialty may also rent or sell mailing lists. The advantage of this type of mailing list is that prospective clients may be members of the organization that publishes the directory. You would therefore be targeting your services to your specific trade or interest market.

There are brokers who represent all the major direct-mail marketing companies. For a fee, they will determine the best mix of mailing lists for your purposes, depending on the amount of money you are prepared to budget. The broker will obtain the best rates for you and charge you a fee.

Mailing lists are generally rented for one-time use, and are "seeded" with the names of fictitious companies or individuals to ensure you do not use the list more than once. However, if someone responds to your mailing, for information or with an assignment, you can add that name to your mailing list.

It is difficult to estimate with certainty, but approximately 1% to 4% of direct-mail marketing ultimately results in assignments. Many factors will determine your response rate, for example, the type of service you provide, the economic climate at the time, the cyclical or seasonal demand for your type of service, and the techniques and format you use in the direct-mail approach. It is important to keep a record of all contacts you make and record the names and particulars. All clients should be added to your mailing list.

There are various stages involved in direct mailing, all of which are equally important to obtain the desired objective. The basic steps are as follows:

(a) Your first mailing should be within the regional area you can realistically service. It is also an opportunity to test market and analyze the effectiveness of your mailings without spending a large sum of money.

(b) Your mailing should consist of a personalized cover letter (printed on a word processor if available) addressed directly to the key decision-maker. Use quality letterhead stationery to create a professional impression. You might also enclose your business card. Enclose a copy of your brochure with your letter. Outline briefly the services you offer and the benefits that will be obtained by the prospective client. State that you will contact the client in ten calendar (or business) days to answer any questions and discuss the matter further at that time.

(c) Keep an accurate filing system of all prospective clients you intend to follow up with. List all pertinent information on the card so you can review it and familiarize yourself with it before you contact the client. Note the date you will contact the prospective client in your daily calendar.

(d) Follow up with a telephone call ten days after you mail the letter. This will give the client a positive impression of your administration and professionalism. Follow the telephone call with a visit to the prospective client if circumstances allow. The next chapter outlines other procedures and techniques to follow before, during, and after the first meeting with the prospective client.

(e) If the response to your mailing is poor, thoroughly review all your techniques and formats. This includes the direct-mail target group, cover letter, brochure, telephone techniques, and meetings.

(f) Constantly revise, refine, and upgrade your mailing list with new prospects.

(g) Send out mailings on a quarterly basis (or more often) as your finances, marketing plan, and other circumstances dictate. This will remind people of your services and expertise, and the repetition ultimately does have an effect. When sending out repetitive mailings, consider enclosing a newsletter, which you could easily prepare, and copies of any articles or other papers pertaining to the industry that is your target base. You may want to have a tear-off coupon in the newsletter that readers can send back if they want to be put on your newsletter mailing list. This way you should be able to track the response. Over time, a large portion of qualified prospects should respond to regular and consistent promotional efforts.

6. Contact network

You need to develop a contact network to develop future prospects and a mailing list. This is a very effective way to acquire clients by referral. Studies have shown that a high percentage of a business's clientele comes from referrals through a contact network or from satisfied clients.

You already have a network, and you can cultivate many more contacts. A partial list includes past and present clients, employees, professional colleagues, business associates, bankers, lawyers, accountants, friends, neighbors, and relatives. Also included are contacts you develop in associations and religious, professional, trade, business, or other organizations. If you sit down and list everyone who comes to mind as a potential contact, the list will be longer than you think.

Developing the contact network is the most effective and inexpensive way of increasing your exposure and credibility. Continually update your network by adding leads and other contacts to your mailing list.

7. Membership in professional, trade, or business associations

Joining a group and then actively participating in meetings and other functions is an effective means of developing leads. Attempt to attend meetings regularly and get involved in discussions. Evaluate a group or association on the basis of potential business prospects who are active in the association. You want to look for members who are likely to give you business opportunities. Because of the time commitment involved in developing your reputation within an organization, you must be very selective in your membership. Limit your memberships to one or two. You may wish to consider civic or trade organizations or associations such as the chamber of commerce, Rotarians, Kiwanis, or associations directly related to your service area. Obtain a list of all the members of the organization and review the list thoroughly. Most lists provide the name, position and company, type of business or profession of the member, and address.

8. Lectures

Many organizations or associations need speakers for breakfast, luncheon, or dinner meetings, conferences, or conventions. Look in the Yellow Pages under "Associations" to obtain appropriate names. Also, review directories of associations available at your local library. Two publications worth checking are *National Trade and Professional Associations and Labour Unions of the United States and Canada* and *Directory of Associations of Canada.*

When you contact the program chairperson, offer your services for free and advise him or her that you have a number of prepared talks you believe would be of particular interest to the membership. Mention that your subject areas are topical and interesting, and your talk can be between 10 and 30 minutes long. This is the normal range of time required for a speaker. Ask about the mix of membership and the number of members who normally attend meetings. Attempt to get in advance a list of members to review so that you can direct your comments more accurately toward your group.

It is helpful to have ready two or three 10- to 20-minute presentations with supporting material. You will then be available on short notice for any presentation.

The object of the presentation is not to make money but to obtain contacts and increase your credibility and exposure for future business opportunities. Those who attend the presentation will probably tell their friends or acquaintances about you if your presentation is interesting. During your presentation, you can give a number of examples or anecdotes based on your experiences. This will reinforce your image as an expert. People will remember you better by the examples or stories that you relate.

You may also wish to consider Dale Carnegie courses, Toastmaster membership, or public speaking workshops offered through continuing education programs of school boards, colleges, and universities to enhance your communication ability.

9. Teaching

There are many opportunities to offer your services as a teacher for school board adult education classes or university or community college continuing education courses. You generally get paid for your time, but ideally the students who attend the course will be potential clients or will recommend you to friends or associates. You are primarily looking for credibility, exposure, and contacts. The preparation required to teach a course also keeps you current on your subject area.

10. Seminars and workshops

You may wish to consider offering your own seminar or workshop. You can offer the seminar for free or for a nominal charge. The people who attend are excellent potential clients. You should try to select a subject that allows you to provide a practical overview of important tips and ideas within your specialty area. You can promote your seminar through your direct-mail list. Allow four to eight weeks lead time to ensure that people can schedule in your seminar.

Other items to consider are the length of the seminar; the location; the time, whether held in the day or evening; when refreshments will be served, if at all; and the number of people you can accommodate. Make sure your announcement states that space is limited and available by advance registration only. In your announcement you can request that registration be made by telephone one week in advance of the seminar. This will give you some idea as to the response and assist you in the preparation of your material. (If your registration deadline is one week before the seminar and not enough people appear to be interested, you can try to negotiate a cancellation arrangement with the seminar room facility by paying a portion of the room rent, or possibly nothing at all, if the facility is able to rebook the room.)

You may also wish to consider the free advertising possibilities in the local newspaper and other monthly or weekly publications. Depending on the number of people and the amount you are charging, you could break even on the seminar.

Make sure you distribute your brochures, newsletters, and any other appropriate material at the seminar. Develop a seminar evaluation form where participants can give their opinions of you and your seminar topic through a rating scale and in space provided for additional comments. Also include questions that will provide you with biographical information on the participants. Attach a coupon to the seminar evaluation form for participants to complete if they wish to be kept on your mailing list for newsletters. You could have draw prizes as an incentive for people to hand in the coupons. Also ask what particular areas of interest or concern a participant has. This should assist you in developing other seminars or improving the existing one.

When a person telephones in to preregister, or on the day of the seminar, make sure that you get the full company name, address, telephone number, and name and position of the person attending. You will want this information for your mailing list.

For further information on conducting seminars and workshops, see *Seminars to Build Your Business,* another title in the Self-Counsel Series.

11. Free media exposure

There are many ways to obtain free media exposure. Exposure provides you with credibility and develops public awareness of you as an expert or authority in one or more areas. If a seminar or presentation is offered, either through your own company or through some other organization, consider preparing a news release. Send it in advance to the appropriate radio, television, newspaper, or magazine contact person. Determine who the contact person is and call in advance so he or she will be expecting your letter or news release. This also gives you an opportunity to introduce yourself and to make sure that the approach you are adopting will obtain the desired free exposure.

Ask the contact person what format is preferred for the information required. Spell out in your letter, and in your conversation, why you feel the topic of the presentation is of interest to the readers, viewers, or listeners. The subject matter may be topical or controversial.

12. Radio and television talk shows

You might also appear in person on a radio or television talk show. The same approach applies as in free media announcements. Locate the appropriate contact person and sell him or her on the benefits to the listeners or viewers of your being interviewed on the program. If possible, try to be on the program a week before your seminar or presentation in order to stimulate attendance. If the talk program is too distant from the seminar date, listeners or viewers may forget about it.

For more information about writing press releases and handling the media, see *Getting Publicity,* another title in the Self-Counsel Series.

13. Writing articles

Writing is an effective way of developing exposure, credibility, and contacts. Once you have developed the format, style, and discipline, you should be able to write three or more articles a year for various publications. All publications are looking for articles; many do not pay very much, if anything, for unsolicited articles — but they will publish your work.

To locate magazines that reach your target audience, look at *Business Publications Rates and Data,* a publication from Standard Rates and Data Service. You should be able to find this publication in your library or university, or through a local advertising agency.

Write an article about your area of expertise that you believe would be of particular interest to the readership of the publication. Use examples and stories in your article. The subject matter could be new trends, the effect of pending legislation, technical information, or any other angle that will enhance your image as an expert.

Contact the publishers of your targeted magazines or journals and obtain free copies so you can review them and familiarize yourself with their style and length. If your article is accepted for publication, request a byline and a brief biographical comment at the end of the article.

There are numerous books on writing style. Have your article reviewed by at least one, if not two, friends or relatives who will candidly comment. Submit a good quality 5" x 7" glossy photograph of yourself and a biography with the article. Submit the article to one trade or business magazine at a time. Keep a list of editors at several trade journals and business magazines whose readership constitutes your potential target base. If one does not publish your article, send it on to the next editor on your list. When it is published, obtain extra copies of the publication to distribute in your next direct mailing or presentation.

Additional benefits to writing articles are the contacts you can make and the credibility you can develop as you go through the research process. For example, you could select 20 or 30 people to interview for background information for the article. These people could include key potential clients. Have a script ready before you telephone them, ask open-ended questions, listen carefully, and note their answers. Ask follow-up questions to their responses. This will show that you are knowledgeable and an intelligent communicator. You can ask their opinion on matters such as the effect of pending legislation, unique problems they encounter in their field of interest, and major opportunities or trends they perceive.

The telephone conversation can be followed by a letter thanking people for their cooperation and assistance. Depending on the responses to your questions, you may see that many business opportunities exist with the people contacted. They may have mentioned some of their problems. At a comfortable time in the future, you may wish to contact these sources and follow up with a personal letter and brochure. You might feel it appropriate to say you will contact them ten days later to ask whether you may be of service. Subtlety is essential.

14. Have articles written about you

Every field of business has news value. By carefully cultivating relationships with editors and reporters, you could be looked on as an expert in your area. They might invite your opinion and quote you in an article on the topic. You could also have articles written about you if you can demonstrate a newsworthy feature, topical benefit, or uniqueness. Attempt to look for news angles that could have a direct or indirect effect on the public at large or your target group in particular. Over time you could build up a reputation as an authority that will generate inquiries from prospective clients.

Part III

GETTING

PREPARED FOR

YOUR

COMPUTER

BUSINESS

13
OFFICE SETUP AND DESIGN

With any business, location is a key to success. It is important to have good access to potential clients and to services you require to conduct your business. Location is also important from a health and safety perspective.

Whether your small business is operated out of an office suite or other commercial location, or from your home, finding a place with proper lighting, ventilation, and room to maneuver will be a hedge against health and safety problems, as well as allow you to work more productively.

A. CHOOSING YOUR WORKSPACE

Special attention should be given to the location of your computer, as this is the heart of your operation, and it will be the place, depending on the type of business you are operating, where you will spend a lot of your time.

If your office is based in your home, the area selected should be free of distractions, especially if you have to work at times when there is plenty of other activity in the home, for example, evenings or weekends. A separate room with a door is ideal. Closing the door will serve many purposes: it shuts off distractions, signals to others that you do not want to be disturbed, and allows you to control the noise if you have to make or take business-related telephone calls.

In considering where you locate in your home, you need to consider whether clients will be coming into your office. Will you be communicating with clients mostly by telephone or e-mail or meeting them at another location? If the type of work you are doing does not require using the computer when

185

you meet clients (e.g., you are presenting them with some type of finished product or a paper-based proposal), you will not necessarily conduct face-to-face business in your workspace. You could make your presentation or have your meeting in an office-like setting of a living room or den.

But if clients do come to you, presenting as professional a workplace as possible is important. This would make rooms like a bedroom or a high-traffic area like the kitchen less suitable. Traipsing down to the basement to a workplace located in between the carpentry bench and the washing machine will also present an unprofessional image.

B. SETTING UP YOUR WORK ENVIRONMENT

Once you have selected the location of your business, it is time to consider how to set it up. The main ingredients will be lighting, storage/shelving, ventilation, desk, chair, and the computer and all of its components.

1. Lighting

In computing, your eyes are your most vital organs. So lessening the strain on them should be a priority. Bad lighting that causes glare on your monitor can tire your eyes and cut down the amount of time you are able to spend working at your computer. Controlling inside and outside sources of light will help reduce glare.

Even though you may have taken care to position your computer so light from a window is not directly hitting the screen (positioning yourself parallel to a window is best), light intensity and direction varies through the day and will also bounce off light-colored surfaces, such as walls or desk surface. Venetian or vertical blinds will help control outdoor sources of light.

In offices or workspaces without such ambient light, the concern is the source of overhead light. Try not to place your desk directly below an overhead source of light, especially rows of fluorescent lighting. You may want to try controlling the lighting intensity with a dimmer or diffusing the brightness with grids that attach to fluorescent lights to control the angle at which the light shines.

Low lighting may also be a problem and is more easily adjusted with a desk lamp. It should be placed to the side and angled away from your eyes.

2. Ventilation

Adequate ventilation is important to a comfortable work environment. And as with lighting, being able to control the ventilation is important to maintaining that comfort.

The simplest method is to have workspace with a window that can be opened and closed as needed. This is not always possible and may not be practical if you are located in a noisy area. Ventilation is something that should be considered when first selecting a location for your workspace, as it is one of the most difficult elements to change. Check to see if you can control the heat and air conditioning in the space.

A ceiling fan is a fairly quiet way of keeping air circulating. Floor or desk fans are noisier and will likely circulate loose papers in addition to the air.

If your workspace is small and enclosed, pay special attention to ventilation. A computer, which generates its own heat, needs fresh air too.

C. SETTING UP EQUIPMENT

1. Desk

You should view your desk as the foundation of your workspace, and as such you should make sure it will accommodate and support you, as well as your computer and its many peripherals.

Tables and older desks are not good substitutes for a proper computer desk. Both are usually too high and older desks do not usually have adequate leg room.

You should look for a desk with a surface that is deep enough to accommodate your keyboard and pointing devices (mouse or trackball), as well as your computer monitor in a position that is far enough away from your eyes (see section **C.3.**).

Depending on the type of work you are doing, you may also need to find room on your desktop for a scanner, printer, and material that you need to access quickly. You may also need space for the computing part of your computer. If your computer is in a tower (vertical) case, rather than in a horizontal unit that usually finds a place beneath the monitor, you can sit it on the floor. However, if you need frequent access to the floppy or CD-ROM drives or need to access the ports at the back of the unit, locating it on your desktop is a better choice.

You may also want to consider using a keyboard tray. It gives you more desk surface and is an option for desks that are too high. A tray can also be tucked away when it isn't in use. It should be wide enough for both keyboard and pointing device, which should be level (see section **C.2.**). A model that can be raised and lowered is the best choice.

2. Keyboard, pointing devices, and wrist rests

Concerns about repetitive strain injuries have fuelled the development of a lot of exotic looking equipment, most of it in the category of keyboards and pointing devices. Keyboards are available that are divided in two while others have a wave-like appearance.

The simple computer mouse is now available with multiple buttons and wheels, and is competing with trackballs and trackpads for the pointing device market.

While these "ergonomic" creations can help prevent repetitive strain injuries with varying success, you should review your posture and the setup of your equipment before investing in expensive equipment. While seated at your computer, your arms should form an L shape with your lower arm perpendicular to the floor, or bent slightly down. Your wrists should be straight, or "neutral." The neutral position should be maintained as you type. Make your bigger, stronger arm muscles do the work, not your wrist muscles.

The pointing device — whether it's a mouse or trackball — should be level and preferably on the same surface as the keyboard. Leaning or reaching forward and up and will cause stress in the shoulder.

A simple tool to keep your wrists in the neutral position is a wrist rest. They are available in a variety of hard and soft models. Soft wrist rests have fallen out of favor, however, because they allow the wrist to sink down out of the neutral position and compress the carpal tunnel (see section **D.2.**).

3. Monitor

Your monitor should be arm's length or a little further from you — usually 18 to 26 inches (45 to 66 cm).

The top of your screen (not the top of the monitor) should be at eye level, allowing your gaze to fall naturally (15 degrees below horizontal eye level) to the center of the screen. And the screen should be tilted up 10 to 20 degrees. You should not be tilting your neck to look at the screen. If you are working on a large monitor — desktop publishers and graphic designers often use 17- to 20-inch models — the top of the screen should be a little higher. The center of the screen should still be 15 degrees below horizontal eye level.

4. Document holder

A document holder is a clipboard that either stands up independently like an easel or has

an arm that fastens to the top of the monitor, so the documents you are reading hang level but to the side of the monitor. They usually have a clear clip the width of the paper that helps hold the paper in place and marks your place if you leave your work for any period. A document holder reduces the movement of your head to a shifting of the eyes (looking at the monitor then at the paper and back again).

This simple and cheap device is suggested for people whose work involves inputting information from paper-based documents or even books.

5. Chair

If you are going to be spending long periods in front of your computer, you should consider investing in a decent chair. Even when seated in a chair you move around quite a lot, and you should look for a chair that moves with you. You should be able to adjust the height so your keyboard is at elbow level and your feet are flat on the floor. It should also swivel (this lessens the amount of twisting you require from your lower back). A separate foot rest is also a good addition as it lets you adjust your posture.

6. Telephone

If you find you are gripping your telephone between your head and shoulder to free your hands to type or take notes (see section **D.3.**), you should consider investing in a headset or a telephone with a good speakerphone function. A headset allows you the most freedom of movement (you don't have to speak into the telephone) and offers the best sound for the person with whom you are communicating.

7. File cabinets, shelves, and storage

A rule of thumb for setting up storage is to keep what you need to access most often closest to you. This rule is obvious in aiding efficiency, but it is also addresses safety. If you put the telephone directory just out of reach on a shelf by your desk, you'll be tempted to reach for it from your seated position. The reaching alone will cause stress to your lower back, and that is only aggravated by the weight of the big thick book you are trying to pick up with your finger tips.

Rank the items in your workspace by importance rather than type and locate them accordingly. You may want to make room on your desk for a few books you frequently refer to, such as a dictionary or directory, rather than putting them on a separate bookshelf.

Your shelving need not be single purpose. Many units now combine filing cabinets with book shelves and general purpose drawers. Desk are also being adapted to the computer age, many with shelving located on top off the desk surface around the monitor.

Wheeled cabinets with drawers or hanging file storage are also very functional. You can roll them next to your chair when you need to access their contents and tuck them away when they are no longer needed. They also supply an extra work surface.

D. ERGONOMIC TERMS AND COMMON INJURIES

The word ergonomics actually refers to the study of the efficiency of workers in their working environment, but in the computer age the word has gained a more particular meaning. It now commonly describes hardware, software, desks, chairs, and lighting designed to prevent or reduce the chance of injury sustained by long hours spent doing repetitive tasks. It is also used to describe preventative exercises and therapies.

1. Repetitive strain injury and cumulative trauma

Like the word ergonomics, repetitive strain injury (RSI) is a term with a broad meaning (any injury caused by a repetitive motion or task) that has narrowed in common usage in the computer age.

There were repetitive strain injuries before the widespread use of computers, but the term has become associated with computer use because computers have become such a common tool and people who use them often spend long hours in front of them without a break, raising their chances of developing such an injury.

Cumulative trauma injury is another term coined since computer use became widespread. The term captures the two important and intertwined elements of computer-related injuries: incorrect use of equipment and over use of equipment.

2. Carpal tunnel syndrome

The carpal tunnel encases the nerves that run down your arm to your hands. The spot that is most vulnerable to this syndrome is on the underside of your wrist, where it bends. It is important not to over extend your wrist in either direction for prolonged periods as it damages the nerves. Symptoms of carpal tunnel syndrome (CTS) are tingling, cold, or numbness in the hands, loss of strength and control in the hands, and pain and stiffness in the hands, wrists, forearms, and elbows. CTS can be avoided by correctly positioning your hands on the keyboard and mouse.

3. Neck strain

The symptoms of neck strain are stiffness, soreness, and/or pain in the neck. These can signal a variety of problems.

Posture is the primary cause. Your head — an eight-pound weight on average — should be held directly over your shoulders. Leaning your head forward throws off the balance and will strain the muscles at the back of your neck. Try to imagine your ears directly over your shoulders when you are seated at your computer: this is the ideal posture.

If you find you are always leaning forward, examine your desk setup. You may be leaning forward because your monitor is too low, or because your chair is not giving you ample support.

Neck strain can also be vision related. You may need to have your eyes checked if you are leaning forward to read small type, or more simply, in most software programs, you can zoom in or change the view on your monitor from 100% to 125% or higher.

Neck strain can also be linked to bad lighting, if you are cocking your head or holding it in an awkward position for a prolonged period to adjust the glare off your computer screen.

Your telephone is another potential source of neck pain and stiffness.

4. Back strain

Back strain has many of the same root causes of neck strain. Your chair may not be offering you enough support, or you may be leaning forward because you can't see the monitor properly. It can also be caused by your movements while you are seated in the chair. If you are twisting and over reaching from a seated position, try to minimize this by keeping everything you use frequently within arm's-length (see section **C.7.**).

5. Eye strain

While there has been no medical proof that staring at a computer monitor for hours permanently damages your eyes, the temporary symptoms can mean a loss of productivity as they decrease your ability to work long stretches at your computer.

If your eyes are irritated and watering, you should first check that your monitor is set up properly for the lighting conditions of your workspace and that the controls on your monitor are properly adjusted (see chapter 14) to control brightness, sharpness, and reduce flicker.

Irritated eyes, along with a sore neck, back, and shoulders; headaches; double vision; and difficulty focusing are most likely the symptoms of too many hours spent in front of the screen.

Studies show that while staring at a computer screen, people tend to blink less frequently and open their eyes more widely — a combination that causes eyes to become drier and irritated. This is aggravated by staring at an object — your monitor — at the same close distance for a long period.

The solution is to take frequent breaks (every 25 to 30 minutes) to focus on something at a distance. You should also consciously try to blink more to keep your eyes moist.

Software is available that will automatically remind you that it is time to take a break and will guide your eyes to look at other objects beyond a screen. This type of software often includes arm, hand, and neck exercise reminders as well. The most aggressive versions of this type of application disable your machine for several minutes so that you can not ignore the warning and keep working. A simple alternative is to use a stove timer or other type of audible alarm set every hour to remind you to take a break from your work.

You should also make sure the type you are looking at is large enough. The letters should be three times larger than the smallest type you can see. Sit at your computer and measure your normal viewing distance from the screen, triple the distance (if you normally sit 20 inches (50 cm) away, step back 60 inches (150 cm) and you should still

be able to read the letters on the screen. Also, dark type on a light background is generally easier for most people to read.

Keep the monitor surface clean. A day of trying to adjust your eyes as they travel past the finger smudge on the screen will irritate your eyes.

If you wear prescription glasses, they may not be designed for computer use. Bifocal wearers especially may have to crane their neck backward to view the screen through the part of the glasses designed for looking at close objects. Glasses are now available for looking directly at the screen so that incidental neck injuries do not become a problem.

6. Time is key

With computer-related injuries, time is key to prevention. By spending too much time at your terminal without taking short breaks, you will create injuries. And like any injury, you run the risk of making it permanently disabling if you do not take the time to let it heal properly and by resuming the patterns that caused the problem in the first place.

If pain or soreness persists or returns after you have made adjustments to your workspace, it is important to see your doctor. Although the discomfort may seem minor, it can cause injury that renders you incapable of working for a prolonged period, or in some cases, permanently.

These same injuries could also prevent you from doing recreational activities or even simple household tasks, so it is critical you understand the potential risks.

14
PURCHASING HARDWARE, SOFTWARE, AND SERVICES

There is a seemingly endless variety of computer hardware, software, and peripherals (e.g., printers, scanners) available. It is so easy to get swept up by the rapid, seemingly daily advances in technology, that buyer's remorse is almost a given when purchasing a computer and its components.

To minimize this postpurchase dread, it is important to begin your search for a suitable system armed with a clear idea of how you plan to use it. The computer you buy should reflect the type of work you plan to do.

A. RESEARCHING YOUR PURCHASE

For hardware, software, and peripherals, find out what the standard is for the type of business you are pursuing. Although it is fairly easy to change file formats or to translate a file made in one software application so it can be read in another, this adds an extra layer to your work that may not be necessary and may be time consuming, especially when trying to meet tight deadlines.

Read computer magazines or on-line publications that include reviews to get other perspectives before purchasing hardware and software. Because they are periodicals, these publications will include up-to-date information on the latest technology. Some publications test software and hardware products and provide comparative data, such as the time it takes various computers to complete a simulated word-processing, spreadsheet, or desktop publishing task.

192

B. HARDWARE

If you are going to be using a computer for a text-based task, such as writing or editing, you need a fairly simple system, with only a few peripherals such as a printer and possibly a modem to communicate, send completed work to clients, or do on-line research.

If you plan to use the computer for more complex tasks, such as desktop publishing, which involves graphics and more sophisticated (memory-hungry) software, you will need a machine that has more memory and a more powerful processor. Spending a little more money at the beginning on added memory and processing power will allow you to spend your working time more efficiently and will lessen the likelihood of frequent crashes by an overburdened computer system.

With more sophisticated tasks come more sophisticated peripherals, including scanners, drawing tablets, and digital cameras. This type of work also brings with it the problem of how to transfer larger files. There are many types of drives that allow you to store more information on their respective medium (e.g., diskettes, tape), including Zip drives, magneto-optic (MO) drives, recordable CDs, and even portable hard drives. These storage options allow you to copy files that are hundreds of megabytes (Mb) in size (options such as a portable hard drive allow you to store gigabytes [Gb] worth of data).

C. COMPUTER COMPONENTS

The following is a list of computer hardware elements that you'll come across and should understand when buying a computer:

1. Central processing unit (CPU)

The central processing unit is the part of the system that does the computing. In a personal computer, this is a chip called the microprocessor. The two key features of a CPU are the speed at which it processes blocks of data and the size of those blocks. The speed, often called clock speed, is measured in megahertz, or MHz. The blocks of data, or word length, are measured in bits, for example, 16-bit or 32-bit. While 16-bit and 32-bit processors of similar clock speeds will process the same number of blocks in, for instance, one second, the blocks processed by a 32-bit chip will be twice as large as those processed by the 16-bit chip.

In addition to clock speed and word length, the design of a CPU can affect the speed of your computer. Chip manufacturers are constantly developing more efficient designs. One of the largest makers of microprocessors, Intel, developed the Pentium chip, which has since been surpassed in efficiency and capability by the Pentium with MMX technology, and then the Pentium II. The other big chip makers are Cyrix, AMD, and Motorola.

If you have a machine that is doing the job, but needs a boost, consider a CPU upgrade. This can be done at your local computer shop, or if you feel confident, you can upgrade the CPU yourself with several kits that are available. Not all systems allow the processor to be upgraded, however. When buying a new computer, find out whether it can be upgraded. If it can, it will allow you to meet your growing computing demands without having to replace your whole system.

There many other factors, in addition to the speed and design of the CPU, that will affect the overall performance speed of your computer (see RAM, section **C.3.**).

2. Motherboard

This is a plastic board with chips and printed circuits on it, including the CPU.

3. Random-access memory (RAM)

Random-access memory (RAM) is measured in megabytes. The amount of RAM you need depends on your business. The RAM in your computer is analogous to the working surface of your desk. When you open a software program or a file, your computer is instructed to go to your hard drive (or to a disk in the floppy drive or other type of drive), retrieve a copy of the application or file, and put in into RAM. Once it is in RAM, you can use the software to change existing files or create new documents. These changes or new documents exist only on the working surface, or RAM, unless you save them to your hard drive (or floppy disk or other media). If your system crashes because of power surges or outages (see UPS, section **D.5.**) or because it is overburdened, you will lose any changes or new files that exist only in RAM.

Having more RAM is like having a bigger working surface: you can have more files and applications open at one time. RAM can easily be added to most computers, in the form of SIMMs (single in-line memory modules).

There are various types of RAM. The most common is dynamic RAM, or DRAM. Static RAM, or SRAM, is faster than DRAM because it uses power more efficiently and does not have to be refreshed as frequently. VRAM, or video RAM, is memory used in some video cards that speeds up the display of images on the monitor. (More VRAM means you can display more colors at a higher resolution.)

4. Hard disk

This the permanent, mass storage area on your computer where data files and software applications reside. It is made up of a number of flat platters coated with magnetic particles. The platters spin and are read, or are written to, by a head that floats closely to, but doesn't touch, the platter surface. The hard disk size is measured in megabytes or gigabytes, which indicate the amount of data it can store.

You can have more than one hard drive in a computer. Hard drives are also available in external, portable models.

5. Sound cards

A sound card or adapter records and plays back sound and outputs it to speakers or an external amplifier.

6. Video cards

A video card controls what you see on your monitor. It determines the resolution (the number of pixels), the refresh rate (the number of times per second the screen renews itself), and the number of colors that can viewed on the screen. Video cards also contain their own memory. More memory means higher resolution, more colors, and faster refresh rates.

7. Expansion slots

Expansion slots allow you to plug extra boards, such as sound cards, video cards, and disk controllers into your computer. The number of slots determines the number of cards you can add. These cards allow you to add extra functions to your computer and to take advantage of technologies developed since you purchased your computer.

8. Monitors

The monitors for most desktop computers are cathode ray tube, or CRT, models. Most laptops use a form of flat panel liquid crystal display, or LCD, technology. Monitor size is determined by the diagonal measurement of the screen. However, this measurement is not necessarily for the viewable area of the CRT or flat panel. The viewable area of a 15-inch monitor, for example, is likely to be smaller than 15 inches.

The quality of a CRT monitor, or screen, is determined by convergence or sharpness, dot pitch, and refresh rate.

Convergence is the intersection of the three color beams (red, green, and blue), or dots, in a pixel. Poor convergence means white pixels will look less pure.

Dot pitch is measured in fractions of a millimeter and indicates the distance between dots of the same color in neighboring pixels. The smaller the distance, the better. A monitor with a dot pitch of .26 mm, therefore, is better than one of .28 mm.

Refresh rate, or frequency, is the speed at which the electron beam in a CRT renews the phosphors on the screen. This is measured in hertz (Hz). A refresh rate of 75 Hz means the screen is renewed 75 times a second. The higher the number the better. A monitor with a refresh rate that is too low will have a visible flicker, which can be irritating to your eyes if you spend long periods in front of your computer.

The quality and size of a monitor will be especially significant for work that requires accurate representation of fine detail or color.

9. Keyboard

The most common layout of an English-language keyboard is QWERTY (the first six letters in the upper left row of letter keys on this type of keyboard). The other, less common, layout is the Dvorak keyboard. The keys on this type of board are laid out so that more words are typed using both hands, with fingers having to travel less. Several manufacturers also make ergonomic keyboards designed to put less stress on wrists and forearms.

10. Pointing device

Also called an input device, a pointing device allows you to move the cursor around the screen. The most popular type of pointing device is a mouse. The second most popular is a trackball, which is like an inverted mouse. Touch pads, toggles (common on laptop computers), and drawing tablets are other, less common pointing devices.

D. PERIPHERALS

1. Printers

The type of printer you need depends on the quality of output required. If you need high-quality output for an annual report or promotional material that will be reproduced on a professional printing press, you'll need a PostScript-compatible laser printer (PostScript, developed by Adobe, is the commercial typesetting and printing standard).

If fine, commercial-quality output is not required, or you need only to print proofs or drafts, an inkjet printer will do the job at a fraction of the price of a laser printer. Inkjet, or bubblejet, printers produce near-laser-quality output by spraying a stream of ink that solidifies when it hits the paper. Color inkjets are also available at very reasonable prices and even some of the cheapest models can have good photographic reproduction (special paper is required for this).

When buying a printer, you should consider the price and availability of ink cartridge replacements. A $300 color inkjet with $30 cartridges is a better bargain in the long run than a $200 color inkjet with $50 cartridges.

With a color inkjet, it is also wise to pick a model with separate color and black cartridges, so that you won't need to replace the colored ink when you run out of black ink. The two cartridges should also reside alongside each other in the printer so you won't have to take one cartridge out and insert the other as you switch from printing full color to black, or vice versa. Each time you switch ink cartridges, the printer runs a cleaning cycle, which wastes ink.

Printer quality is also determined by its resolution, which is expressed in dots per inch, or dpi. The higher the dpi number, the finer the quality of the output.

PPM, or pages per minute, refers to the speed at which a printer outputs pages in a particular mode, such as high resolution, draft, or color. Printing speed is also affected by the processing power of the computer and the type of cable connecting the printer to the computer.

2. Modems

Because telephone lines are analog and computer data is digital, a modem is needed to change or modulate, then demodulate the data you are trying to send across the analog lines. Modems are distinguished by their data transfer rate, which is measured in kilobits per second, or Kbps. Common sizes are 28.8, 33.6, and 56 Kbps. Modems are also available in internal and external models. A faster modem is a good idea if you spend a lot of time on-line doing research, dealing with graphics, or if you send and receive large files. If you are frustrated by the speed of even the fastest modem, you might want to consider other, higher speed connections to the Internet (see Buying services, section **I.**).

3. Scanners

There are several types of scanners, including flatbed, slide, sheetfed, and handheld, which digitize images and documents.

Flatbed scanners, which resemble small photocopiers, are the type of scanner preferred by graphic artists, desktop publishers, and designers because of their versatility. Items scanned by a flatbed don't need to be completely flat. You can scan pages in a book or magazine, or even a range of small three-dimensional objects. (For inputting images from slides or film negatives, a separate slide scanner is needed.) Because the scanning mechanism moves rather than the item being scanned, flatbeds provide higher quality images but are also more expensive.

With a sheetfed scanner, you can scan only single sheets of paper. This is a useful tool if you have to input a lot of text that already exists in a printed form. For this purpose, a sheetfed scanner would be used in conjunction with optical character recognition, or OCR, software, which translates the digitized page into a text format that can be edited or manipulated.

A handheld scanner is another cheaper alternative to a flatbed model. It too allows you to scan pages in a book, in addition to flat sheets of paper. But because the scanning head is controlled by the user, the quality of the scanned image depends largely on the steadiness of the hand.

4. Drives

To store or transfer data to clients or service bureaus, or to read a variety of media, there are several types of drives, including CD-ROM, CD-R, CDRW, Zip, and MO.

A lot of software developers are now delivering their product on CD-ROMs rather than floppy diskettes, because CD-ROMs can hold more data. CD-ROM drives are distinguished by their speed, such as 8x, 12x, or 24x, which indicates that they transfer data 8 times, 12 times, or 24 times as quickly as the original 150 Kb per second, or 1x, CD-ROM drives. Higher speed drives are necessary for multimedia reference books, or CD-ROMs that contain full-motion video. A CD-ROM is not a storage option, because you can only read it, not write to it.

If you want to use CD-ROM technology but you want to be able to write to the diskettes, you need a CD-R or CDRW drive. These allow you to create your own CD-ROMs.

CD-R stands for CD-recordable, but unlike a floppy diskette which can be updated, you can record to the blank CD only once. The finished product can be read in a common CD-ROM drive. CD-R drives can also be used to read CD-ROMs. CD-R is a good option for storing material that has to be archived.

CDRW drives, however, allow you to update information on the recordable CDs, making it a good option for backing up data. The RW in the abbreviation stands for *rewriteable*.

Zip and MO (magneto-optic) drives are other storage options that each have their own proprietary media — diskettes or cartridges — that can be read or written to by their particular drives only. These also good options for backing up large amounts of data or for transferring large files to clients or service bureaus. (Check with the client or service bureau to make sure they have the same types of drives.)

5. Uninterruptible power supply (UPS)

A uninterruptible power supply, or UPS, provides protection against sudden power outages or surges that can do permanent damage to your computer system. A UPS provides enough power to shut down your computer properly when the power fails. Cheaper UPS units, which are adequate for a single computer, use a battery for power. More expensive models, suitable for a network of computers, employ a generator and can supply power for a longer period. Most UPSs also have some form of power surge filter.

E. PORTABLE COMPUTERS

The idea of portability is an attractive one. A laptop or notebook computer allows you to take your work with you when you visit clients and to input information at remote locations. But portability comes at a cost.

Because a laptop computer needs to be more durable and lighter than a desktop system, you will pay a minimum of twice the price for the same technology in the more compact form. Also, upgrading a laptop is more expensive and less easy than a desktop system for the do-it-yourselfer.

You will pay a premium for external or portable peripherals, because they, like the laptops, must be more durable and lighter than their internal, desktop peers.

If, after assessing your needs, you plan to buy a laptop, it is important to consider the expandability options of the system. Is the laptop equipped with an expansion bay? Do you have the option of purchasing a docking station for the system? Both of these options will cost more but will make your system more versatile and possibly give you years more use of your expensive portable unit.

F. HANDHELD COMPUTERS

If you already own a desktop computer and don't want to purchase a full-fledged laptop for use on the road, you may want to consider a handheld computer. There are now several models from name brand manufacturers that are small enough to fit in a pocket, purse, or briefcase. And they are significantly cheaper to buy and to run than a laptop computer. Most handhelds operate for a significantly longer amount of time on common, easy-to-find batteries.

Depending on the model, a handheld computer usually has functional, but less fully featured, versions of desktop software, including databases, word processing, e-mail, Web browsers, and spreadsheets. The information gathered on the road can then be uploaded to your desktop computer to update your files. The connection to the desktop computer can be made via a docking station, a cable, or sometimes through an infrared signal (this requires infrared ports on both computers, of course).

Most handheld models look like tiny laptops and have small keyboards in addition to a stylus for entering information. Other simpler models, have the option of an on-screen keyboard or a system of simplified symbols for entering letters or numbers.

G. SECURITY

1. Backing up data

If you are running a business that uses a computer, the most valuable thing to you is not the hardware or software, it's the data. The most valuable thing to a thief, however, is your computer, so it is important to back up your data daily, and it is a very good idea to keep a copy of the data in another location.

If you work in an office, that other location can be your home. If you work at home, however, other solutions are necessary. The safest solution is to use a safety deposit box in your bank. This may not be practical, however, if you back up large amounts of data daily and your bank is not easily accessible.

You can also leave the backup copy of your data with someone you trust, such as a relative, who can store it in a secure, dry place. Another solution is a remote backup service that backs up your data on-line. This can also be a time saver because you don't have to do the back up yourself, and you can specify that it be done at a time when you are not using the computer, such as the middle of the night. This service is available through some Internet service providers (see section **I.**).

Back ups are also essential in case of catastrophes, such as fire or hard drive crashes. Data recovery specialists can work miracles with machines that have crashed and even those ravaged by fire or water, but these miracles come at a price. Backing up the data and having your insurance company replace the computer system is cheaper in the long run. The sooner you can get your system up and running means less wasted work time for you.

2. Virus protection

Data can also be damaged by viruses, and there are a number of strategies and software applications that can prevent or limit this potential damage.

A virus is code embedded in a program which, once launched, will attach itself to existing applications in the computer system. The damage wrought can range from annoying to serious, including data erased permanently from the hard drive.

The first step to limiting damage, as noted above, is to make frequent backups of your data.

Another important step is installing an antivirus utility application on your computer to automatically detect viruses. As new viruses frequently appear, look for an antivirus utility that includes updates.

Also be careful of what you put into your computer. An illegal or pirate copy of an application is of unknown origin. And while it is cheaper than buying legal, licensed software, it may be a lot more costly if the data is corrupt and it damages your system.

H. BUYING SOFTWARE

The primary piece of software for your computer is the operating system, or OS. An operating system is also referred to as the platform, as it is the base from which all other programs and hardware function. The operating system you use will largely depend on the computer you use and the work you do.

Most Apple computers use the Macintosh operating system. Most PCs (personal computers) come with some version of the Microsoft Windows operating system. Most computers come with an operating system installed. Make sure your hardware vendor provides the user manual and CD-ROM or diskettes for the operating system in case you have to reinstall it.

You should also check that you have a legitimate license rather than a pirated version of the software. While a pirated version will likely work as well as a legitimate copy, you will not have the benefit of technical support from the software developer, and you will not be eligible for upgrades or patches (small programs that fix a problem in the operating system or other programs). Upgrades are made available to licensees when a new version of an operating system is developed. Upgrades are much cheaper than the cost of a full version of the program and provide you with the new features.

There is also a range of niche or less widely used operating systems that may be more suitable to your needs. For example, if your work involves developing or administration of a network, you would want a network operating system, or NOS.

One important consideration in choosing an operating system is whether there is a standard in your industry. If you are frequently exchanging files with clients or service bureaus, it will make your life a lot easier if you are using the same system.

The same rule applies for the software tools you select. Find out what the industry standard is. This is more important for complex or graphic-oriented tasks. If your work is text-based or if you are presenting clients with a finished product, compatibility is less important.

More common software, such as word processors, spreadsheet programs, and even Web page creation programs, are often available in suites. With a suite you have the advantage of integration. A suite allows you to easily move from program to program and use data from one application in another. For example, you can create a letter or form in the suite's word processor and then fill in the address via a link to the contact database. The same letter or form can also be saved in a format for posting on your Web site. Buying a suite can also be cheaper than buying the same set or a set of similar programs separately.

Don't limit your software choices to what you can find on the shelf of your local computer store. Several software developers allow you to download programs from their Web sites. And an increasing number of developers now offer try-before-you-buy incentives. These are either time-limited or demo versions of the program that can be downloaded from the company's Web site.

There is also a wealth of shareware and freeware available on-line. These programs are developed by enthusiasts and not for commercial considerations and are available for free or for a small fee. Web sites that specialize in promoting these kind of niche programs are a good place to find out what is available.

And with certain programs, usually office suites or graphics software, developers will try to buy your loyalty. If you use a competitor's program, they will sell you the full version of their software at the upgrade price in the hope of securing your future business.

I. BUYING SERVICES

The decisions don't stop after you've picked the perfect computer and the software that is suitable for your business needs. If your work involves the Internet in any way, you will also need to pick an Internet service provider, or ISP. Although the cost of this service is a usually a monthly expense rather than a large one-time purchase, it is important to choose wisely.

As with the physical location of a business, every time you move your location on-line (your e-mail address or the address of your Web site) you are in danger of losing customers who aren't aware of the change unless you spend money and effort informing them about it. Moving also requires changing business cards, stationery, and forms.

One way around this is to register your own domain name, such as *http://www.my business.com*, which you can take with you if you change your ISP. Domain name registration has an annual charge.

There is a wide range of companies that provide Internet access. There are content providers, such as Microsoft Network, America Online, and CompuServe, which have Web pages and chat groups that are available only to subscribers, in addition to providing access to the Internet and the World Wide Web. The value of that content is entirely subjective, but is usually presented in a polished, easy-to-navigate format. Content providers often offer free trials, so it is possible to use the service for a few weeks to see if it suits your needs. This type of service is usually more expensive than the ISPs described below, and, if you are in Canada, find out whether the monthly fee and hourly charges you are quoted are in American or Canadian dollars.

201

ISPs provide access to the Internet and the World Wide Web only. ISPs can be further divided into national services and local or regional services. National ISPs are a good option if you travel frequently, as you won't pay long distance charges to access the Internet from another city. Your ISP will be able to supply you with local dial-up numbers for the cities you are visiting. Local ISPs may also have options for travelers.

There are also options beyond the common telephone line connection. These include ISDN (integrated service digital network), ADSL (asymmetrical digital subscriber line), cable, and satellite. All these services are more high speed and more expensive modes of connection, but if your work involves a lot of on-line access or transfer of large files, they are options worth considering. Some of these services are available through ISPs.

ISPs and content providers usually have a range of charges and fees depending on the type of service selected. The most common is a monthly fee that includes a limited number of hours of on-line access. You then pay per hour for use over and above the limit. Many ISPs offer an unlimited access rate, which is not the same as a dedicated connection. With an unlimited account, you may be disconnected.

ISPs often have business rates that offer services not available in packages for individual users, such as electronic commerce services. These packages are worth checking into, and also ask if there are discounts for paying quarterly or semiannually instead of monthly.

Have a clear idea of what you plan to do with your Internet connection. If you are designing and maintaining Web sites or spending long hours doing on-line research, your needs will be very different from those of someone who wants only to send and receive e-mail.

In operating a Web site you also need to consider the amount of traffic that will be attracted to it. Traffic is the total amount of time visitors spend accessing a site over a certain period, usually a month. ISPs limit the amount of traffic included in their monthly charge for hosting a Web site. If the traffic to your site exceeds the limit, you will be charged a certain amount per gigabyte for the extra access. This is an important consideration because you can't control the amount of access to your site. If you expect a lot of traffic, you may want to arrange with your provider to raise the traffic limit and pay a little extra in advance.

Personal references should also play a role in choosing a service provider. While there are many reputable ISPs, the business in general has a slightly tarnished image. A lot of people have jumped on the ISP bandwagon, including those with technical enthusiasm but no business sense, and those with sharply honed marketing skills and a desire to make a quick buck. Neither is likely to be in business for the long run, but you don't want to be subject to declining service or nonexistent technical support as their business collapses.